"Teachers of comparative politics, students of democratic processes, and researchers on extremist parties will find in this book a precious treasure of data, analysis, and comprehension. Through the case of VOX, its authors, a bright team of young scholars, offer a rigorous examination of Spanish democracy and an invaluable contribution to the literature on populist radical right parties".

— **José Ramón Montero**, *Universidad Autónoma de Madrid, Spain*

"With its comprehensive coverage of VOX's origin, growth, organization, manifestos and voters, this is a much-needed contribution to our understanding of the rise of the radical right. A must-read for those interested in party system change, Spanish and European politics".

— **Eva Anduiza**, *Universitat Autònoma de Barcelona, Spain*

"The first systematic analysis of the Spanish VOX in the English language … a comprehensive account of the party's origins, ideology, organizational structure and social base. This book is a valuable resource for scholars and students of the radical right in Spain and beyond".

— **Daphne Halikiopoulou**, *University of Reading, UK*

"This very timely book offers intriguing analyses of VOX's origins, positions and voters. It provides keen insights into the radical right party, helping readers understand why Spain is no longer an outlier in Europe. It is essential reading for anyone interested in contemporary Spanish and European politics".

— **Bonnie N. Field**, *Bentley University, USA*

"In 2019 Spain was the next country to elect populist radical right party to parliament. Where many others had failed, VOX succeeded. This study of the Spanish populist radical right upstart explains how it has been able to impact Spanish politics within years of its founding … essential reading for scholars of Spanish politics and of the far right".

— **Cas Mudde**, *University of Georgia, and Center for Research on Extremism (C-REX), University of Oslo, Norway*

VOX

This book examines VOX, the first major and electorally successful populist radical right-wing party to emerge in Spain since the death of General Franco, and the restoration of parliamentary democracy in the late 1970s.

In December 2018, VOX, a new party on the populist radical right, entered the Andalusian regional parliament, and played the role of kingmaker in the ensuing government formation discussions. Since then, under the leadership of Santiago Abascal, VOX has earned political representation in numerous local, regional and national elections. The party attracted more than 3.6 million votes in the November 2019 general election, making VOX the third largest party in the Spanish Congress. In two years, the party has become a key political challenger and an important player in Spanish politics. This book explains the origins of the party, its ideology and relationship with democracy, its appeal with voters, and its similarities with (and differences from) other populist radical right parties in Europe. It draws upon a rich source of domestic as well as cross-national survey data and a systematic analysis of party manifestos which provide a detailed account of the rise of VOX and what its emergence means for Spanish politics.

This volume will be of interest to scholars of comparative politics, political parties, voters and elections, Spanish politics, the populist radical right and populism in general.

José Rama is a Lecturer in the Department of Political Science & International Relations at Universidad Autónoma de Madrid (UAM), Spain. He holds a PhD in Political Science at UAM. He has published in a number of leading journals including, amongst others, *Journal of Democracy*, *Government and Opposition*, and *European Political Science Review*.

Lisa Zanotti is an Associate Researcher at Instituto de Investigación en Ciencias Sociales – Universidad Diego Portales (UDP), Chile. She holds a joint PhD in Political Science from Diego Portales University and in Humanities from Leiden University, the Netherlands. She has recently published in *Political Studies Review*, and *Comparative European Politics*.

Stuart J. Turnbull-Dugarte is an Assistant Professor at the University of Southampton, UK. He holds a PhD in Political Science from King's College London, UK. He has published in a number of leading journals including, amongst others, the *European Journal of Political Research*, *Journal of European Public Policy*, *West European Politics*, and *Electoral Studies*.

Andrés Santana is an Assistant Professor of Political Science at Universidad Autónoma de Madrid, Spain. He researches in voting behaviour (populist parties, turnout and the decision to vote), women's political representation, and research methodology. He has recently published in the *Journal of Elections*, *Public Opinion and Parties*, *Social Politics*, *Politics & Gender*, and *East European Politics*.

ROUTLEDGE STUDIES IN EXTREMISM AND DEMOCRACY

Series Editors: **Caterina Froio,** *Sciences Po, Paris, France,* **Andrea L. P. Pirro**, *Scuola Normale Superiore, Florence, Italy* and **Stijn van Kessel**, *Queen Mary University of London, UK*

Founding Series Editors: Roger Eatwell, *University of Bath, UK* and **Cas Mudde**, *University of Antwerp-UFSIA, Belgium*

This series covers academic studies within the broad fields of 'extremism' and 'democracy', with volumes focusing on adjacent concepts such as populism, radicalism, and ideological/religious fundamentalism. These topics have been considered largely in isolation by scholars interested in the study of political parties, elections, social movements, activism, and radicalisation in democratic settings. A key focus of the series, therefore, is the (inter-)relation between extremism, radicalism, populism, fundamentalism, and democracy. Since its establishment in 1999, the series has encompassed both influential contributions to the discipline and informative accounts for public debate. Works will seek to problematise the role of extremism, broadly defined, within an ever-globalising world, and/or the way social and political actors can respond to these challenges without undermining democratic credentials.

The books encompass two strands:
Routledge Studies in Extremism and Democracy includes books with an introductory and broad focus which are aimed at students and teachers. These books will be available in hardback and paperback.

Routledge Research in Extremism and Democracy offers a forum for innovative new research intended for a more specialist readership. These books will be in hardback only.

VOX
The Rise of the Spanish Populist Radical Right
José Rama, Lisa Zanotti, Stuart J. Turnbull-Dugarte and Andrés Santana

For more information about this series, please visit:
https://www.routledge.com/Extremism-and-Democracy/book-series/ED

VOX

The Rise of the Spanish Populist Radical Right

*José Rama, Lisa Zanotti,
Stuart J. Turnbull-Dugarte and
Andrés Santana*

LONDON AND NEW YORK

First published 2021
by Routledge
2 Park Square, Milton Park, Abingdon, Oxon OX14 4RN

and by Routledge
605 Third Avenue, New York, NY 10158

Routledge is an imprint of the Taylor & Francis Group, an informa business

© 2021 José Rama, Lisa Zanotti, Stuart J. Turnbull-Dugarte and Andrés Santana

The right of José Rama, Lisa Zanotti, Stuart J. Turnbull-Dugarte and
Andrés Santana to be identified as authors of this work has been asserted
by them in accordance with sections 77 and 78 of the Copyright,
Designs and Patents Act 1988.

All rights reserved. No part of this book may be reprinted or reproduced or utilized
in any form or by any electronic, mechanical, or other means, now known or
hereafter invented, including photocopying and recording, or in any information
storage or retrieval system, without permission in writing from the publishers.

Trademark notice: Product or corporate names may be trademarks or registered trademarks,
and are used only for identification and explanation without intent to infringe.

British Library Cataloguing-in-Publication Data
A catalogue record for this book is available from the British Library

Library of Congress Cataloging-in-Publication Data
Names: Rama, José, author. | Zanotti, Lisa, 1982– author. |
Turnbull-Dugarte, Stuart J., author. | Santana, Andrés, author.
Title: VOX : the rise of the Spanish populist radical right /
José Rama, Lisa Zanotti, Stuart J. Turnbull-Dugarte and Andrés Santana.
Description: Abingdon, Oxon ; New York, NY : Routledge, 2021. |
Series: Extremism and democracy | Includes bibliographical references and index.
Identifiers: LCCN 2020055437 (print) | LCCN 2020055438 (ebook) |
ISBN 9780367502416 (hardback) | ISBN 9780367502430 (paperback) |
ISBN 9781003049227 (ebook)
Subjects: LCSH: Vox (Political party : Spain)–History. |
Right-wing extremists–Spain. | Democracy–Spain. |
Spain–Politics and government.
Classification: LCC JN8395.V6 R36 2021 (print) |
LCC JN8395.V6 (ebook) | DDC 324.246/03–dc23
LC record available at https://lccn.loc.gov/2020055437
LC ebook record available at https://lccn.loc.gov/2020055438

ISBN: 978-0-367-50241-6 (hbk)
ISBN: 978-0-367-50243-0 (pbk)
ISBN: 978-1-003-04922-7 (ebk)

Typeset in Bembo
by Newgen Publishing UK

To the workers, volunteers and families, both native-born and foreign, whose everyday efforts, be that at home in Spain or abroad, help to make Spain great.

Es preferible meterse las manos en los bolsillos y echar a andar por el mundo (…) aún a sabiendas de que en esta época de estrechos y egoístas nacionalismos el exiliado, el sin patria, es en todas partes un huésped indeseable que tiene que hacerse perdonar a fuerza de humildad y servidumbre su existencia.
Chaves Nogales, A Sangre y Fuego. Héroes, bestias y mártires de España

CONTENTS

List of figures	*xiv*
List of tables	*xvi*
Acknowledgements	*xviii*
Foreword	*xx*
Cristóbal Rovira Kaltwasser	

1 Introduction: from pariah to the institutions   1
What happened: explaining the rise of VOX 2
VOX as a populist radical right party 4
Outline 6
References 7

2 Genesis and expansion of VOX: from a people's party split to the
third largest party in Spain   10
Spain: no country for old parties? 10
Patterns of party system and electoral cycles 11
Party system dimensions 15
VOX origins: a PP split 17
VOX electoral growth 23
VOX internal organization 26
How does VOX select its candidates? 28
Conclusions 30
References 33
Appendix 36

xii Contents

3 A question of supply: what does VOX want? A party
  manifesto analysis in comparative perspective   42
  The electoral manifesto of VOX 43
    National way of life: positive 45
    Law and order 46
    Immigration 48
    Traditional morality 51
    Welfare state: expansion 52
  The emergence of VOX: a cleavage-based analysis 54
    Polarization in the left–right divide 55
  VOX in comparative perspective 59
  Conclusion 63
  References 65
  Appendix 68

4 A question of demand: who votes for VOX?   69
  Who votes for VOX? 69
    Gender 70
    Age 72
    Class 74
    Education 77
    Modelling socio-demographic support for VOX 79
  What do VOX's voters want? 81
    Ideology 82
    It's (not) the economy, stupid! 84
    Socio-cultural preferences: Europe, gays, and green politics 87
    Voting for VOX: nativism vs nationalism 93
    Modelling ideological support for VOX 100
  VOX voters compared: still an Iberian exception? 102
    Modelling support for the populist radical right 105
  Conclusions 108
  References 109

5 VOX and support for democracy: legacies from an
  authoritarian past   114
  Democracy and the populist radical right 115
  VOX and democracy 117
  Attitudes towards democracy and vote for populist radical
    right parties in comparative perspective 123

Contents **xiii**

Modelling support for VOX as a function of non-democratic regime preferences 126

Distribution of voters' regime preference in Spain 126

Measuring the effect of regime preference upon the probability to vote for VOX 128

Conclusion 132

References 135

Appendix 137

6 Conclusions 139

Who is VOX? 139

How did Spain get here? 140

What does VOX want? 141

Who votes for VOX? 142

Is VOX a threat to democracy? 143

Consequences of the rise of VOX 144

VOX and Spain tomorrow: where do we go from here? 145

References 148

Index 150

FIGURES

2.1	Party system indicators	16
3.1	Evolution of immigration saliency in the Spanish party system	50
3.2	Trend of programmatic polarization in post-democratic Spain	56
3.3	Trend of the RILE index for the five main parties in Spain, 1977–2019	57
3.4	Centre–periphery index	60
A3.1	Concerns about immigration compared with other issues in Spain	68
4.1	Marginal effect of age and electoral support for VOX	74
4.2	Income distribution of voters	76
4.3	Average marginal effects on the probability of voting for VOX	80
4.4	Support for state intervention	85
4.5	VOX supporters on immigration and European Union	86
4.6	Left–right ideological values and support for Spexit	90
4.7	VOX supporters on environment and LGBT+ rights	92
4.8	Voters who think the Catalan problem is the most important issue	95
4.9	Voters who claim the Catalan referendum affected their vote	96
4.10	Voters who think immigration is the most important issue	98
4.11	Partisan preferences for different immigration types	99
4.12	Average marginal effect of political determinants	101
4.13	VOX supporters versus those of other PRRPs	103
4.14	Sociological profile of VOX compared	106
4.15	Political profile of VOX compared	107
5.1	Populist radical right ideological traits	116
5.2	Electoral support for far-right parties in Spain	121
5.3	The democratic/undemocratic and satisfied/unsatisfied voter	124
5.4	Attitudes towards democracy and support for populist radical right parties	125

5.5	Regime preferences in Spain	127
5.6	Regime preferences in Spain by party	128
5.7	Probability to vote for VOX instead of other parties	130
5.8	Effect of regime support on the propensity to vote for VOX	130
5.9	Probability of voting for VOX instead of other right-wing parties	131
5.10	System preferences, age and voting for VOX	132

TABLES

2.1	Government formation in Spain	12
2.2	Main founders of VOX	18
2.3	Political landmarks related to the emergence of VOX, 2012–2020	20
2.4	VOX's electoral performance since December 2018 Andalusian elections	24
2.5	VOX's electoral performance, by region	25
2.6	Electoral performance of UPyD and Cs in regions with competing national identities	26
2.7	Members of VOX's internal organs	27
2.8	Summary of VOX candidate selection	30
2.A1	Vote shares in the Congress of Deputies	36
2.A2	Seats in the Congress of Deputies	39
3.1	Five most salient categories in VOX programme	44
3.2	National way of life: positive mentions	45
3.3	Law and order index	47
3.4	Strict law enforcement and tougher action against crime: positive mentions	47
3.5	Salience of traditional values: positive and negative mentions	52
3.6	Traditional values: positive mentions	52
3.7	Welfare state: positive and negative mentions	53
3.8	Market liberalism, welfare state and centre–periphery indexes	58
3.9	Salient categories for the populist radical right	61
4.1	Gender gap in support for VOX	70
4.2	Age distribution of Spanish party voters	73
4.3	Subjective class identities	75
4.4	Importance of being rich, having money and owning expensive things	77

4.5	Educational profiles of Spanish party support	78
4.6	Partisan supporters' ideological position	83
4.7	Distribution of ideological placement by parties	84
4.8	Support for Spain's exit from the European Union	89
4.9	Religious profile of party supporters	93
4.10	Support for European Union exit compared	104
4.11	Religiosity compared	104
5.1	Scheme of the democratic/undemocratic and satisfied/unsatisfied voter	123
5.A1	Probability of voting for VOX instead of other parties	137
5.A2	Probability of voting for VOX instead of other parties, merged dataset	138

ACKNOWLEDGEMENTS

This book is the product of months of debate, analysis, and deliberation with colleagues and peers, to whom we are both indebted and extremely grateful.

We are thankful to the participants of the virtual workshop held on 1 September 2020 when a draft version of the manuscript was subjected to a rigorous review amongst scholars of Spanish politics and populism. We are immensely grateful to Cristóbal Rovira Kaltwasser (Universidad Diego Portales-COES), Astrid Barrio (Universitat de València), and Bonnie Field (Bentley University) for their outstanding comments and recommendations. Their feedback, guidance, and direction have helped in clarifying and refining our arguments.

Some chapters benefitted from the feedback of participants at a presentation given at the Faculty of Social Sciences of the University of Nottingham on 13 March 2020. We are grateful for the invitation by Fernando Casal Bértoa, co-director of the Research Centre for the Study of Parties and Democracy (REPRESENT). The suggestions of the attendees helped us with the elaboration and development of the ideas presented in the pages that follow in significant and substantive ways.

We also thank Pola Lehmann and the Manifesto Project (MARPOR-CMP) for providing us with the pre-release data for the April 2019 Spanish general election.

Individually, we express our gratitude to *our* institutions during the time that we spent writing this book: King's College London, University of Southampton, Universidad Autónoma de Madrid, University Carlos III, and Diego Portales University. Without doubt, the interaction with our colleagues has allowed us to refine and improve the arguments in this book.

José particularly acknowledges the Department of Political Science at the Universidad Autónoma de Madrid, and especially José Ramón Montero and Guillermo Cordero. Both have served as an example and motivation to carry out this project. Thanks to conversations with them about Spanish politics, José was able to develop part of the contents of this book. He also expresses his gratitude to the

Department of Political Economy at King's College London, where, supported by leading researchers, he was able to write and develop various ideas for the book. Last but not least, he also acknowledges José Javier Olivas (UNED) for his support during *unpredictable times*.

Lisa acknowledges the support of the Research and Expertise Centre for Survey Methodology (RECSM) at Pompeu Fabra University in Barcelona, and of Mariano Torcal. The research stay she undertook in September/October 2020 was crucial for the last phase of the writing of this book. She also specifically acknowledges the unconditional support and aid of Cristóbal Rovira Kaltwasser whom she is lucky enough to call her mentor.

Stuart also specifically acknowledges the aid and support provided by the Juan March Institute in Madrid where he undertook a research stay in 2019. Much of the motivation and interest in launching a book project on the rise of VOX in Spain was gleaned from interactions with colleagues. In particular, he recognizes the close mentorship afforded him by Pablo Simón, whose critical eye was ever useful in correcting and developing his reasoning.

Andrés expresses his gratitude to José Ramón Montero for his sustained, inspiring and supporting role, as well as to Susana Aguilar, Mariano Torcal, Santiago Pérez Nievas, Xavier Coller, Piotr Zagórski, and Carlos Fernández-Esquer for the countless lively discussions on Spanish politics.

This book is a product of our previous work and research on populism, radicalism, and Spanish politics that anonymous reviewers helped to substantially improve.

Finally, we are grateful to all academics and scholars in the field of political and electoral behaviour, populism, radicalism, parties, and party systems who, with their previous work, have provided us the ideas to contribute, with this book in the case of VOX, to a more widely developed literature.

FOREWORD

For a long period, Spanish politics appeared to have followed a different path from most Western European countries. While the fragmentation of the electoral space into different political forces and the emergence of populist radical right parties have become increasingly common across Western European societies, Spain appeared immune to these trends. After the transition to democracy in the late 1970s, Spain's two main parties – the socialist PSOE and the conservative PP – were able to become truly catch-all parties at the national level. Although it is true that regional parties have always played an important role, the PSOE and the PP were ideally conditioned to become hegemonic actors at a national level.

However, this comfortable situation ended abruptly with the onset of the Great Recession of 2008. One of the consequences of the latter was the emergence of the Indignados Movement, which paved the way for the rise of the populist radical left party Podemos. The latter aggressively confronted the PSOE and it took a long struggle and numerous electoral contests before both parties were prepared to form a national-level coalition government, which is presently headed by Pedro Sánchez from the PSOE. At the same time, the rise of the liberal party Ciudadanos contested the PP's historical supremacy on the right-wing block. On top of this, the more recent appearance of the populist radical right party VOX further complicated the PP situation, since the right-wing block is now divided into three different political parties. In summary, contemporary Spain has become far more similar to most Western European party systems, which are increasingly fragmented into different political formations and have at least one reasonably well-established populist radical right party.

By taking into account this transformation of the Spanish political system, the authors of this book not only offer a fascinating account of contemporary Spain, but also view the situation of the country in comparative perspective. In fact, those interested in Spanish politics and in the populist radical right will learn much from this book. Without intending to provide a detailed list of the lessons one can draw from this book, there are at least three foci that are worth highlighting.

First, the book does a fine job in revealing the characteristics of VOX voters as well as the ideas espoused by the party. This analysis helps demonstrate that VOX is anything but a mainstream right party. Indeed, it should be classified as a populist radical right party. Interacting with academic literature on the topic, the book shows that the profile of VOX voters is not too different from most populist radical voters across Western Europe. The same can be said about VOX's policies, which are indeed similar to populist radical rights' across the continent, characterized, among other issues, by strong rejection of immigration, harsh rhetoric on law and order, as well as the defence of the traditional interpretation of the nation.

Second, the empirical analysis undertaken by the authors is careful enough to show that despite important similarities between VOX and the populist radical right, there are certain elements that make VOX a peculiar member of this party family within the Western European context. After all, the academic literature has pointed out that in order to adapt to the national context, populist radical right parties can end up giving more emphasis to certain issues that are relevant in some areas but not in others. In the case of VOX, this account reveals that their voters come mainly from the middle-upper class and that the party spares no effort in presenting a romanticized image of Francoist Spain. Moreover, the authors also indicate that in contrast to most populist radical right parties in Western Europe, VOX affords much attention to the defence of the integrity of the Spanish nation (i.e. radical condemnation of regionalist forces) and to the protection of traditional values (i.e. frontal attack against feminism). This means that in some aspects VOX is closer to exponents of the populist radical right beyond Western Europe, such as Donald Trump in the United States and Jair Bolsonaro in Brazil.

Third, the book provides enough empirical evidence to argue that VOX is a new party whose origins are deeply related to the main conservative party of the country. Most of the key leaders of VOX have made a political career within the PP and not a few VOX voters are former PP supporters. In other words, despite its newness, VOX relies on well-trained personnel who have experience in elections and in government. Therefore, it is not far-fetched to suggest that VOX will not be an ephemeral phenomenon. Seen in this light, VOX represents a major challenge to the PP, which sooner or later will have to make the difficult decision: either adapt to segments of the Spanish electorate that express the liberal and progressive values of the so-called silent revolution, or give voice to those Spanish voters who sympathize with the authoritarian and nativist ideas associated with the so-called silent counter-revolution. As the experience of other countries in Western Europe and the world reveal, the future of liberal democracy and the success of the populist radical right hinges on the approach taken by the mainstream right. Therefore, academics and pundits alike should carefully analyse the behaviour of the PP in the coming years.

In summary, this book addresses an important research gap. By providing a detailed analysis of VOX and studying this political party in a comparative fashion, the authors offer a much-needed contribution on the transformation of Spanish politics, its increasing similarities with the political landscape of Western Europe and the challenges that democracy faces in the country.

Cristóbal Rovira Kaltwasser
Santiago de Chile, November 2020

1

INTRODUCTION

From pariah to the institutions

> If you feel gratitude and honour for those who wear a uniform and guard the wall;
> If you remember those who have fallen so that they do not fall into nothing;
> If you respect the history of your elders;
> If you are willing to push yourself to protect your future and the wealth of your children;
> If you love your country as you love your parents;
> If you bless beauty, the good and truth;
> If you are willing to fight in an eternal fight for freedom;
> If you take part and get your hands dirty to fight injustice;
> If you think that in risk, there is hope;
> Then believe me, if you do all of this day and night;
> During the storm and during peace times;
> In the days of misery and in the days of abundance;
> Then you will know that you are succeeding in helping to:
> MAKE SPAIN GREAT AGAIN.
>
> *(Santiago Abascal, from VOX election campaign video, 2018)*[1]

More than 9,000 VOX sympathizers filled the Vistalegre Stadium in Madrid in October 2018. A former bullring was the selected venue for the first big demonstration of the depth and breadth of the support enjoyed by Spain's new populist radical right party. Born in 2013, without any notable electoral success, VOX [Latin: voice] looked set to join the graveyard full of failed radical and extreme right-wing parties that had fallen short of their goal of rupturing Spain's exceptional status as a country free of the radical or extreme right since the transition to

2 Introduction

democracy. Fast-forward to 2018 and, in the lead-up to the regional elections of Andalusia, all political pundits could talk about was whether or not VOX would win a seat in the regional parliament.

The party's rallying cry to "Make Spain Great Again!", which they announced alongside their 100-measure plan "for a living Spain" [*por la España viva*] at Vistalegre, took some commentators by surprise: supporters of the radical right were no longer disorganized and dispersed, but could be mobilized under one roof and behind one political party. In the lead-up, the polls, namely that administrated by Spain's national polling agency,[2] estimated that, at best, VOX would take one seat in the Andalusian regional parliament. The polls, however, failed to estimate the latent support for the ultra-nationalist party, whose electoral gains were bolstered by their dominance over the issue of national unity and the defence of the Spanish nation against internal and external threats in the form of (pro-Catalan independence) secessionists and immigrants, respectively. Just two months after the Vistalegre rally, VOX surpassed the polls and won 11 per cent of the popular vote and 12 out of 109 seats in the Andalusian parliament. Spanish exceptionalism (Alonso and Rovira Kaltwasser, 2015) had come to an end.

One year later, in October 2019, *Vistalegre II Plus Ultra*[3] took place with VOX only a few short weeks away from consolidating its expanding position to become the third largest party in Spain. Greeted by shouts of "Long live Spain!" [*Viva España!*], the party's leader and president, Santiago Abascal, alongside his four henchmen – Iván Espinosa de Los Monteros, Rocío Monasterio, Javier Ortega Smith, and Jorge Buxadé Villalba – were introduced by Spanish songs interpreted by a collection of famous artists. The party conference attracted more than 12,000 people; the party promised to defend and love the nation. Before *Vistalegre I*, VOX, the party leader and his four henchmen were barely known to the wider population. Shortly after *Vistalegre II*, VOX would become Spain's third largest party and a key right-wing government-supporting partner across different layers of government in Spain's multilevel governance structure, and Santiago Abascal, alongside his inner circle, would all become household names.

What happened: explaining the rise of VOX

So how did we get here? The birth of VOX predates 2018 with the party establishing itself in 2013 as a result of an internal split from the mainstream right-wing party, the People's Party [*Partido Popular*] (PP). 2017, one year before VOX's virgin success in 2018, is, however, undeniably when political events in Spain lit the flame that would embolden VOX and bring it out of the electoral wilderness. One year before VOX's infamous mass rally in *Vistalegre I*, Spain entered uncharted constitutional territory when the regional government in Catalonia unilaterally declared independence from Spain following the results of an unauthorized plebiscite on Catalan self-determination. The territorial conflict between proponents and opponents of decentralized decision-making and governance is nothing new in Spanish politics (Dowling, 2018; Gray, 2020): political parties at the national and subnational levels have long danced around the issue, leaning to leniency and opposition to sub(national) party agendas that best suit their own governing ambitions (Field, 2014).

What marks the events of 2017 apart, however, is that the actions of the regional government in pursuing its secessionist agenda, violating both the regional laws (*Estatuto de Autonomía*) and the Spanish Constitution, and the response of the government in seeking to i) squash participation in the unauthorized plebiscite by force, and ii) dismantle the regional government and impose direct rule from Madrid, aided to engender further polarization and heightened territorial tensions across the country (Simón, 2020; 2021).

VOX, much like one of Spain's earlier party entrepreneurs, Citizens [*Ciudadanos*] (Cs),[4] leveraged popular concerns over the issue of regional statehood and the ambitions of independent statehood of the Catalan government to enter the political arena. VOX built upon its unapologetic Spanish nationalism and its reliance on national symbols to present itself as the sole political party disposed to advocate, with sufficient aggression, the unity of Spain.

The message of being "tough on Catalonia" played out well for the party. Their inaugural success in the Andalusian elections, which brought 36 years of socialist-led rule in the region to an end, was in large part attributed to the fact that the second-order elections became, to an important extent, a quasi-plebiscite on the national government's handling of the Catalan crisis. The data on this is clear: those who wanted devolution to be reduced or reversed were significantly more likely to support VOX (Turnbull-Dugarte, 2019). One of the main strategies adopted by mainstream parties to diminish electoral opportunities of emerging challengers is to lean into their "competency advantage" gained from their experience in government (De Vries and Hobolt, 2020). The competency advantage of government experience, however, requires demonstrated successes to signal competency and, in the case of Catalonia, the responses of successive governments have remained wanting. VOX's stance on the question of devolution and its treatment of secessionism was therefore a particularly effective wedge issue with which it was able to attack all of the established parties, as no left- or right-leaning government had been able to resolve the issue.

Shortly after VOX's maiden success in Andalusia, on 10 February – alongside the other right-wing parties – VOX called for the now infamous Demonstration for the Unity of Spain, which took place on Madrid's well-known Colón square.[5] The rally, organized by the three right-wing parties in response to what they penned as the socialist-led government's "betrayal" of Spain, called for the resignation of Pedro Sánchez's government (Forrest, 2019). When Catalan regionalist parties refused to back the government's budget bill in February (they conditioned their support to the celebration of a legitimate independence referendum in Catalonia), the Prime Minister, of the Spanish Socialist Worker's Party [*Partido Socialista Obrero Español*] (PSOE), called for new elections. Only five days had elapsed since the Colón rally. The results of the 28 April polling day are well known: VOX achieved nearly 2.7 million votes or 10.26 per cent of the ballots cast and took home 24 of

4 Introduction

the 350 seats in the Spanish Congress. VOX entered national level representative institutions for the first time.

From the initial success in December 2018 and its eruption into the national parliament in April the party has gone from strength to strength. The inability of the PSOE to gather enough support from other parties on either the left (*Unidas Podemos*), the right (Cs), or among the other minor parties needed in order to form a government led to a repetition of Spain's general elections in November. One year and one month since they first gained electoral representation (beyond the 22 testimonial councillors in the 2015 local elections), VOX overtook the support enjoyed by Spain's other two new parties and emerged as the third largest political force, only after the PP and the PSOE.

VOX has made it into the mainstream of Spanish politics. The party currently boasts 52 out of 350 MPs in Spain's national Congress and has supported the formation of several PP-led governments at the regional level, namely those in the Madrid, Murcia, and Andalusia regions, and at the local level, such as those in the cities of Madrid, Santander, and Córdoba, via a number of confidence and supply agreements. VOX's rise is clear, but what type of party is VOX?

VOX as a populist radical right party

The categorization of populist radical right parties is controversial. We maintain, like the vast body of empirical literature, that VOX belongs to the populist radical right (Mudde, 2019; Mendes and Dennison, 2021; Norris, 2020; Ribera Payá and Díaz Martínez, 2020; Rooduijn et al., 2020; Turnbull-Dugarte et al., 2020; Vampa, 2020; Rama and Zanotti, 2020).[6] Also, in the words of Norris (2020), VOX is essentially a "classic example of a populist radical right party".

Populist radical right actors share, at least, three ideological features: nativism, authoritarianism, and populism (Mudde, 2007). Nativism holds that states should be inhabited exclusively by members of the native group (the nation), whereas non-native (or alien) elements, whether persons or ideas, are fundamentally threatening to the homogenous nation-state (Mudde, 2007). Nativism is the core ideology of populist radical right parties. As Mudde (2016) pointed out, within the ideology of the populist radical right, populism comes second to nativism. This is particularly evident in the case of VOX. VOX's discourse focuses on the primacy of Spain as a nation, exalting and glorifying the alleged characteristics of the true Spaniards in opposition to the out-group, i.e. the non-native population. Nativism is a combination of xenophobia and nationalism (Mudde, 2019) and as far as VOX is concerned, the nationalist component is particularly relevant. Indeed, at least to the present day, the discourse of the party focuses more on the exaltation of the inner group (nationalism) than on the exclusion of the out-group (xenophobia).

Second, populist radical right actors are authoritarian. This understanding of authoritarianism is not inherent to their support of a specific political regime. Instead, authoritarianism, in this case, refers to the belief in a strictly ordered society in which infringements on authority are to be severely punished (Mudde

2019: 29). This translates into "stricter law and order policies which call for more police with greater competencies and less political involvement in the judiciary" (Mudde, 2015: 296). This defence of a more ordered society can be observed in the party's approach to certain phenomena that allegedly aim at the disruption of this order. To give an example, in a video on the party's official YouTube channel, Abascal defends the need of life imprisonment for certain criminal offences, like rape; the video is accompanied by the following description, elaborated by the party itself: "Santiago Abascal demands life imprisonment without any type of rehabilitation for certain crimes, to protect society, to punish the offender, and to compensate the victim".[7] Some months later, Rocío Monasterio defended the same ideas in another video entitled, as the first one, "Life imprisonment now", and accompanied by the following description: "We won't take a step back. In VOX we demand the Congress to be tough on criminals and murderers".[8]

Finally, populist radical right parties share a populist ideology. Populism is one of the buzzwords of this century and, to some extent, is still a contested concept (Aslanidis, 2016; Laclau, 2005; Panizza, 2005; Mudde, 2004; Weyland, 2001). Scholars, however, seem to be converging towards the so-called ideational definition. The ideational definition focuses on one particular feature of populists: their ideas (Mudde, 2004). These ideas manifest themselves in a "shared way of seeing the political world as a Manichean struggle between the will of the people and the evil, conspiring elite" (Hawkins and Rovira Kaltwasser, 2018: 2). Populism, then, is seen as "first and foremost a moral worldview that is used to both criticize the establishment and construct a romanticized view of the people" (Rovira Kaltwasser, 2014: 496). Even if, as mentioned before, populism is not the primary characteristic of the populist radical right, the appeal to the people characteristic of populism is bridged with the more traditional frames of the radical right, such as the nativist definition of us and them (Caiani and della Porta, 2011). This dualistic and moral vision of society is present in VOX's discourse. For example, Ribera Payá and Díaz Martínez (2020), in an empirical assessment of VOX's written and spoken communication, conclude that "[VOX] fits the populist radical right party scheme", and evince this by showing how the party "builds a populist narrative of Manichean conflict between the virtuous Spanish people/nation (which are one and the same) and the evil globalist and progressive elites, surrounded by a myriad of threats to the Spanish nation".

We observe this also in their rhetoric used in *Vistalegre I*, where Abascal claimed:

> *Either them or us, either the same or something new, either the progressive consensus or VOX; either the regional division or the national unity; either the tyranny of the left or freedom; either regional privilege or equality; either the politicians', the parties,' the trade unions', and the NGOs' welfare state or the one of the Spaniards, of the early risers; either the state of the autonomies or the pensions; either the Spaniards (first) or the illegal immigrants; either living wages for our policemen, for our guards or swimming pools and gyms for the criminals.[9]*

6 Introduction

This extract highlights the understanding of society and politics as a moral contra-position which is typical of populism. Both "the people" and "the elite" are floating signifiers that can be filled with different content (Laclau, 2005). Together they form a chain of equivalence which represent a collective identity (Errejón and Mouffe, 2015).

Outline

We hope that this book will be of interest to scholars and students with a desire of understanding the populist radical right as well as the changes in the Spanish party system and electorate. Our primary goal is to offer an accessible and digestible contribution that provides individuals outside of academia with an enjoyable read. Political scientists (we included) have a strong penchant of relying on statistical modelling and advanced quantitative methods to present their arguments. Whilst the main body of our book relies on quantitative datasets of national and cross-national survey data, as well as on other data sources, we have aimed to keep any advanced modelling to the appendices. Where statistical tests are reported, these are presented with an accompanying description of how they may be interpreted without, we hope, too much effort.

Our journey to understand VOX's rise begins in Chapter 2. Here we give an account of the evolution of the Spanish party system since the return to democracy in 1977 and we present the milestones, since 2012, necessary to understand the upsurge and the features of VOX. Moreover, this chapter furnishes an initial assessment of the organizational structure of VOX, examining its internal statutes and its rank and file.

In Chapter 3, we take a look at the supply side and ask, "What does VOX want?" Relying on longitudinal data on parties' ideological positions from Spain's transition to democracy up to the present day, as well as on comparative data from the manifestos of populist radical right-wing parties from across Europe, we provide a rich empirical discussion of which positions matter for the party and how these compare both across time and space.

Chapter 4 takes the opposite approach and focuses on the demand-side factors. Essentially this chapter asks, "Who votes for VOX?" Relying on both national and cross-national survey data, we assess the socio-demographic makeup of VOX's supporters to appraise the extent to which they diverge from the average Spanish voter and from those of the established right-wing parties. Are VOX's voters an electoral breed in their own right, or are they a Spanish iteration of an archetypical populist radical right-wing voter profile observed across the rest of Western Europe?

In Chapter 5, we take a closer look at the relationship between VOX and democracy. While it is true that populist radical right parties' ideology is not at odds with democracy, it is also true that at the empirical level both populisms, left and right, put a strain on the internal contradictions of democracy with its liberal component, while nativism has inherently exclusionary features. Having said this, in

Chapter 5 we analyse the democratic profile of VOX's voters comparing them with the supporters of the other main Spanish parties. Here we also assess the relationship between attitudes towards democracy at the individual level and the vote for VOX from a comparative perspective, analysing populist radical right parties in different regions.

Finally, we tie the strings together in Chapter 6. Our concluding chapter recaps on our main research findings and lays out a vision of what VOX's rise means for Spanish politics in the turbulent political years to come.

Notes

1 See: www.youtube.com/watch?v=RaSIX4-RPAI&t=51s
2 *Centro de Investigaciones Sociológicas* (CIS).
3 *Plus ultra* is the Latin for further beyond. Additionally, the Plus Ultra appears in the coat of arms of Spain, written in the Hercules columns. It was first used in 1516 by King Carlos I of Spain, who employed it as his personal motto to symbolize the dynamism of the new Spanish Empire, in which the sun never set. This is one of the many examples (see Chapter 5) that illustrates the allusions of VOX to a "better" pre-democratic Spanish past.
4 Here we are referring to Ciudadanos's initial success at the regional level in Catalonia. Their later success on the national stage was also fuelled by their promise of democratic renewal and regeneration. See for example, Orriols and Cordero (2016).
5 Never one to lose the opportunity to take advantage of symbolic settings, Plaza Colón is a national monument to Christopher Columbus [*Cristóbal Colón*], who "discovered" the Americas. The square is host to a monumental 294m² Spanish flag which was installed by the PP's former prime minister, José María Aznar, as part of his attempt to rekindle a feeling of national pride that, in his eyes, was underdeveloped in Spain (Díez and González, 2002).
6 This categorization is not uniform. Ferreira (2019), for example, does not observe a populist component and defines the party as a radical right-wing party of the non-populist variety.
7 See: www.youtube.com/watch?v=UhPdci-3yJ0&ab_channel=VOXEspa%C3%B1a
8 The discourse of VOX as regards gender issues (clearly oriented toward the rejection of feminism and the understanding of society as male oriented) could also be understood in this light, insofar as party leaders perceive feminism – or, as they have called it, "the feminist jihad" – as a challenge to the supposed predetermined order in society which the party aims at counter arrest.
9 See: www.youtube.com/watch?v=0yjHe0h3UmY&ab_channel=VOXEspa%C3%B1a and www.youtube.com/watch?v=L95ilYuqrSU.

References

Alonso S and Rovira Kaltwasser C (2015) Spain: No Country for the Populist Radical Right? *South European Society and Politics* 20(1): 21–45.
Aslanidis P (2016) Is Populism an Ideology? A Refutation and a New Perspective. *Political Studies* 64: 88–104.
Caiani M and della Porta D (2011) The elitist populism of the extreme right: A frame analysis of extreme right-wing discourses in Italy and Germany. *Acta Politica* 46(2): 180–202.

8 Introduction

De Vries CE and Hobolt SB (2020) *Political Entrepreneurs: The Rise of Challenger Parties in Europe*. Princeton: Princeton University Press.

Díez A and González M (2002) Polémico homenaje a la bandera. *El País*. 3 October.

Dowling A. (2018) *The Rise of Catalan Independence: Spain's Territorial Crisis*. London: Routledge.

Errejón Í and Mouffe C (2015) *Construir pueblo: Hegemonía y radicalización de la democracia*. Más Madera 116. Barcelona: Icaria.

Ferreira C. (2019) Vox como representante de la derecha radical en España: un estudio sobre su ideología. *Revista Española de Ciencia Política* 51: 73–98.

Field B. (2014). Minority parliamentary government and multilevel politics: Spain's system of mutual back scratching. *Comparative Politics* 46(3): 293–312.

Forrest A (2019). "More than 40,000 Spanish nationalists protest against government talks with Catalan leaders". www.independent.co.uk/news/world/europe/spain-catalonia-protest-madrid-pedro-sanchez-socialists-plaza-de-colon-a8772401.html

Gray C. (2020) *Territorial Politics and the Party System in Spain: Continuity and change since the financial crisis*. London: Routledge.

Hawkins KA and Rovira Kaltwasser C (2018) Introduction: The ideational approach. Carlin RE, Hawkins KA, Littvay L, and Rovira Kaltwasser C (eds) *The Ideational Approach to Populism: Concept, Theory, and Analysis*. Extremism and Democracy 42. London; New York: Routledge, pp. 1–24.

Laclau E (2005) *On Populist Reason*. London; New York: Verso Books.

Mendes MS and Dennison J (2021) Explaining the emergence of the radical right in Spain and Portugal: salience, stigma and supply. *West European Politics* 44(4): 752–775. Online First: 10.1080/01402382.2020.1777504.

Mudde C (2004) The Populist Zeitgeist. *Government and Opposition* 39(4): 541–563.

Mudde C (2007) *Populist Radical Right Parties in Europe*. Cambridge, UK; New York, NY: Cambridge University Press.

Mudde C (2015) Populist radical right parties in Europe Today. Abromeit J, Norman Y, Marotta G, et al. (eds) *Transformations of Populism in Europe and the Americas: History and Recent Tendencies*. At the heart of research. London: Bloomsbury Academic, pp. 295–307.

Mudde C (2016) Introduction: The Populist Radical Right Today. Mudde C (ed.) *The Populist Radical Right: A Reader*. Routledge Studies in Extremism and Democracy. London; New York: Routledge, pp. 1–10.

Mudde C (2019) *The Far Right Today*. Cambridge: Polity Press.

Norris P (2020) Measuring populism worldwide. *Party Politics* 26(6): 697–717. Online First: 10.1177/1354068820927686.

Orriols L and Cordero G (2016) The Breakdown of the Spanish Two-Party System: The Upsurge of Podemos and Ciudadanos in the 2015 General Election. *South European Society and Politics* 21(4): 469–492.

Panizza F (ed.) (2005) *Populism and the Mirror of Democracy*. London; New York: Verso Books.

Rama J and Zanotti L (2020) ¿Radical o extremo? *El País*, 9 January. Madrid. Available at: https://elpais.com/elpais/2020/01/08/opinion/1578508347_621843.html (accessed 17 March 2020).

Ribera Payá P and Díaz Martínez J I (2020) The end of the Spanish exception: the far right in the Spanish Parliament. *European Politics and Society*. Online First: https://doi.org/10.1080/23745118.2020.1793513

Rooduijn M, Van Kessel S, Froio C, et al. (2019) The PopuList 2.0: An Overview of Populist, Far Right, Far Left and Eurosceptic Parties in Europe. Available at: https://popu-list.org/ (accessed 16 June 2019).

Rovira Kaltwasser C (2014) The Responses of Populism to Dahl's Democratic Dilemmas. *Political Studies* 62(3): 470–487.

Simón P (2020) The Multiple Spanish Elections of April and May 2019: The Impact of Territorial and Left–right Polarization. *South European Society and Politics*. DOI: 10.1080/13608746.2020.1756612

Simón P (2021): Two-bloc Logic, Polarisation and Coalition Government: The November 2019 General Election in Spain, *South European Society and Politics*, DOI: 10.1080/13608746.2020.1857085

Turnbull-Dugarte SJ (2019) Explaining the end of Spanish exceptionalism and electoral support for Vox. *Research & Politics* 6(2). DOI: 10.1177/2053168019851680.

Turnbull-Dugarte SJ, Rama J and Santana A (2020) The Baskerville's dog suddenly started barking: voting for VOX in the 2019 Spanish general elections. *Political Research Exchange* 2(1). Routledge: 1781543. DOI: 10.1080/2474736X.2020.1781543.

Vampa D (2020) Competing forms of populism and territorial politics: the cases of Vox and Podemos in Spain. *Journal of Contemporary European Studies*. Online First: 10.1080/14782804.2020.1727866.

Weyland K (2001) Clarifying a Contested Concept: Populism in the Study of Latin American Politics. *Comparative Politics* 34(1): 1–22.

2

GENESIS AND EXPANSION OF VOX

From a people's party split to the third largest party in Spain

This chapter aims to briefly place the surge and growth of VOX within the wider Spanish electoral context. After describing the Spanish party system and its electoral cycles since the restoration of democracy in 1977, it focuses on the origins of VOX and its electoral success in recent elections. To that end, the second part of the chapter presents the emergence of VOX in 2013 as a conservative People's Party split, summarizing the milestones of its development and its electoral results in different levels of power: local, regional, European and national. Finally, we dedicate a few paragraphs to understanding VOX's internal organization, as well as its methods of candidate selection.

Spain: no country for old parties?

Spain used to be labelled as a polity plagued with contradictions, including volatile parties and stable voters, weak parties enjoying strong results, bright and grey party leaders, a two-party-plus system with low fragmentation but many regionalist and nationalist parties, party strategies zigzagging between moderation and polarization, consistency of ideological preferences by voters, and policy packages in a continual state of change (Linz and Montero, 2001).

In Spain, the Great Recession of 2008 initially produced an electoral overturn which only eroded slightly the pre-eminence of the two largest parties, the Spanish Socialist Workers' Party [*Partido Socialista Obrero Español*] (PSOE), and the conservative Popular Party [*Partido Popular*] (PP), leading to an absolute majority for the latter in the 2011 general elections (see Anduiza et al., 2014).

Hence, in Spain, the first elections after the beginning of the crisis were normal elections, i.e. they brought about the expected replacement of the governing party, the PSOE, for the main political force of the opposition, the PP. This is at odds with the developments in other Southern European countries which, like Spain, were hardest hit by the economic crisis: the party systems changed in a notable way, with the emergence and electoral success of new (populist) radical parties, like the 5 Star Movement [*Movimento 5 Stelle*] (M5S) in the 2013 Italian general elections and SYRIZA in the 2012 Greek ones.

This pattern changed in the 2014 European Parliament (EP) and 2015 general elections. Two new nationwide parties, We Can [*Podemos*] and Citizens [*Ciudadanos*] (Cs), entered the national Parliament, giving place to a moderately pluralist party system. For the first time in almost 40 years, government formation proved impossible (Rodríguez Teruel et al., 2016; Rodríguez Teruel and Barrio, 2016; Simón, 2016; Orriols and Cordero, 2016), so six months later, in June 2016, new elections were celebrated and the PP ruled with the external support of Cs.

However, less than two years later, in June 2018, the PSOE rallied opposition parties to bring the government down in a censure vote. The ensuing PSOE government depended on the support of Together We Can [*Unidos Podemos*] (UP)[1] and the external support of regionalist parties so, when Catalan parties refused to back the government's budget bill in February, the PSOE called for an early election, thereby putting an end to the shortest Spanish government since the return of democracy in 1977.

The story of the 2019 April Spanish general elections is well known (Rama and Santana, 2019): the big winner was the PSOE and the big loser, the PP, partly because of the growth of Cs and partly due to the entrance of a new nationalist, nativist and anti-immigration party, VOX.[2] Far from being the end of turbulent times, the lack of agreement between PSOE and UP led to new elections in November 2019, which gave place to an even more fragmented parliament, in which the PSOE won again and VOX ascended to the third position.

Patterns of party system and electoral cycles

Although the last years have been politically wise turbulent, the truth is that politics in Spain are better characterized by the term *stability* than by change. In this regard, there is certain consensus on the different electoral cycles in which we can divide Spanish politics since 1977. Thus, four cycles may be differentiated, each one of them characterized by peculiar combinations of the levels of electoral support for the main parties, the format of the party system, the patterns of competition among its members, and its main voting dimensions, especially electoral fragmentation, electoral volatility, and ideological polarization (Montero, 1988; Linz and Montero, 2001). Table 2.1 summarizes the electoral cycles.

The first electoral cycle is the one of *democratic transition* and comprises the first two democratic elections after the restoration of democracy, held in 1977 and 1979. They gave place to a moderate and pluralist party system which facilitated the development of democratic institutions after the four decades-long dictatorship of General Francisco Franco (Montero and Lago 2010). Adolfo Suárez's centre-right Union of the Democratic Centre [*Unión de Centro Democrático*] (UCD) comfortably won the 1977 elections (see Table 2.1), and led a minority single-party government

12 Genesis and expansion of VOX

TABLE 2.1 Government formation in Spain

Legislature and years[a]		Government type[b]	Governing parties			External support[e]	Months[f]
			Party[c]	Prime Minister	Seats[d]		
First period							
0	1977–1979	spmg	UCD	Suárez	166	47.4 No	25
I	1979–1981	spmg	UCD	Suárez	168	48.0 No	22
	1981–1982			Calvo-Sotelo			21
Second period							
II	1982–1986	SPMG	PSOE	González	202	57.7 No	44
III	1986–1989	SPMG	PSOE	González	184	52.6 No	40
IV	1989–1993	SPMG	PSOE	González	175	50.0 No	44
V	1993–1996	spmg	PSOE	González	159	45.4 Yes	33
Third period							
VI	1996–2000	spmg	PP	Aznar	156	45.6 Yes	48
VII	2000–2004	SPMG	PP	Aznar	183	52.3 No	48
VIII	2004–2008	spmg	PSOE	Zapatero	164	46.9 Yes	48
IX	2008–2011	spmg	PSOE	Zapatero	169	48.3 No	44
X	2011–2015	SPMG	PP	Rajoy	186	53.1 No	48
Fourth period							
XI	2015–2016	ngf	–	–	–	– –	10
XII	2016–2018	spmg	PP	Rajoy	137	39.1 Yes	19
	2018–2019	spmg	PSOE	Sánchez	85	24.3 Yes	11
XIII	2019–2019	ngf	–	–	–	– –	6
XIV	2019– /	mcg	PSOE	Sánchez	120	34.3 No	–
			UP		35	10.0	

a: The 1977–1979 legislature is traditionally referred to as the 'Constituent legislature'.

b: SPMG: single-party majority government, smpg: single party minority government, MCG: majority coalition government, mcg: minority coalition government, ngf: no government formed.

c: UCD: Unión de Centro Democrático, PSOE: Partido Socialista Obrero Español, PP: Partido Popular, UP: Unidas Podemos.

d: The first figure is the number of seats, and the second the percentage out of the 350 seats of the Spanish Congress.

e: External support means that a general agreement was reached that some parties, despite not entering a formal coalition government, provided stable support to governing party or coalition, whether the agreement involved a formal pact, like in 1996, or not, like in 1993. In the V legislature, the government was supported by CiU (Convergència i Unió); in the VI, by CiU, PNV (Partido Nacionalista Vasco) and CC (Coalición Canaria); in the VIII, by ERC (Esquerra Republicana de Catalunya), IU (Izquierda Unida), CC, BNG (Bloque Nacionalista Galego) and CHA (Chunta Aragonesista); in the first part of the XII, by Cs (Ciudadanos) and CC, and in its second part, by UP.

f: The figures for the XI and XIII legislatures reflect the number of months with an interim government.

Source: Own elaboration of the authors based on Ministry of Interior data (1977–2019).

whose main task was to deliver a democratic constitution: it was endorsed by a supermajority of almost 90 per cent of the voters in December 1978, and the so-called Constituent legislature was dissolved.

UCD revalidated its victory in the 1979 elections, established a second single-party minority government, and initiated the process of territorial decentralization. However, due to several factors, including a complicated economic situation and disagreements within the governing party, Suárez resigned and Leopoldo Calvo-Sotelo served as prime minister the second half of the term (which receives the name of legislature I, as it was the first one with the new constitution).

The second cycle is the one of *democratic consolidation* and encompasses four elections (1982, 1986, 1989, and 1993) marked by the *political hegemony* of Felipe Gonzalez's socialist PSOE. Spain joined supranational organizations like the North Atlantic Treaty Organization (NATO) and the European Union (EU), and its economy underwent a process of internationalization and modernization.

The 1982 contest amounted to an electoral earthquake (Santamaría, 1984) that dramatically redrew the political landscape: the PSOE boomed (from 121 to 202 seats, the highest figure ever achieved by a party in Spain), the UCD collapsed (from 168 to 11) and the conservative Popular Alliance [*Alianza Popular*] (AP), the predecessor of the PP, emerged as the main opposition party (from nine to 107). The losers acknowledged their defeat and peacefully transferred the government to the PSOE, attesting to the consolidation of the young democratic regime.

The critical 1982 elections brought about a predominant party system in which the PSOE occupied an exceptionally favourable place and faced a fragmented and weak opposition (Linz and Montero, 2001). Thence, González concatenated three absolute majorities of seats (in 1982, 1986, and 1989) and a final simple majority in 1993.[3]

In 1993, González renewed his mandate with the crucial external support of a centre-right Catalan nationalist coalition, Convergence and Union [*Convergència i Unió*] (CiU), and the Basque Nationalist Party [*Partido Nacionalista Vasco*] (PNV), which is ideologically quite close to the centre. However, after the increasing unwillingness of CiU to back the government's legislative proposals, González decided to call for early elections, thus giving way to the next cycle.

The third cycle is characterized by the *extraordinary intensification* of electoral competition between PSOE and PP, as well as by the *alternation in power* of these two parties. It covers five elections: 1996 (minority government of José María Aznar's PP), 2000 (majority government of Aznar), 2004 and 2008 (minority governments of José Luis Rodríguez Zapatero's PSOE), and 2011 (majority government of Mariano Rajoy's PP).

Again, in the three instances which did not produce an absolute majority, the winner needed to gather the support of regional nationalist parties to become invested and seize government, although in none of these occasions did the nationalists' backing translate into a coalition government. In 1996, after complicated negotiations, Aznar secured the support of CiU, PNV, and Canarian Coalition [*Coalición Canaria*] (CC), which continued backing most of the government's proposals

14 Genesis and expansion of VOX

throughout the legislature. In 2004, Zapatero governed with the blessing of the traditional radical left party, United Left [*Izquierda Unida*] (IU), and a left Catalan nationalist coalition, Catalan Republican Left [*Esquerra Republicana de Catalunya*] (ERC). Finally, in 2008, Zapatero's investiture was possible thanks to the abstention of IU, CiU, PNV, and three smaller regionalist or regional nationalist parties, the abovementioned CC, the left-wing Galician National Block [*Bloque Nacionalista Galego*] (BNG), and Navarre Yes [*Nafarroa Bai*] (NaBai), a left-wing pro-Basque nationalist party operating in Navarre.

Throughout this cycle, the combined seats of the two major parties tended to be larger than in the other three periods, and the legislatures lasted longer, in spite of the substantive variations in the levels of participation, in government policies, in opposition strategies and in the alignments of the main parties with their voters (Montero 2008).

The precise boundaries of this cycle may be debated. On the one hand, several of its characteristics are already present in the 1993 election. On the other hand, the 2011 election witnessed some changes that were forcefully amplified in the fourth cycle. The support for the PSOE suffered a sharp decline, much in line with the trend for many members of the Socialist and Social Democratic party family in other European countries (Hanretty, 2015), and a centre-left party, Union, Progress and Democracy [*Unión, Progreso y Democracia*] (UPyD), as well as the traditional radical left party, IU, experienced a significant surge in their vote share.

The fourth and last cycle is the one of the *demise of bipartisanship* and opens a new scenario of *precarious governance*. The new electoral earthquake of the 2015 general elections (with more than 35 per cent volatility, only comparable to the one experienced in 1982) supposed a sharp cut in the combined share of PP and PSOE votes (down to 51.1 per cent from 74.4 in 2011) and seats (60.9 from 84.6), sent IU and UPyD to the morgue, and left behind the irruption of two new relevant national players: We Can (with more than five million votes and 69 out of the 350 seats) and Cs (three and a half million votes and 40 seats).[4] The combination of a balanced distribution of seats of the national parties in each ideological block (PP plus Cs had 163 seats and PSOE plus We Can 159) and the difficulty of obtaining enough support from regional parties (given the complicated situation in Catalonia) precluded the formation of any government.

Thus, new elections were called for 20 June 2016. The full results of these (and all the other elections) are reflected in Table 2.A1 (in terms of vote shares) and Table 2.A2 (in terms of seats). Again, the distribution of votes was similar for both ideological blocks, but the belief that citizens would be outraged if negotiations failed again to yield a government allowed Mariano Rajoy to set up the government with lower parliamentary muscle (only 39.1 per cent of the seats share) since 1977. Hence, less than two years later Pedro Sánchez was able to overthrow it with a censure vote, only to install an even weaker government (24.3 per cent of the seats) which had to call for early elections given the obstacles it faced for passing legislation.

It is in this context, in the two elections celebrated in 2019, that VOX surged as one of the new key political players on the board, as we have already commented above. As Table 2.1 reveals, the XIV legislature has brought about the first (minoritarian) coalition government at the national level in Spanish post-Francoist history.

Party system dimensions

Figure 2.1. summarizes four indicators commonly used to understand the stability or change of party systems: electoral volatility, electoral fragmentation, levels of turnout, and electoral competitiveness. Bartolini and Mair (1990: 19) defined electoral volatility as the "net electoral change between two consecutive elections". In this sense, Lane and Ersson (2007) established a threshold of the 15 per cent of electoral volatility to talk about high levels of changes among parties between elections.

In Spain, these digits were just achieved in four (1982, 2011, 2015, and April 2019) elections: one belonged to the first electoral cycle, one to the third one and two to the most recent (fourth) electoral cycle. With the exception of the 1982 "critical elections", the most remarkable one is the election of 2015, which supposed the end of the intensified competition between PSOE and PP during the third electoral cycle and the beginning of unstable voters supporting new party brands.

As Montero (2008) and recently Rama (2016) underlined, most of these changes of voting preferences took place within blocks, i.e. among electors that support the same family of parties (from a left to another left party or from a right to another right party). Thus, although the fourth electoral cycle displays higher levels of instability, most of the changes are transfers among parties that belong to the same ideological family: PSOE and Podemos in 2015 and 2016; and PP, VOX and Cs in April and November 2019.

Regarding the trends of electoral fragmentation (an index that considers the number of parties with electoral support as well as their percentage shares of votes), three periods are clearly distinguishable. The first one coincides with the foundational elections, with high levels of electoral fragmentation, and without any majority party. The second one corresponds with the second and third electoral cycles: the dominance of PSOE and the intensification in the competition between PSOE and PP. Not in vain, from 1982 to 2011, the two major parties combined (PSOE and PP) obtained a mean of 75.9 per cent of the votes and 86.2 of the seats. The third one starts in 2015, with the beginning of the last electoral cycle.

Since 2015, the party system turned from a two-party-plus system (in which PSOE and PP enjoyed a dominant position; IU was, with varying degrees of success, the third most voted party, and several subnational regionalist and nationalist parties obtained seats in their constituencies) to a more fragmentated one. At the begging of the cycle (2015 and 2016), the party system was headed by four major national parties (PSOE, PP, Podemos, and Cs) which, in the April 2019 elections, became

16 Genesis and expansion of VOX

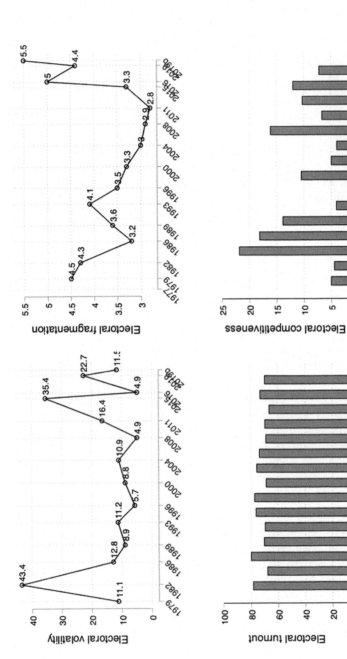

FIGURE 2.1 Party system indicators

Source: Elaboration of the authors based on Rama (2019).

five, given the ascent of VOX. However, the November 2019 elections returned to a format with four large parties, given the spectacular loss of seats of Cs (from 57 to ten).

Subnational parties retained and even increased their presence in the Spanish Congress in this cycle, further contributing to the fragmentation of the Spanish party system. Within the nationalist camp, at least two relevant developments took place: in Catalonia, ERC caught up and even surpassed CiU and its successors, establishing itself as the main Catalan force in the Spanish parliament.[5] In a similar vein, in the Basque Country, the left-wing nationalist party Basque Country Unite [*Euskal Herria Bildu*] (EH Bildu) managed to reduce the distance from PNV in the two 2019 elections.

Hence, while in most of the previous legislatures the dominance of the two main national parties was so notorious that Spain was often referred to as a case of an imperfect bipartisan or a two-party-plus system, its current party system fits better a new definition: extreme pluralism (Rama, 2019: 108).

In this regard, the evolution of the levels of electoral competitiveness, measured by the difference in the percentage of votes between the first and second most voted political parties (UCD and PSOE in 1977 and 1979, and PSOE and PP since 1982), demonstrates that while the first electoral cycle was characterized by high levels of competitiveness, the second one, at least until its last elections (1993), exhibits clearly the dominance of PSOE. Then, from 1996 to 2008, the electoral competitiveness intensified, thanks to the growth of the PP, which emerged as a viable alternative to substitute the PSOE in the government. The most recent elections (2015, 2016, and April and November 2019) display moderate levels of competitiveness. Thus, while in the first ones (2015 and 2016) the PP achieved a significant difference with regard to the PSOE, in the last two, both of them celebrated in 2019, it was the PSOE, the political option with the highest support, followed at a certain distance by the PP (in the April elections, the PP obtained its worst result since its refunding in 1989: 66 seats).

Finally, with the exception of the first elections (1977) and the ones of the earthquake (1982), the rest of the elections exhibit moderate levels of electoral participation (the mean was 72 per cent), being the ones with the highest levels of competitiveness and also those with the higher levels of turnout: 1993 with 76.4 per cent; 1996 with 77.4 per cent, and 2004 with 75.7 per cent.

The recent elections of April 2019 meant, as well, an increase in the levels of participation. Although the competitiveness was not intense, a new political option, VOX, could mobilize some sectors of the electorate that, until recent elections, had preferred to stay at home instead of going to the polls to cast a vote (Pirro and Portos, 2020; Anduiza et al., 2019).

VOX origins: a PP split

The story of VOX is the story of its leader. Santiago Abascal, VOX's current president, occupied relevant positions in the PP since he was 18, when he enrolled in

18 Genesis and expansion of VOX

the party's youth wing. At the age of 20, he joined the PP's provincial committee in Álava, entering the executive committee just a few years later. Then, he was designated president of the party's youth wing in the Basque Country, member of the national directive of PP, and member of the PP's executive in the Basque Country.

However, in 2013 Abascal decided to abandon the PP and, just one month later, he contributed to launch VOX. Behind his choice were disagreements with Mariano Rajoy, who led the PP from 2004 to 2018, on some policies related to ETA[6] prisoners and the allegedly permissive attitude of the PP towards the Catalan secessionist movement (Sangiao, 2018).[7] Indeed, in the letter that Abascal wrote to justify his decision to exit the PP, he blamed the European Court of Human Rights' sentence that put an end to the "Parot doctrine"[8] and, as a consequence, the automatic release of ETA prisoners (Queralt Jiménez, 2018). The perceived inaction of the PP against both this sentence and against a battery of repeated allegations of systemic corruption affecting the PP were the straw that broke the camel's back (Sangiao, 2018).

VOX was officially founded in December 2013 and presented to the press in January 2014 with the intention of competing in the forthcoming European elections of May 2014. Within the circles of the party's hierarchy, the origins of VOX are clearly linked to the PP. As Table 2.2 shows, several of their main founders came from the PP or from foundations or institutes linked to it, such as

TABLE 2.2 Main founders of VOX

	Relationship with VOX	*Origin*
Alejo Vidal-Quadras	First party President and Candidate for the 2014 European Parliament elections	President of the Catalan branch of the PP, member of its national executive, Director of FAES, *DENAES*
Ana Velasco Vidal-Abarca	Militant	Villacisneros Foundation[a]
Cristina Seguí	Ex-militant	–
Enrique Álvarez López	Militant	–
Ignacio Camuñas Solís	Ex-Vice-President and ex-militant	Co-founder and ex Minister of UCD
Iván Espinosa de los Monteros	Spokesman, former Vice-President, ex-General Secretariat	Ex-Secretary of *DENAES*
José Antonio Ortega Lara	Militant	Ex-militant of the PP
José Luis González Quirós	Second President (ad interim), ex-militant	UCD, CDS, ex-militant of the PP, FAES
María Jesús Prieto-Laffargue	Ex-militant	General Direction in the first Aznar Government (PP)
Santiago Abascal	President	PP, President of *DENAES*

a: Online access: www.fundacionvillacisneros.es/

Source: Elaboration of the authors, on the basis of Sangiao (2018) and www.voxespana.es.

the right-wing think tank founded by Abascal in 2006, DENAES[9] [*Fundación para la Defensa de la Nación Española*] and the PP's main think-tank FAES[10] [*Fundación para el Análisis y el Estudio*].

Just to give an example, Alejo Vidal-Quadras, first president of VOX, and well known for his participation in right-wing national political talk shows like Intereconomía or 13tv, had been the president of the PP in Catalonia and a member of the party's National Board of Directors, while Santiago Abascal, as we previously mentioned, had held relevant positions in the Basque Country's PP. Additionally, Abascal occupied a discretionally appointed position in the Community of Madrid, becoming the Director of the Data Protection Agency from 2012 to 2013, and in April 2013 he was appointed, thanks to the intervention of the former President of the Region of Madrid, Esperanza Aguirre (PP), as Director of the Foundation for Patronage and Social Sponsorship. In sum, VOX can be considered as a scission of the mainstream PP (Döring and Manow, 2020).

Table 2.3 summarizes the relevant milestones to understand VOX's development from 2012 to 2020. We highlight four of the most important ones, starting with VOX's first electoral participation in the May 2014 European elections, only some months after the party's public presentation in January 2014. In those elections, its top candidate Vidal-Quadras, who at the time served as president of the party, obtained 246,833 votes and almost gained a seat: with just 50,000 votes more, the coalition European Spring [*Primavera Europea*] took home a seat. Shortly after the elections, there was a reshuffling of the party elite: Vidal-Quadras resigned to prevent the fragmentation of the vote for the right and to combat the upsurge of radical left formations like the also newly founded Podemos,[11] and Santiago Abascal was designated as president.

The second relevant milestone was the implication of VOX as a popular prosecutor in the trial of Catalan independence leaders, commonly known as the *Procés*, alluding to the process envisioned by these leaders for the creation of a new Catalan state. The process itself was the consequence of a series of developments that were set in motion in the beginning of the 2010s. Facing several judicial trials because of large political corruption scandals, CiU, headed by its new leader Artur Mas, embarked Catalan nationalists on a series of anti-constitutional activities, including an unauthorized unilateral consultation in 2014, the proclamation of a so-called rupture or transitional law by the regional parliament in September 2017, the holding of a second unauthorized plebiscite on 1 October, and the regional government's subsequent and ephemeral unilateral declaration of independence on 27 October (Montero and Santana, 2020).

Catalan separatist leaders underwent trial for misuse of public funds, disobedience, and either sedition or rebellion, depending on the case. The role of VOX as a popular prosecutor against Catalan independence leaders gave notoriety to the party, which started to attract relevant presence in the media (Turnbull-Dugarte et al., 2020). It suffices to say that, during these times, at least in the eyes of an important section of right-wing voters, VOX represented the sole Spanish political party able to stand up to the Catalan independence movement.[12]

20 Genesis and expansion of VOX

TABLE 2.3 Political landmarks related to the emergence of VOX, 2012–2020

2012	
	Website reconversion.es established. Several of the founders of VOX participated in this platform, which advocated for recentralizing the state.
2013	
17 December	VOX (voice in Latin) was founded by former members of the PP (Alejo Vidal-Quadras; Santiago Abascal, and José Antonio Ortega Lara).
2014	
16 January	VOX was formally presented at a conference with invited media delegates.
8 March	Alejo Vidal-Quadras elected as President of VOX.
25 May	Elections to the European Parliament (VOX obtained 246,833 votes and 1.6% of the vote).
20 September	Abascal installed as the party's new president and Espinosa de los Monteros named the new secretary general.
2015	
22 March	VOX won 0.23% of the vote in the Andalusian regional elections.
24 May	VOX won 0.29% of the vote in the local elections.
24 May	VOX participated in 9 of the 13 regions and one of the two autonomous cities that held regional elections and won a simple average of 0.62% of the vote.
27 September	Regional elections in Catalonia took place, but VOX did not participate.
20 December	VOX participated in the general elections and won 0.23% of the vote.
2016	
26 June	VOX participated in the general elections and won 0.20% of the vote.
25 September	VOX participated in the Basque regional elections, with Abascal as leading candidate, and obtained 0.07% of the vote; the party did not participate in the concurrent Galician regional elections.
2017	
6 November	VOX joined lawsuit against the Catalan independence leaders in the case of the Procés as a popular prosecutor.
21 December	Regional elections in Catalonia took place, but VOX did not participate.
2018	
10 September	A regional MP from the parliament in Extremadura left the PP and joined VOX.
6 October	VOX held a national rally in the Vistalegre Palace.
2 December	VOX participated in the Andalusian regional elections and won 10.96% of the vote.
2019	
10 January	PP and Cs agreed to form a coalition government in Andalucía. VOX gave external support to this coalition government.
16 January	Juan Manuel Moreno (PP), elected president of the regional government of Andalucía with the support of Ciudadanos and the external support of VOX.
10 February	VOX, PP and Ciudadanos held a rally in Plaza Colón (Madrid) calling on early elections under the banner "For a united Spain, elections now!".
12 February	Trial against Catalan secessionists began in the Spanish Supreme Court.

Genesis and expansion of VOX **21**

TABLE 2.3 Cont.

15 February	Pedro Sánchez announced early elections to take place on 28 April.
22 April	First televized debate between four presidential candidates: Pedro Sánchez (PSOE), Pablo Casado (PP), Albert Rivera (Ciudadanos), and Pablo Iglesias (Unidas Podemos). VOX excluded from participating.
28 April	VOX participated in the concurrent Spanish general elections and the Valencian regional elections and won 10.26% and 10.59% of the vote, respectively.
21 May	Inauguration of the 13th Spanish legislature. Meritxell Batet (PSOE) elected president of the Congress and Manuel Cruz (PSOE) of the Senate.
26 May	Super Sunday: European Parliament elections, regional elections in 12 of Spain's 17 regions, and local elections took place. VOX obtained 6.21% of the vote in the European elections, a simple mean of 6.97% in the regional elections, and 3.57% in the local elections.
7 June	Pedro Sánchez invited to seek to form a government by King Felipe VI.
24 June	Toni Roldán (Economics spokesperson and head of party programme) and Javier Nart (European Parliament deputy) resigned from Ciudadanos as they disagreed with Albert Rivera's refusal to negotiate a government with the PSOE and with the party's association with VOX.
22 July	Beginning of the investment debates for the presidency of Spain.
23 July	Pedro Sánchez failed to be invested as president after being unable to gain an absolute majority of supporting votes in Congress.
25 July	Pedro Sánchez failed to gain a simple majority in a second voting round and was unable to be invested as the country's president.
26 July	The PP's candidate in Murcia, Fernando López Miras, was designated President of the Region with the support of Cs and the external support of VOX (with whom a legislature agreement was signed).
14 August	The PP candidate in Madrid, Isabel Díaz Ayuso, was designated President of the Region with the support of Cs and the external support of VOX.
23 September	Without any agreement among parties regarding the formation of a government, the legal timescales expire leading to the automatic call for new general elections on 10 November.
14 October	The Spanish Supreme Court published the sentence of the case against Catalan separatists.
24 October	Remains of the former dictator, Francisco Franco, were exhumed from the Valley of the Fallen [Valle de los Caídos].
27 October	Massive demonstrations in Barcelona for "la Concordia" (the concord) and against secessionism.
10 November	VOX participated in the general elections and won 15.09% of the vote.
12 November	PSOE and Unidas Podemos unexpectedly announced they that had reached a "pre-agreement" leading to formal coalition talks.
30 December	PSOE and Unidas Podemos published their coalition agreement.
2020	
7 January	Pedro Sánchez failed to be invested as president after failing to gain an absolute majority of support in Congress.

(continued)

22 Genesis and expansion of VOX

TABLE 2.3 Cont.

10 January	Pedro Sánchez was elected President of Spain after gaining a simple majority in Congress with the support of his coalition partner, UP, and the external support of regional minority parties.
12 July	VOX participated in the concurrent Basque and Galician regional elections, and won 1.26% and 2.03 of the vote, respectively.
29 July	VOX announced a vote of no confidence against Pedro Sánchez.
2021	
14 February	VOX won 7.69% of the vote and 11 of 135 seats in the Catalan regional elections.

Source: Elaboration of the authors.

The third relevant milestone is the national rally held by the party on 6 October 2018, in which it managed to fill the Vistalegre Palace with more than 9,000 supporters, in what can be regarded as the party's first show of force. The success of the rally and the ensuing media attention it received served to signal to eventual voters of the party that VOX could become a relevant player in the Spanish political arena, and that their potential vote for it would not be wasted. The leadership of the party is fully aware of the relevance of the Vistalegre rally, as the letter of invitation to the 2019 rally, also in the Vistalegre Palace, attests:

> […] we met in Vistalegre prepared to defend and strengthen Spain, our home-land. Until then, the progressive dictatorship thought that we the Spanish had surrendered, and that we would allow the Nation to be broken down, our children to be indoctrinated, […] and fiscally plundered to sustain their decentralized system of government […] (Santiago Abascal 2019, www.voxespana.es/noticias/plus-ultra-vox-vuelve-a-vistalgre-un-ano-despues-20190906).

The fourth and last milestone we intend to highlight here is the formation of a coalition government between PP and Cs in Andalusia with the external support of VOX in January 2019. This is important because the reaction of other political forces to the appearance of populist radical right parties varies from country to country, as many works, several of them concerned with radical parties' mainstreaming, attest (Akkerman et al., 2016a; Mudde, 2019).

Some of these parties, like the Austrian Freedom Party [*Freiheitliche Partei Österreichs*] (FPÖ), have formed part of the cabinet; others, like the Danish People's Party [*Dansk Folkeparti*] (DF), have provided external support to minority governments without forming part of them, and still others, like the French National Rally [*Rassemblement National*] (RN), have been subjected to a cordon sanitaire that has kept them away from office (Akkerman et al., 2016b).

As VOX is the first successful party of the kind in Spain, the position adopted by the two mainstream parties on the right and centre-right side of the political spectrum was crucial for the party's long-term prospects of having an influence on policy-making. The negotiations for the Andalusian government fit into the second, intermediate case: although VOX is not a member of the governing coalition, which is restricted to PP and Cs, these parties accepted its support to seize government, and accepted several conditions as well in exchange for VOX's support. The Andalusian model has moreover been emulated in July in Murcia and in August in Madrid, consolidating the figure of VOX as a potential external supporter of right-wing minority cabinets.

VOX electoral growth

Only some months after its foundation, VOX participated for the first time in the 2014 European elections and received 1.57 per cent of the vote, failing to gain any representation in the European legislature. In 2015, the party ran for the first time in a national election, obtaining only 0.23 per cent (58,114 votes). Then, in the snap election of June 2016, the party's electoral support decreased slightly to 0.20 per cent (47,182 votes).

The party remained marginal until the 2018 Andalusian elections, in which its support suddenly mounted to 10.97 per cent of the votes (395,978), gaining 12 of 109 seats available in the regional parliament. As mentioned before, this success seems to be grounded on the events related to the Catalan pro-independence movement that gained salience in the aftermath of late 2017 (Turnbull-Dugarte 2019). In the lead-up to the Andalusian elections, Abascal made a clamorous speech in front of thousands of Spaniards convened by DENAES for a demonstration in favour of a united Spain.

Following the success in Andalusia, VOX consolidated its presence in all levels of government, as shown in Table 2.4. Thus, in April 2019, it won 10 per cent of the vote and 24 out of 350 seats in the National Congress (and 10 out of 99 seats in the parliament of the region of Valencia). This result allowed the party to jump to the national level and partially reshape the Spanish party system. Just one month later, on 24 May 2019, the party obtained 6.21 per cent of the votes in the European elections, which translated into four of the 54 seats assigned to Spain in the European Parliament. In the concurrent regional elections, VOX's electoral fortunes varied across the regions. Crucially, however, the party was able to signal its political significance, surpassing the electoral threshold for representation in seven out of the 12 autonomous communities that held elections that day. Across the different regions, the party increased its number of regional seats from zero to 49 (plus 8 in the two autonomous cities).

The electoral ascent of VOX across the different regions in Spain is significant given the high levels of devolved powers that the regions enjoy (Hooghe et al. 2016). Importantly, the existing right-wing parties (PP and Cs) were unwilling to enter coalition talks with the new right-wing challenger but, as explained above, they were ready to accept their external support. Although formally excluded from right-leaning coalition governments, VOX's support to them played a crucial role in several important regions like the abovementioned cases of Madrid (home to the country's capital city), Murcia and Andalusia.

Finally, the outcome of the November 2019 snap general election is well known, as VOX raised 15.09 per cent of the votes and 52 out of 350 seats in the Congress

24   Genesis and expansion of VOX

TABLE 2.4 VOX's electoral performance since December 2018 Andalusian elections

Elections	Date	Institution	Seats	Seats	% seats	Votes	% votes
General	28/04/2019	Congress	350	24	6.86	2,688,092	10.26
	10/11/2019	Congress	350	52	14.86	3,640,063	15.09
		Senate	208	2	0.96	3,204,496	5.12
European	26/05/2019	European Parliament	54	3	5.56	1,393,684	6.21
Regional	02/12/2018	Andalusia	109	12	11.01	396,607	10.96
	28/04/2019	Valencia region	99	10	10.10	278,947	10.59
	26/05/2019	Aragon	67	3	4.48	40,671	6.08
		Asturias	45	2	4.44	33,784	6.42
		Balearic Islands	59	3	5.08	34,668	8.12
		Cantabria	35	2	5.71	16,392	5.05
		Castile and León	81	1	1.23	75,331	5.49
		Madrid region	132	12	9.09	285,099	8.86
		Murcia region	45	4	8.89	61,591	9.46
	12/07/2020	Galicia	75	0	0	26,485	2.03
		Basque Country	75	1	1.3	17,517	1.96
void	14/02/2021	Catalonia	135	11	8.15	217,371	7.84
Local	26/05/2019	City of Madrid	57	4	7.02	124,252	7.63
		City of Valencia	33	2	6.06	28,126	7.25
		City of Seville	31	2	6.45	25,122	7.95
		City of Zaragoza	31	2	6.45	20,392	6.15
		City of Murcia	29	3	10.34	21,078	10.17
		Palma	29	4	13.79	19,111	13.11
		City of Alicante	29	2	6.90	8,578	6.38
		City of Córdoba	29	2	6.90	11,788	8.04
		City of Valladolid	27	1	3.70	10,665	6.33
		Gijón	27	2	7.41	9,517	7.01
		City of Granada	27	3	11.11	10,203	9.42
		Elche	27	2	7.41	6,024	5.93

Source: Elaboration of the authors, based on Santana and Rama (2019).

of Deputies, which placed it as the third largest party of the country. Table 2.4 summarizes the results of VOX since its entrance in the Andalusian Parliament in December 2018, including the 2020 regional elections of Galicia and the Basque Country and the 2021 ones of Catalonia. VOX was only able to achieve one seat in the Basque Country, while Galicia remained free of any (neither left nor right) populist party. In Catalonia, VOX obtained 11 out of 135 seats.

VOX has grown rapidly, and the party has managed to enter all institutional levels, but it is important to remark that its territorial penetration is markedly unequal. To appreciate this, we have gathered data from its electoral performance at the regional level in different types of elections. Table 2.5 displays the electoral support of the party in the 17 autonomous communities and the two autonomous cities of the country. We display the results of the two 2019 general elections, the 2019 elections to the European Parliament, and the two last regional elections which, in most regions, where held in 2019 and 2015.

TABLE 2.5 VOX's electoral performance, by region

Region	General elections		European elections	Regional elections	
	November 2019	April 2019	May 2019	May 2019 [a]	May 2015 [a]
Ceuta (autonomous city)	35.19	23.93	20.58	22.37	1.22
Murcia (region)	27.95	18.62	11.12	9.46	0.87
Castile-La Mancha	21.90	15.28	8.21	7.02	0.48
Andalusia	20.36	13.37	7.56	10.96 [b]	0.45 [b]
Valencia (region)	18.46	12.01	7.23	10.59 [c]	0.41 [c]
Melilla (autonomous city)	18.40	17.20	10.50	7.76	NP
Madrid (region)	18.34	13.86	9.89	8.86	1.17
Balearic Islands	17.07	11.30	7.66	8.12	NP
Aragón	16.97	12.19	7.91	6.08	NP
Extremadura	16.82	10.77	5.65	4.00	0.28
Castile-Leon	16.61	12.28	7.18	5.49	0.68
Asturias	15.86	11.49	7.45	6.42	0.59
Cantabria	14.39	11.18	6.83	5.05	0.34
Canary Islands	12.45	6.56	3.31	2.47	0.20
La Rioja	11.46	8.99	5.22	3.86	NP
Galicia	7.82	5.29	2.60	2.03 [d]	NP [d]
Catalonia	6.29	3.59	1.99	7.84 [e]	NP [e]
Navarre	5.80	4.86	4.22	1.29	NP
Basque country	2.45	2.21	1.22	1.96 [d]	0.07 [d]

Notes: Key: NP = VOX did not run in these elections. Table sorted from highest to lowest vote shares in the November 2019 general elections.

a: The regional elections of Andalusia, Galicia, Catalonia, and the Basque Country are celebrated in different dates and, in 2019, this was also the case in the Valencian region.

b: Andalusian elections were held on December 2018 and March 2015.

c: Valencian elections were held on April 2019, concurrently with the general elections.

d: Galician elections were held on July 2020 and September 2016, concurrently with Basque elections.

e: Catalonian elections were held on February 2021 and December 2017 (and September 2016).

Source: Elaboration of the authors, on the basis of data from the Spanish Ministry of the Interior (www. infoelectoral.mir.es).

To be true, holding the electoral level constant, VOX has grown throughout the whole Spanish territory: its results in the 2019 November general elections outperformed those of the April elections in all the regions without exception, and likewise its results in the last regional elections systematically improved those of the former ones.

There is nonetheless considerable disparity among regions. VOX systematically attains its best results in the North African autonomous city of Ceuta, whereas its worst results tend to be those of the Basque Country. For instance, in the November 2019 general elections, VOX's vote share ranged from a high of 35.19 per cent in Ceuta to a low of 2.45 in the Basque Country. The limited success of VOX in the

26 Genesis and expansion of VOX

TABLE 2.6 Electoral performance of UPyD and Cs in regions with competing national identities

Party	Spain, average	Basque Country	Navarre	Catalonia	Galicia	Balearic Islands	Valencia (region)
UPyD, 2011	4.70	1.80	2.06	1.15	1.21	4.23	**5.60**
Cs, 2015	13.94	4.11	7.07	13.05	9.06	**14.78**	**15.84**
Cs, 2016	13.06	3.53	6.11	10.94	8.62	**14.57**	**14.96**

a Highlighted in bold those regions where parties obtained higher than average results.

Source: Elaboration of the authors, on the basis of data from the Spanish Ministry of the Interior (www.infoelectoral.mir.es) for the 2011, 2015 and 2016 general elections.

Basque Country is especially noteworthy, given the relevance of Basque politicians and intellectuals in the foundation of the party and the Basque origin of its leader. Indeed, it was Abascal's candidacy where VOX received the worst result: 0.07 per cent of the votes in the 2015 Basque regional election. Murcia, Castile-La Mancha, and Andalusia also surpassed the 20 per cent threshold in the last general election, while Navarre, Catalonia and Galicia did not reach the 10 per cent one. Interestingly, VOX did not attempt to compete in Navarre, Catalonia, and Galicia in the first regional elections in which it could have done so.

Notice that the four regions where the results of VOX are more modest all have strong national identities that compete with the Spanish one. However, its results are above the average in two other regions that share this trait, the region of Valencia and the Balearic Islands.

To dig a bit further into this issue, we gathered the electoral results of UPyD in 2011 and Cs in 2015 and 2016, i.e. when VOX was still small and had little effect on the performance of Cs. As in the case of VOX, the reason for the foundation of UPyD and Cs had much to do with the national question in the Basque Country and Catalonia. Table 2.6 shows that both UPyD (which was more concerned with the Basque case) and Cs (which has a closer relationship with the Catalan one) obtained worse than average electoral results in the Basque Country, Navarre, Catalonia, and Galicia, but better than average results in the Balearic Islands and Valencia. This matches the patterns of results for VOX presented above.

Hence, the lower appeal in the former four regions and the greater allure in the latter two does not seem to be a peculiar characteristic of VOX or of a given election. On the contrary, this territorial pattern of support has been shared during a decade by the three parties that have aimed to combat what they regard as the evils of decentralization and regionalism: UPyD, Cs, and VOX. The results of the 2021 Catalan elections suggest that VOX may break this pattern.

VOX internal organization

According to VOX's webpage (www.voxespana.es/espana/organos-internos), the party is structured in three major organs: the National Executive Committee,

TABLE 2.7 Members of VOX's internal organs [a]

Organ	Current member	Profession
National Executive Committee		
President	Santiago Abascal	Sociologist
Political Vice-President	Jorge Buxadé	Lawyer
Economic Vice-President	Víctor González	Business administration
Social Vice-President	Reyes Romero	Saleswoman
Treasurer	Pablo Sáez	Auditor, consultant
Secretary General	Javier Ortega Smith	Lawyer
Member 1	Rocío de Meer	Lawyer
Member 2	Ignacio Garriga	Dentist
Member 3	Enrique Cabanas	Businessman
Member 4	Juan Luis Steegman	Physician, researcher
Member 5	María Ruiz	Journalist, businesswoman
Member 6	Pedro Fernández	Lawyer
National Vice-Secretariats		
of the Presidency	Enrique Cabanas	Businessman
of the Spokesperson	Patricia Rueda	Public Relations
of Relations with the Courts	Macarena Olona	Lawyer
of Communication	Manuel Mariscal	Journalist
of Institutional Relations	Ana Velasco	Journalist
of International Relations	Iván Espinosa	Business administration, businessman
of Management	Juan José Aizcorbe	Lawyer
of Organization	Tomás Fernández	Lawyer, business management
of Affiliation	Virginia Martínez	Computing
of Resources	Víctor González	Computing
of Legal Issues	Marta Castro	Lawyer
of Training	Begoña Conde	Political scientist

a Data presented in the table reflect the positions as of August 2020.

Source: Elaboration of the authors, on the basis of www.voxespana.es/espana/organos-internos (consulted on August 18 2020).

the National Vice-Secretariats, and the Electoral Committee. Table 2.7 shows the current members of the first two; the Electoral Committee is conformed by the members of the party's Guarantee Commission (who must have law degrees), but their members have yet not been revealed. The National Executive Committee is the most relevant organ and defines the party's strategy. It is comprised of a president, three vice-presidents, a treasurer, a secretary general, and six members.

There are 12 national vice-secretariats, which manage specific functions and act following the instructions of the president and the secretary general. The aforementioned vice-secretaries or deputy secretaries are not part of the National Executive Committee, but their presence may be required by the president or by the general secretary to report on matters within their competence.

The Electoral Committee is the guarantor of the internal democracy of the party, including the transparency, objectivity, and effectiveness of VOX's electoral processes. Since the approval of the current Internal Regulation of Election Procedures, the Electoral Committee is constituted following the National Executive Committee's calls for internal election processes. During them, the Electoral Committee is the highest decision-making body, with decision-making and sanctioning power in electoral matters. It exercises its functions autonomously and independently of the rest of the party's organs, adopting its decisions in a collegiate manner. To ensure their independence, members of the Electoral Committee may not simultaneously belong to any executive body of the party, unless they expressly agree to abstain from resolutions that affect the executive body to which they may belong.

How does VOX select its candidates?

Since the beginning of the century, there is a general trend towards more participatory mechanisms of selecting candidates and leaders by political parties (Cross and Katz, 2013; Cross and Pilet, 2015; Hazan and Rahat, 2010). Democracy within parties has increased from the beginning of the economic crisis as a reaction to anti-party feelings and political disaffection (Cordero et al., 2016). In this sense, new parties are putting forward more inclusive selection methods to improve their electoral expectations and decrease the gap between citizens and politics.

In the case of Spain, although the constitution formally states that the parties' internal structure and functioning must be democratic, the lack of specific regulations has allowed party elites to dominate the rules selecting party candidates.[13] With the exception of Podemos, none of the main parties has held any primaries to select the whole list of candidates running in any election. Thus, their leaders have been able to retain the control over candidate selection (Hopkin, 2001). Moreover, the closed electoral lists in all types of elections (but the Senate) confer an enormous power to national or, in some instances, regional party leaders in the selection of candidates and, consequently, in the composition of those who will later hold a seat in a representative chamber (Cordero et al., 2016). However, in recent years the use of primaries as a method of selecting party leaders and candidates is becoming more common, especially among new parties, like Cs, UPyD and Podemos (Barberá et al., 2014; Rodríguez Teruel and Barberà, 2017; Pérez-Nievas et al., 2018).

The two main political parties, PP and PSOE, have traditionally suffered from weak internal democracy (Pérez-Moneo, 2012). Although they have introduced some internal democracy provisions as well, their reach has been rather limited. The only primaries held by the PP took place in July 2018 for the national leadership of the party, and were to some extent *sui generis* in that they comprised two rounds, the first one among the affiliates (58,305 voted), but the second one only among the 3,184 party delegates, which handed the leadership to Pablo Casado (thereby *amending* the affiliates' vote, which had placed Soraya Sáenz de Santamaría first and Casado second).[14]

The PSOE has a longer tradition of primaries to select some of its local, regional, and national leaders. However, these primaries are sporadic and intermittent, instead of systematic: most of its leaders are not selected by them, and some of those who are, like Gabilondo in the also *sui generis* 2018 primaries in the region of Madrid, run as sole, uncontested candidates. Moreover, the PSOE first introduced primaries among delegates: this was the case of the process to select Alfredo Pérez Rubalcaba as National Secretary instead of Carmen Chacón. The first primary among all its affiliates took place in 2014, whereby Pedro Sánchez was elected as Secretary General of the PSOE.

In the case of Podemos, the study conducted by Pérez-Nievas and collaborators (2018) demonstrates that, while in terms of candidacy, i.e. those liable to be eligible as candidates in party for elections, Podemos is inclusive (party membership is not required: it suffices to register oneself on the party's website and obtain the endorsement of at least one of the party's local clubs or *Círculos*), the voting procedures significantly distort the voters' preferences over candidates. On top of voting for individual candidacies, it is possible for those who are registered in Podemos's website to vote for lists of candidacies: the existence of block voting enables the best-known candidates to drag with them other candidates who are within their list and who are of their confidence. Moreover, the voting system is far from providing the expected proportional representation, given that the preferences expressed by the voters in the primaries suffer a three-fold revision: they are superseded by the inclusion of some candidates from other parties, due to the regional agreements of Podemos to present joint lists with them; refined by the inclusion of the so-called *fichajes*, i.e. relevant personalities that the leaders of the party allocate in different positions of the list; and corrected by the gender quotas.

In sum, while in the last few years the procedures to select candidates have improved in terms of their democratization, it is also true that new parties, which usually are considered the most internally democratic ones (or those that make more public claims about it), are far from perfect examples of a democratic way to select candidates in general, regional or local elections.

We briefly analyse the candidates' selection procedure followed by VOX in the April 2019 general elections through the operationalization proposed by Hazan and Rahat (2010: 18) based on four dimensions, each of which provides information on the following questions: (a) who can be selected as the party's candidate? (Candidacy); (b) who selects the candidates? (Selectorate); (c) where (at which level) does the selection take place? (Decentralization); and (d) how are the candidates selected? (Voting systems). Table 2.8 summarizes our analyses.

Initially, candidate selection in VOX followed the procedures of its Foundational Manifesto, which envisioned the selection of both internal positions and of candidates for public offices in conferences opened to all party members; however, these procedures were no longer efficient when the party grew, so its General Assembly altered it in February 2019 (Barrio, 2020).

Currently, the way to select candidates for the different elections in VOX is defined in the Statutes (Norms) of the Party, Article 24 "Procedure for the

30 Genesis and expansion of VOX

TABLE 2.8 Summary of VOX candidate selection

Candidacy	To be appointed as a candidate, you should be a member of the party. [a] The candidacy is restricted to those members of VOX (the National Executive Committee has the capability to refuse the membership)
Selectorate	Regional and local committees select the candidacy with the final approval of the National Executive Committee.
Voting system/ appointment system	Regional and local committees propose a list of candidates and the National Executive Committee validates it.
Decentralization	Selection is theoretically decentralized (at regional and local level), although the final decision is made by the National Executive Committee.

a: See the requisites to be a member of VOX in the article 6: www.voxespana.es/wp-content/uploads/2020/04/ESTATUTOS-CAMBIOS-PROPUESTOS-CEN-02-03-2020-1.pdf

Source: Elaboration of the authors.

appointment of candidates to elected public offices".[15] Article 24.1 is about the candidates for general, regional and local elections. According to it, the Provincial Executive Committee and the autonomous cities Executive Committee propose the candidates for specific elections to the National Executive Committee from among the affiliates who meet the requirements established by the National Executive Committee. The National Executive Committee reviews, modifies and, where appropriate, approves the final electoral list.

Regarding the candidates for general elections (Congress of Deputies and Senate) and European (European Parliament) ones, and after consulting the regional and local committees, the National Executive Committee approves the lists of the final candidates who meet the requirements established in Article 24.2.

Article 24.3 determines that all those affiliates who are legitimized by the current and internal legislation of the party as candidates for public office may participate as members of a candidacy, in each electoral process, and this without prejudice of the fact that the National Executive Committee, in certain situations, approves the concurrence of independent candidates.

Thus, our analysis of VOX's statutes suggests that its internal procedures to select candidates for the different elections closely resemble what would be expected from a system of direct appointment by the leader. More generally, it appears as though the important decisions in VOX are restricted to a reduced group of insiders, much in line with the oligarchic trends in political forces predicted long ago by Michels (2001 [1911]).

Conclusions

Our analysis of the evolution of the Spanish party system and the characteristics of the surge and rise of VOX have sought to provide a picture of the reasons for the success of the new populist radical right-wing birth and success, and to answer the question: "Why did VOX succeed where all previous like-minded parties in Spain failed?"

We have outlined a picture of the Spanish party system liable to be divided into four cycles: transition, democratic consolidation and Socialist dominance, intensified competition and alternation in power between socialists and (conservative) populars, and demise of partisanship and precarious governance.

Vox was born as a PP-split in 2013, towards the end of the third cycle. Contrasting with the developments in many other European polities, the consequences of the Great Recession had not yet had significant effects on the Spanish party system, and had only given place to another replacement of the Socialist incumbent by the Popular Party, which in 2011 had managed to accumulate an impressive amount of institutional power.

After the electoral earthquake of 1982 (Santamaría, 1984), which marked the transition between the first two cycles, and up to the second quake to the system in 2015, Spain was characterized by producing monotonous patterns of centripetal party competition. Soon after the birth of VOX, the Spanish party system entered the fourth cycle, which could be described as an *open electoral market*. Citizens, who in 2011 had punished the PSOE for its management of the crisis, were deeply unsatisfied with the PP for its management of the post-crisis and for its serious corruption scandals. They started to turn their eyes to new political entrepreneurs. Levels of electoral volatility and partisan fragmentation soared, ideological polarization rose, and the electoral competition became more centrifugal. Political instability mounted as well, and access to the government, one of the main characteristics of party systems (Mair, 1997), became more open.

A window of opportunity for new nationwide parties of medium size started to open. Nonetheless, the infancy of VOX was a tough one: its electoral results in all the contests from 2014 to 2017 were, at best, humble, and in many regional elections and city councils the party simply did not even attempt to run. It remained a marginal party without institutional representation at the national, regional and European level, and with a testimonial number of councillors at the local level.

This is so because, at the beginning, the aforementioned window of opportunity was concentrated in the ideological space at the flanks of the PSOE, so it comes as no surprise that the parties that initially took advantage of the deterioration of the former two-party-plus system were left-wing populist parties like Podemos (Rodríguez-Teruel, Barrio, and Barberà 2016; Santana and Rama 2018) and parties placed close to the centre like UPyD or Cs (Rodríguez Teruel and Barrio, 2016).

However, aided by the corruption scandals that had already aggravated the erosion of the PP's image, and by the motion of no confidence that removed PP's Prime Minister Rajoy from government and further debilitated the main right-wing party, VOX was able to capitalize on the territorial crisis and present itself as the ultimate and most credible line of defence of Spanish nationalism.

Given the overwhelming salience of the territorial issue following the challenge of Catalan secessionist leaders and, most importantly, after the failed (and unlawful) declaration of independence, many of the citizens concerned with the issue decided

32 Genesis and expansion of VOX

to give VOX an opportunity. The role of VOX as a popular prosecutor of the Catalan independentist leaders gave the party media attention, and the show of force in the Vistalegre rally served to present it as a credible alternative.

Starting with the maiden success in the December 2018 Andalusian regional elections, the rest of the story is a sweet one for VOX: they have increased their support in all the regions of Spain and gained access to all the institutional levels of representation. They are currently the third largest party in the country and although they have not been able to enter coalition governments at the regional level or in the city councils of the largest cities, the other right-wing parties, PP and Cs, have accepted their external support in exchange for certain policy conditions.

The future developments of the party are, of course, uncertain, but given its territorial penetration (with representation in most of the Spanish regions) and its role as coalition government facilitator in several regions and in some relevant town halls, VOX meets all the conditions not to be a flash party.

Santiago Abascal and his front-line lieutenants (Rocío Monasterio, Javier Ortega-Smith, Iván Espinosa de los Monteros, Macarena Olona, Jorge Buxadé, and Ignacio Garriga, among others) seem willing to fight in the next elections and present themselves (as they have already done leading a motion of no confidence in the PSOE government in October 2020) as the true alternative to socialism.

Notes

1 The coalition of Podemos with United Left [*Izquierda Unida*].
2 The PSOE obtained 38 seats more than its otherwise lowest mark of 85 in 2016. The PP lost 71 of the 137 seats it held in 2016, obtaining its worst electoral results so far. Cs grew from 32 to 57 seats, UP (now Unidas Podemos instead of Unidos Podemos) fell from 71 to 42, and VOX obtained 24 of the 350 seats.
3 Strictly speaking, in 1989, the PSOE obtained 175 of the 350 seats. In practical terms, this amounted to an absolute majority, as the MPs of Herri Batasuna (HB), a Basque independentist party which was later outlawed due to its connections with the Basque secessionist terrorist organization ETA, never went to the Congress.
4 We Can's main source of voters were former supporters of the PSOE and IU; while Cs came to occupy the centre position that UPyD had had since 2008, although, unlike Rosa Díez's party, it was somewhat more to the right and managed to enter several electoral districts, favoured by disgruntled PP and, to a lesser extent, PSOE former voters.
5 Due to several factors, including legal problems related to corruption scandals, personal frictions among leaders, and differences in the approach regarding the relationship between Catalonia and the rest of Spain, former CiU politicians concurred under several brands in the 2015–2019 period: still CiU in 2015, Democracy and Freedom [*Democràcia i Llibertat*] (DiL) in 2016, and Together for Catalonia [*Junts Per Catalunya*] (JxCAT-JUNTS) in the two 2019 elections. In 2015 and 2016, it obtained eight seats as compared to the nine of ERC; in April and November 2019, the figures are seven versus 15 and eight versus 13, respectively. This is at odds with the dominance that CiU had enjoyed in almost all the previous national elections (in 2011, for instance, it obtained 16 seats, while ERC gained only three).

6 ETA (Euskadi Ta Askatasuna – Basque Country and Liberty) was a Basque nationalist terrorist organization that proclaimed itself independent, nationalist, socialist, and revolutionary. During its 60-year history, between 1958 and 2018, its main objective was the construction of a socialist state in Euskal Herria and its independence from Spain and France.

7 Abascal and his family were threatened by ETA on several occasions.

8 The Parot doctrine is a jurisprudence, following a Sentence of the Spanish Supreme Court, to apply (in cases of serious crimes) the reductions of sentences not to the maximum accumulative sentence of 30 years but to the total term of the Sentence.

9 Online access: https://nacionespanola.org/

10 Online access: https://fundacionfaes.org/es

11 See Vidal-Quadras declarations in one of the TV shows were he usually participated: / www.youtube.com/watch?v=LooOQsVph4o

12 See the report in *El País Semanal* with several interviews to VOX voters: https://elpais.com/elpais/2020/02/07/eps/1581073136_206237.html

13 An exception to the lack of specific regulation on candidate selection is the so-called Equality Law, which requires candidate lists to preserve a gender balance. Its proper name is Ley Orgánica 3/2007, and it was issued on 22 March 2007, during Zapatero's first cabinet. The regulation affecting electoral competition is developed in the Second Additional Provision. www.boe.es/buscar/pdf/2007/BOE-A-2007-6115-consolidado.pdf

14 Four other candidates participated in the first round but lagged behind Santamaría and Casado and therefore did not make it to the next round.

15 See: www.voxespana.es/wp-content/uploads/2020/04/ESTATUTOS-CAMBIOS-PROPUESTOS-CEN-02-03-2020-1.pdf

References

Akkerman T, De Lange SL and Rooduijn M (eds) (2016a) *Radical Right-Wing Populist Parties in Western Europe: Into the Mainstream?* London: Routledge.

Akkerman T, De Lange SL and Rooduijn M (2016b) Inclusion and mainstreaming? Radical right-wing parties in the new millenium. Akkerman T, De Lange SL, and Rooduijn M (eds) *Radical Right-Wing Populist Parties in Western Europe: Into the Mainstream?* London: Routledge, pp. 1–28.

Anduiza E, Bosch A, Orriols LL and Rico G (2014) *Elecciones Generales 2011.* Madrid: Centro de Investigaciones Sociológicas.

Anduiza E, Guinjoan M and Rico G (2019) Populism, participation, and political equality. *European Political Science Review* 11(1):109–124.

Barberà O, Rodríguez Teruel J, Barrio A, et al. (2014) The selection of party leaders in Spain. Pilet J-B (ed.) *The Selection of Political Party Leaders in Contemporary Parliamentary Democracies: A Comparative Study.* London: Routledge, pp. 108–123.

Barrio A (2020) Vox y la irrupción de la derecha radical en España. València: Manuscript.

Bartolini S and Mair P (1990) *Identity, Competition and Electoral Availability: The Stabilization of European Electorates 1885–1985.* Cambridge, UK: Cambridge University Press.

Cordero G, Jaime-Castillo AM and Coller X (2016) Candidate Selection in a Multilevel State: The Case of Spain. *American Behavioral Scientist* 60(7): 853–868. DOI: 10.1177/0002764216632823.

Cross WP and Katz RS (2013) *The Challenges of Intra-Party Democracy.* Oxford, UK: Oxford University Press.

34 Genesis and expansion of VOX

Cross WP and Pilet J-B (2015) *The Politics of Party Leadership: A Cross-National Perspective.* Oxford, UK: Oxford University Press.

Döring H and Manow P (2020) Parliaments and Governments Database (ParlGov): Information on parties, elections and cabinets in modern democracies. Development version. Available at: www.parlgov.org/ (accessed 16 June 2019).

Hanretty C (2015) Electorally, West European social democrats are at their lowest point for forty years. *Medium.* Available at: https://medium.com/@chrishanretty/electorally-west-european-social-democrats-are-at-their-lowest-point-for-forty-years-ac7ae3d8ddb7 (accessed 19 August 2020).

Hazan RY and Rahat G (2010) *Democracy within Parties: Candidate Selection Methods and Their Political Consequences.* Oxford, UK: Oxford University Press.

Hooghe L, Marks G, Schakel AH, et al. (2016) *Measuring Regional Authority.* Oxford, UK: Oxford University Press.

Hopkin J (2001) Bringing the members back in? Democratizing candidate selection in Britain and Spain. *Party Politics* 7(3): 343–361.

Lane J-E and Ersson S (2007) Party System Instability in Europe: Persistent Differences in Volatility between West and East? *Democratization* 14(1): 92–110. DOI: 10.1080/13510340601024322.

Linz JJ and Montero JR (2001) The party systems of Spain: Old cleavages and new challenges. Karvonen L and Kuhnle S (eds) *Party Systems and Voter Alignments Revisited.* London: Routledge, pp. 150–196.

Mair P (1997) *Party System Change: Approaches and Interpretations.* Oxford: Oxford University Press.

Michels R (2001 [1911]) *Los Partidos Políticos: Un estudio sociológico de las tendencias oligárquicas de la democracia moderna.* Buenos Aires: Amarrortu Editores.

Montero JR (1988) Elecciones y ciclos electorales en España. *Revista de Derecho Político* 0(25): 9–34. DOI: 10.5944/rdp.25.1988.8358.

Montero JR (2008) Elecciones y sistemas de partidos. Vallespín F and Jiménez de Parga M (eds) *La política.* Biblioteca España Siglo XXI. Madrid: Biblioteca Nueva.

Montero JR and Lago I (2010) *Elecciones generales 2008.* Madrid: Centro de Investigaciones Sociológicas (CIS).

Montero JR and Santana A (2020) Elections in Spain. Muro D and Lago I (eds) *The Oxford Handbook of Spanish Politics.* Oxford Handbooks. New York: Oxford University Press, pp. 347–369.

Mudde C (2019) *The Far Right Today.* Cambridge: Polity Press.

Orriols L and Cordero G (2016) The Breakdown of the Spanish Two-Party System: The Upsurge of Podemos and Ciudadanos in the 2015 General Election. *South European Society and Politics* 21(4): 469–492. DOI: 10.1080/13608746.2016.1198454.

Pérez-Moneo M (2012) *La selección de candidatos electorales en los partidos.* Madrid: Centro de Estudios Políticos y Constitucionales.

Pérez-Nievas S, Rama J and Fernández-Esquer C (2018) New Wine in Old Bottles? The Selection of Electoral Candidates for General Elections in Podemos. Cordero G and Coller X (eds) *Democratizing Candidate Selection: New Methods, Old Receipts?* New York, NY: Palgrave Macmillan, pp. 123–146.

Pirro ALP and Portos M (2020) Populism between voting and non-electoral participation. *West European Politics* 0(0). Routledge: 1–27. DOI: 10.1080/01402382.2020.1739451.

Queralt Jiménez A (2018) Chronicle of an Enforcement Foretold: The Effectiveness of the Del Río Prada ECtHR Judgement in Spain. Pérez Manzano M, Lascuraín Sánchez JA, and Mínguez Rosique M (eds) *Multilevel Protection of the Principle of Legality in Criminal Law*. Cham: Springer, pp. 195–212.

Rama J (2016) Ciclos electorales y sistema de partidos en España, 1977–2016. *Revista Jurídica Universidad Autónoma de Madrid* 0(34): 241–266. Available at: https://revistas.uam.es/revistajuridica/article/view/7738 (accessed 16 October 2020).

Rama J (2019) *Parties and economic crisis in Europe: a comparative analysis of new parties and changing party systems*. Universidad Autónoma de Madrid, Madrid. Available at: https://repositorio.uam.es/handle/10486/690277 (accessed 2 September 2020).

Rama J and Santana A (2019) The electoral fragmentation on the right side: 2019 Spanish general elections. *Who Governs Europe*. Available at: https://whogoverns.eu/the-electoral-fragmentation-on-the-right-side-2019-spanish-general-elections/ (accessed 29 May 2019).

Rodríguez Teruel J and Barberà O (2017) *Modelos, alternativas y consecuencias de la participación directa de las bases en los partidos*. Zoom Político 31/2017, 23 January. Madrid: Fundación Alternativas. Available at: www.fundacionalternativas.org/laboratorio/documentos/zoom-politico/modelos-alternativas-y-consecuencias-de-la-participacion-directa-de-las-bases-en-los-partidos (accessed 16 October 2020).

Rodríguez Teruel J and Barrio A (2016) Going National: Ciudadanos from Catalonia to Spain. *South European Society and Politics* 21(4): 587–607. DOI: 10.1080/13608746.2015.1119646.

Rodríguez-Teruel J, Barrio A and Barberà O (2016) Fast and Furious: Podemos' Quest for Power in Multi-level Spain. *South European Society and Politics* 21(4). Routledge: 561–585. DOI: 10.1080/13608746.2016.1250397.

Sangiao S (2018) Los orígenes de Vox: el aznarato y la lucha contra ETA. *ctxt.es | Contexto y Acción*. Available at: http://ctxt.es/es/20181129/Politica/23127/vox-aznar-eta-esperanza-aguirre-sergio-sangiao.htm (accessed 29 March 2020).

Santamaría J (1984) Elecciones generales de 1982 y consolidación de la democracia: A modo de introducción. *Revista Española de Investigaciones Sociológicas* 28: 7–17. DOI: 10.2307/40183098.

Santana A and Rama J (2018) Electoral support for left wing populist parties in Europe: addressing the globalization cleavage. *European Politics and Society* 19(5): 558–576. DOI: 10.1080/23745118.2018.1482848.

Santana A and Rama J (2019) El perfil del votante de Vox. Welp Y (ed.) *El auge la extrema derecha en Europa*. Madrid: Comisiones Obreras - Agenda Pública, pp. 17–24. Available at: https://docs.google.com/document/d/134l-gXkHQIEOUpObORj6pn P2knzqyUfTpaEtCqvHNDc/edit?usp=embed_facebook (accessed 23 February 2020).

Simón P (2016) The Challenges of the New Spanish Multipartism: Government Formation Failure and the 2016 General Election. *South European Society and Politics* 21(4): 493–517. DOI: 10.1080/13608746.2016.1268292.

Turnbull-Dugarte SJ (2019) Explaining the end of Spanish exceptionalism and electoral support for Vox. *Research & Politics* 6(2). DOI: 10.1177/2053168019851680.

Turnbull-Dugarte SJ, Rama J and Santana A (2020) The Baskerville's dog suddenly started barking: voting for VOX in the 2019 Spanish general elections. *Political Research Exchange* 2(1). 1781543. DOI: 10.1080/2474736X.2020.1781543.

Appendix

TABLE 2.A1 Vote shares in the Congress of Deputies

Parties	1st Cycle		2nd Cycle				3rd Cycle					4th Cycle			
	1977	1979	1982	1986	1989	1993	1996	2000	2004	2008	2011	2015	2016	2019	2019
Nationwide parties															
PCE/IU [b]	9,37	10.82	4.04	4.45	9.14	9.31	10.65	6.06	5.04	3.81	7.02	3.70			
Podemos/Unidos Podemos [c]												20.83	21.31	14.3	12.8
Más País															2.3
PSOE [d]	29.20	30.54	48.33	44.33	39.89	39.09	38.00	34.71	43.27	44.36	29.16	22.16	22.8	28.7	28
PSP-US	4.47														
UPyD										1.20	4.76	x			
CDS			2.87	9.16	7.95	x	x	x	x	x					
Cs												14.05	13.16	15.9	6.8
UCD	34.52	35.08	6.47												
AP/PP [e]	8.05	5.97	26.46	26.13	25.97	35.04	39.17	45.24	38.31	40.39	45.25	28.92	33.26	16.7	20.8
UN		2.12													
VOX														10.3	15.1
Nationalist and regionalist parties															
Andalusia															
PSA/PSA-PA/PA		1.82	x	x	1.05	x	x	0.90	x	x	x				
Aragon															
CHA					x			0.33	0.37	x		x			
CAIC/PAR/PA [f]	0.20	0.21		0.36	0.35	0.62									
Teruel Existe															0.1

Asturias															
FAC/FORO [g]											0.41				
Basque Country															
HB		0.96	1.01	1.07	1.07	0.88	0.73								
EH-Bildu												0.88	0.77	0.99	1.2
Amaiur											1.39				
EA [h]					0.67	0.55	0.47	0.44	0.32	x					
EE	0.34	0.48	0.48	0.53	0.52										
PNV	1.62	1.54	1.89	1.54	1.24	1.25	1.29	1.55	1.65	1.20	1.35	1.21	1.20	1.51	1.6
Canary Islands															
UPC		0.33	x												
CC [i]				0.33	0.32	0.88	0.89	1.09	0.92	0.69	0.60	0.33	0.33	0.53	0.51
Cantabria															
PRC														0.2	0.3
Catalonia															
CUP															1
ERC [j]	0.79	0.69	0.66	x	x	0.81	0.68	0.85	2.56	1.17	1.07	2.4	2.65	3.89	3.6
CiU/DL/CDC/JxCat [k]	2.82	2.61	3.69	5.05	5.07	4.98	4.64	4.25	3.28	3.06	4.23	2.27	2.03	1.91	2.2
UDC-IDCC	0.95														
Galicia															
BNPG/BNG [l]	x	x	x	x	x	x	0.89	1.34	0.82	0.84	0.77	x	x	x	0.5
CG				0.40	x										
Navarre															
Na-Bai/Geroa-Bai									0.24	0.25	0.18	x	x		
UPN [m]		0.16												0.41	0.41
Valencian Community															
CIC	0.16														
Compromís-EUPV											0.52			0.66	

(continued)

TABLE 2.A1 Cont.

Parties	1st Cycle		2nd Cycle					3rd Cycle				4th Cycle			
	1977	1979	1982	1986	1989	1993	1996	2000	2004	2008	2011	2015	2016	2019	2019
UV				0.32	0.71	0.48	0.37	x							
Others	7.51	6.67	4.10	6.33	6.05	6.11	2.22	3.24	3.22	3.03	3.29	3.25	2.49	4	2.8
Total	100	100	100	100	100	100	100	100	100	100	100	100	100	100	100
Turnout	78.80	68.00	80.00	70.50	69.70	76.40	77.40	68.70	75.70	73.80	68.90	69.70	66.50	71.76	66.2

a: Parties with parliamentary representation at least in one general election; parties are ordered from left to right. An x denotes parties fielding candidates who did not get representation.

b: PCE until 1983, IU since 1986 with several minor parties, above all in Catalonia; in 2016, IU merged with Podemos as Unidos Podemos.

c: Podemos in 2015 and Unidos Podemos in 2016 after merging with IU; in both years, with regional branches in Catalonia, Galicia, and Valencian Community.

d: Including its Catalan branch, PSC; sometimes in coalition with regionalist parties in the Canary Islands, Catalonia, and Extremadura.

e: AP until 1986, as the main party of several coalitions, and PP since 1989, in coalition with many regionalist parties.

f: CAIC in 1977, PAR between 1979 and 1989, and PA since 1993, sometimes in coalition with PP.

g: In coalition with PP in 2015 and 2016.

h: It split from PNV in 1986.

i: A coalition of several Canarian parties in 1993, later in coalition with several other regionalist parties.

j: In coalition with several nationalist parties between 1977 and 1979 and since 2011.

k: In 1977, PDC; CiU as a coalition between CDC and UDC since 1979 through 2011; in 2015, DL, in 2016 CDC and in 2019 (both April and November) JxCat (Junts per Catalunya).

l: From 1977 through 1982, BNPG; afterwards, BNG.

m: In coalition with PP in many elections. In fact, NA⁺ is an electoral coalition between PP, UPN, and Cs.

Source: Electoral Results, Ministry of Interior (www.infoelectoral.mir.es), complemented by the authors (1977–2019).

TABLE 2.A2 Seats in the Congress of Deputies

Parties	1st Cycle		2nd Cycle									3rd Cycle				4th Cycle			
	1977	1979	1982	1986	1989	1993	1996	2000	2004	2008	2011	2015	2016	2019	2019
Nation-wide parties															
PCE/IU/IU-ICV	20	23	4	7	17	18	21	9	5	2	11	2			
Podemos/Unidos Podemos												69	71	42	35
Más País															3
PSOE	118	121	202	184	175	159	141	125	164	169	110	90	85	123	120
PSP-US	6														
UPyD										1	5				
CDS/UC-CDS/CDS			2	19	14	0	0	0	0	0					
Cs												40	32	57	10
UCD	165	168	11												
AP/CD/AP-PDP/CP/PP	16	9	107	105	107	141	156	183	148	154	186	123	137	66	88
VOX														24	52
UN		1													
Independiente	1														
Nationalist and regionalist parties															
Andalusia															
PSA/PSA-PA/PA		5	0	0	2	0	0	1	0	0	0				
Aragon															
CHA				0	0	0	1	1	0			0			
CAIC/PAR/PA	1	1		1	1	1		0	0	0					
Teruel Existe															1
Asturias															
FAC/FORO											1				

TABLE 2.A2 Cont.

Parties	1st Cycle		2nd Cycle					3rd Cycle				4th Cycle			
	1977	1979	1982	1986	1989	1993	1996	2000	2004	2008	2011	2015	2016	2019	2019
Basque Country															
HB		3	2	5	4	2	2								
EH–Bildu												2	2	4	5
Amaiur											7				
EA				2	1	1	1	1							
EE	1	1	1	2	2										
PNV	8	7	8	6	5	5	5	7	7	6	5	6	5	6	7
Canary Islands															
UPC		1	0												
AIC/CC				1	1	4	4	4	3	2	2	1	1	2	2
Cantabria															
PRC														1	**1**
Catalonia															
CUP															2
EC-FED/ERFN/ERC-CAT SÍ	1	1	1	0	0	1	1	1	8	3	3	9	9	15	13
PDPC	11														
CiU/DL/CDC/JxCat		8	12	18	18	17	16	15	10	10	16	8	8	7	8
UDC-IDCC	2														
Galicia															
BNPG/BNG	0	0	0	0	0	0	2	3	2	2	2				1
CG				1	0										
Navarre															
Na-Bai/Geroa-Bai									1	1	1	0			

UPN/Na+	1												2	2
Valencian Community														
Compromís-EUPV											1		1	
UV			1	2	1	1	0							
Total	350	350	350	350	350	350	350	350	350	350	350	350	350	350

PODEMOS/UNIDOS PODEMOS: In 2015, it ran in coalition with EQUO and was part of EN COMÚ in Catalonia, PODEMOS-COMPROMÍS in the Valencia region, and EN MAREA in Galicia. In 2016, the coalition also included IU, and the coalition in the Valencia region was called A LA VALENCIANA.

PCE/IU: From 1977 to 1982, PCE; from 1986, IU; in Catalonia, it ran in coalition with the PSUC from 1977 to 1982, and with ICV in 2004 and 2008; other years, it was represented by EUiA. It also ran in coalition with other subnational and green parties, such as *EG* in Galicia or *Los Verdes de Andalucía* in 1996 and 2000. In 2011, it was the leading partner of the IU–LV coalition; and in 2015, of the UP coalition. In Galicia and Catalonia, it joined Podemos-led EN MAREA and EN COMÚ in 2015. In 2016, it joined Podemos-led UP as well as EN MAREA and EN COMÚ.

The PSOE ran in coalition with SIEX and NC in 2015 and with NC in 2016 in the Canary Islands; with ICV-EUiA in Catalonia in 2011; and with PREx-CREx in Extremadura from 2004 to 2011.

CDS/UC-CDS/CDS: CDS from 1982 to 1995; UC from 1995 to 1998; UC-CDS from 1998 to 2002; and CDS since 2002.

AP/CD/AP-PDP/CP/PP: In 1977, AP; in 1979, CD; in 1982, AP-PDP; in 1986, CP; since then, PP. The PP (or its former brands) joined forces with several subnational parties: PAR in Aragón in 1982, 1996, 2011, 2015 and 2016; FAC/FORO in Asturias in 2015 and 2016; CCN in Canarias in 2011; EU in Extremadura in 2011; UPN in Navarra since 1982; and UV in Valencia in 1982.

PSA/PSA-PA/PA: Created as PSA; from 1979 to 1984, PSA-PA; from 1984 to its dissolution, in 2015, PA.

CAIC/PAR/PA: In 1977, CAIC; from 1977 to 1990, PAR; and from them on, PA.

AIC/CC: In 1986 and 1989, AIC; since 1993, CC.

PSUC/PSUC-ENE: From 1979 to 1982, PSUC; in 1986, PSUC-ENE.

EC-FED/ERFN/ERC/ERC-CAT SÍ: In 1977, EC-FED; in 1979, ERFN; from 1982 to 2011, ERC; in 2015 and 2016, ERC-CAT SÍ.

CiU/DL/CDC: From 1979 to 2011, CiU; in 2015, DL; in 2016, CDC.

BNPG/BNG: In 1977, 1979 and 1982, BNPG. After the 1982 elections, BNG.

Source: Electoral Results, Ministry of Interior (www.infoelectoral.mir.es), complemented by the authors (1977–2019).

3

A QUESTION OF SUPPLY

What does VOX want? A party manifesto analysis in comparative perspective

> *"We are the Spain that does not need to look at polls or read a newspaper to know what the fashionable discourse is. Our speech is born from our convictions, regardless of whether they are more or less popular. In short, VOX is the party of Spain alive, free and brave"*
>
> *(VOX electoral manifesto)*[1]

In this chapter, we assess the discourse of VOX in various dimensions, relying on the systemic analysis of its electoral manifesto. In the introduction to this book, we have gauged the ideology of the party, concluding that it can be characterized as a populist radical right party (PRRP). The objective of this chapter is to analyse in a more detailed fashion the characteristics of VOX's ideology through the examination of the electoral programme of the party, the one written up with the occasion of the April 2019 election. Through the analysis of the most salient issues for VOX and the main parties from the return to democracy in 1977, we offer an overview of the dynamic of the competition within the Spanish party system. This analysis is relevant for a better understanding of the reasons behind the emergence of VOX in a political system that, until recent times, constituted an exception in Western Europe due to the lack of populist radical right parties (Alonso and Rovira Kaltwasser, 2015).

To the best of our knowledge, this chapter represents the very first analysis of VOX's electoral manifesto in a systematic way. Previous studies analyse VOX's manifesto in a non-systematic fashion and offer neither (1) a longitudinal analysis of the dynamic of competition within the party system nor (2) a comparative assessment (see Gould, 2019; Ferreira, 2019). On the contrary, in this chapter, we study the salience of the main issues raised by VOX in its manifesto, focusing on how the other political party alternatives have addressed these issues. Moreover, we examine the evolution of the relevant cleavages from the return to democracy in 1977 until VOX's national upsurge in 2019.

The chapter is divided into four sections. First, relying on the manifesto data provided by the Manifesto Project (MARPOR) – former Comparative Manifestos Project (CMP)[2] – we assess the political positions promoted by VOX, focusing on the categories that are more salient in its April 2019 electoral programme. The second part of the chapter is dedicated to the analysis of the lines of conflict that have structured the Spanish party system. This analysis is useful to better understand the emergence of VOX in a party system that until recent years has not seen the presence of any successful populist radical right party. The third section focuses on a comparison of VOX's programme with those of other well-known populist radical right parties in Europe as well as populist leaders in other countries such as (former president) Donald Trump in the United States, Jair Bolsonaro in Brazil, and José Antonio Kast in Chile. In the fourth and last section, we draw a short conclusion in which we synthesize and assess the main findings of the chapter.

The electoral manifesto of VOX

The aim of this section is to analyse VOX's discourse looking specifically at its political programme. Party manifestos are published by the official organs of the party and represent the official vision of parties. They are published for each election, allowing an analysis of the evolution of the party's positions over time and a comparison of their treatment of political issues with those of other parties (Alonso, Volkens and Gómez, 2012). Relying on coded manifesto data provided by MARPOR,[3] we assess the political positions promoted by VOX, paying particular attention to how these compare with those of traditional parties in Spain across several issues. This, in turn, can contribute to shedding light on the reasons behind the emergence of VOX at this particular time. For a party to emerge, there must be some programmatic or policy free space in the system. By owning this void in the political space, a party can attract a portion of voters to which its programmatic offer is appealing (De Vries and Hobolt, 2020: 5).

As briefly mentioned, we decided to use party manifestos to analyse VOX's discourse for three main reasons. First, we argue that electoral programmes matter to politics. Manifestos are theoretically relevant for the theory of prospective voting as well as the mandate theory and the concept of accountability. As stated by Downs (1957), the theory of prospective voting states that citizens evaluate parties' proposals and choose to vote for the political formation closer to their preferences: the electoral programme is the document that embodies those proposals. Electoral programmes are also crucial for the accountability of governments: they represent the mandate that citizens uphold for their representatives in office (Manin, Przeworski, and Stokes, 2001; Körösényi and Sebók, 2013:12). Second, electoral programmes are the only written document systematically produced by parties and reflect their ideology, preferences, or interests. They are approved by elected committees and/or

44 What does VOX want?

are ratified by parties' congresses. They therefore constitute official declarations on behalf of the whole party and not just a faction (Debus, 2009: 289). Third, they are published at regular intervals by incumbents as well as opposition parties, allowing for comparisons along time and among parties; given their coverage of a wide range of issues, they are liable to comparisons among parties, party systems, and countries (Alonso, Volkens, and Gómez, 2012).

We analyse parties' manifestos using the MARPOR database. This is a quantitative, long-run cooperative project based on the codification of political parties' electoral programmes as a way to measure the salience of different issues within the political space. This dataset continues to be the best one available so far, allowing for longitudinal as well as international comparison of parties' positions. Moreover, its convergence validity with other measures has extensively been examined on different dimensions and topics (Dinas and Gemenis, 2010; Hutter and Kriesi, 2019). The data measure the salience of issues in addition to the position of parties. Salience theory argues that the policy space is not fixed: it changes over time with the capacity of parties to process voter demands and their ability to make specific issues relevant through electoral propaganda (Adams et al., 2005). As Madariaga and Rovira Kaltwasser (2020) pointed out, this is relevant since it assumes that while some issues, such as the so-called valence issues, are relevant for all the parties within the system, specific parties put more emphasis on the issues they are more credible on.

Table 3.1 summarizes the five most salient categories in VOX's electoral programme. The left-hand (or first) column lists the five most salient issues in the programme, i.e. the five issues that received more attention. Most issues in the MARPOR project are defined both in terms of their topic (e.g. national way of life) and polarity (e.g. positive). The second column refers to the code of the categories. Finally, the values in the right (or third) column show the percentage of the document dedicated to the issues in the left-hand column. What seems to be the most noticeable factor is the percentage of the manifesto dedicated to sentences that defend the national way of life (10.3). This is then followed by favourable stances on law and order (9.5), immigration (8.8), traditional morality (7.9), and welfare state expansion (7.5).

TABLE 3.1 Five most salient categories in VOX programme

Top five issues in the programme	VOX 2019	Values
National way of life: positive	per 601.1	10.3
Law and order: positive	per 605.1	9.5
Immigration negative/assimilation	per 608.1 + 601.2	8.8
Traditional morality: positive	per 603	7.9
Welfare state: expansion	per 504	7.5

Source: Elaboration of the authors, based on MARPOR data

National way of life: positive

Table 3.1 shows that positive references to the national way of life occupies more than 10 per cent of VOX manifesto.[4] This category picks up all the "favourable mentions of the manifesto country's nation, history and general appeals for established national ideas, general appeals to the pride of citizens appeal to patriotism, nationalism, and support to some freedoms to protect the state against subversion" (MARPOR, Handbook).

The numerous references in the manifesto to the homogeneity of the Spanish culture in contrast to the sub-cultures present in the country can shed light on the high salience of this particular issue for VOX. The percentage of the programme devoted to this issue is high in comparison with the other political formations in the Spanish party system (see Table 3.2) and, as we show later in this chapter, also with regard to the space allotted to the issue by other populist radical right parties in Europe and beyond (see Table 3.9). In Spain, the average of the salience of this issue for *all* the parties in the system in both 2015 and 2016 was 0.23 (MARPOR data). The higher percentage for this category, 1.39, was scored by the People's Party (PP) PP in both elections. When VOX competed at the national level as a major player for the first time, it scored 10.3 per cent on this specific category (notice, incidentally, that the entrance of VOX in 2019 is accompanied by a sharp rise of the frequency allocated to the national way of life also by Ciudadnoas (Cs) Cs and PP). This is an outstanding percentage both in Spain and abroad. For instance, a radical right party ideologically similar to VOX, Brothers of Italy [*Fratelli d'Italia*], devoted just 3.3 per cent of its programme to this category in 2018 (MARPOR data).

Positive stances on the country's history and culture indeed go hand in hand with nativism, which is the primary ideological trait of the populist radical right (Mudde, 2007). Claiming that the state should be inhabited only by the members of the nation, nativism assumes a hierarchy among states and, as a result, among cultures. Behind this, there is another assumption: national culture is perceived and depicted as homogeneous.

This aspect has relevant consequences in the case of Spain. A high decentralization characterizes the country with the presence of 17 regions, the so-called autonomous communities [*Comunidades Autónomas*], as well as two autonomous cities (Ceuta and Melilla) in the North African territory. Each one of these regions features distinct cultural traits that, in most cases, somehow overlap with the Spanish

TABLE 3.2 National way of life: positive mentions

Election year	UP	PSOE	Cs	PP	VOX
2015	0.34	0.34	0.09	1.39	–
2016	0.34	0.27	0.36	1.39	–
2019	0.44	0.22	1.20	3.67	10.27

Source: Elaboration of the authors, based on MARPOR data (2015–2019)

46 What does VOX want?

cultural tradition (see Linz, 1973). For example, in regions such as Galicia, Catalonia, the Valencian Community, the Balearic Islands, the Basque Country, and Navarre, many people speak local languages, which are constitutionally recognized as co-official state languages.[5] The emphasis that VOX puts on the unity of the country is openly expressed through the whole manifesto, especially in the first part called "Spain, Unity, and Sovereignty".[6]

The aversion toward the autonomies is also patent regarding the symbols of unity. For example, VOX advocates *"giving the highest legal protection to the nation's symbols: The Flag, the Anthem, and the Crown. Increased penalties for offences and outrages against Spain and its symbols. No affront to them should go unpunished"* (VOX manifesto: 2).

Even if in the majority of the regions the local culture is not openly in conflict with the Spanish culture, there are some exceptions. Thus, dual identification as Spaniards together with one from the autonomous community is not unusual in the country but, in regions such as Catalonia (and also the Basque Country), a significant percentage of citizens identifies only with the region (Pérez Nievas and Rama, 2018: 324–327).

According to VOX, another stepping stone for the defence of Spanish unity is the protection of the national language. Thus, its electoral programme states:

> *"No administration or private individual can disparage the standard language: Spanish. Much less discriminate against it. We need to comply with the constitutional mandate that all Spaniards have the right to use the Spanish language, and the duty to know it. Also, there is the need to delete the requirement of knowledge of the co-official language* [the languages spoken in the autonomies] *in accessing the public function to avoid any type of discrimination* (VOX manifesto: 2).

Then again, VOX finds it necessary to *"guarantee the right to be educated in Spanish throughout the national territory. Spanish should be a compulsory vehicle language and co-official language [should be] optional. Parents should have the right to choose their children's language in school"* (VOX manifesto: 15).

In sum, the high level of decentralization and the consequential dual identification seem to be crucial to the importance that VOX gives to the defence of the national way of life. It contraposes the national values to those particular forces that allegedly aim at destroying the Spanish identity.

Law and order

Security is one of the more recurrent topics promoted by the radical right (see below). PRRPs express their discursive authoritarianism (Mudde, 2007; 2019) through policy proposals related to law and order (Alonso and Rovira Kaltwasser, 2015). This is because "every political issue is perceived through the lens of a 'threat to the natural order', creating insecurity, which has to be dealt with an iron hand" (Mudde, 2019: 33). It is essential to underline that security issues in general terms refer both to individuals and to the idealized collective, most notably the nation or race, and have a cultural, economic, and physical component (Mudde, 2019: 33).

In this respect, VOX does not constitute an exception. Looking back at Table 3.1, we can see that 9.5 per cent of the electoral programme is dedicated to supporting law and order. To analyse the level of politicization of security issues in the Spanish party system before the entrance of VOX, we created a "law and order" index (see Table 3.3). This index captures the salience of the law and order issue by counting both the positive and negative references to law and order. While this is one of the issues which has been more politicized by VOX, if we observe the Spanish party system from a longitudinal perspective, it is patent that this was not a primary issue for the main parties in the system, at least until 2016.

Indeed Table 3.3 shows that the centre-right PP scored in just 3.28 in both the 2015 and 2016 elections, while the other parties dedicated to law and order issues less than the two per cent of their political programmes. Things changed in 2019. Coincidentally, with the entrance of VOX in the electoral competition, the share dedicated to law and order within the political programmes of all four main parties increased and, in some instances, in a significant manner (see in Table 3.1 the values of PP and, above all, the liberal Cs).

Additionally, Table 3.4 shows the percentage of the parties' manifestos dedicated to positive assessments of law and order policies. This means that Table 3.4 presents the same information as Table 3.3. but without taking into account the non-favourable mentions of law and order. More in detail, the table shows the percentage of the main parties' programmes dedicated to "favourable mentions of strict law enforcement and tougher action against domestic crime" (MARPOR, Handbook).[7]

TABLE 3.3 Law and order index [a]

Election year	UP	PSOE	Cs	PP	VOX
2015	0.40	1.62	1.09	3.28	–
2016	0.40	1.50	0.60	3.28	–
2019	1.57	1.51	5.12	6.83	9.49

a: Per605.1 + Per605.2.

Source: Elaboration of the authors, based on MARPOR data

TABLE 3.4 Strict law enforcement and tougher action against crime: positive mentions

Election year	UP	PSOE	Cs	PP	VOX
2015	0.11	0.80	1.09	3.28	–
2016	0.11	0.84	0.60	3.28	–
2019	0.96	1.42	4.97	6.83	9.49

Source: Elaboration of the authors, based on MARPOR data

48 What does VOX want?

On the one hand, as mentioned above, in the first election in which VOX participated as a major contender at the national level, almost 10 per cent of its manifesto was composed of favourable mentions to law and order[8] (see Table 3.1).

On the other hand, all the other major parties in the system incremented the percentage of their programme dedicated to this issue. For Cs and the PP, the share of quasi-sentences dedicated to supporting more law and order policies increased respectively 4.3 percentual points (from 0.6 to 4.97) and more than 3.5 percentual points (from 3.3 to 6.8). It looks like VOX acted as a driver for the other main parties, altering the salience and talking the ownership of the law and order issue (Meguid, 2005: 347).

Meguid's (2005) assessment of niche parties maintains that mainstream parties have a choice whether competing on the issue politicized by the newcomer. They can either ignore the issue, adopting a so-called dismissive strategy, or adopt a position on the issue dimension.[9] If they choose to adopt a position, it can be accommodative or adversarial. In the case of law and order in Spain, mainstream parties preferred to adopt the issue. On the one hand, both the PP and Cs adopted an accommodative strategy given that the salience of law and order increased between 2016 and 2019. On the other hand, UP and the PSOE increased their manifestos' share dedicated to security, but in a much slimmer percentage. The strategy of adopting the newcomer's issue has the consequence of reinforcing the challenger, as it validates its agenda choice (Krause et al., 2019).

Immigration

Taking the proportion of the electoral programme dedicated to a particular issue as an indicator of issue salience considering single categories, immigration is *not* present in the top five categories. This may sound surprising since anti-immigration stances are a common feature of populist radical right parties (Mudde and Rovira Kaltwasser, 2018). This is a consequence of the fact that nativism is a core ideological tenet of this party family. However, this is, at least in part, the result of different coding categories relative to anti-immigration in the MARPOR dataset. In fact, two categories are dedicated to unfavourable stances on immigration: immigration: assimilation and immigration: negative.

A closer look at the manifesto reveals that these two different categories together are salient for VOX. On the one hand, category 608.2 (see Table 3.1) refers to opposing stances on those immigrants who are already present in the country for whom VOX demands assimilation to the Spanish culture. This category represents the 4.4 of the manifesto of the party. This is not surprising since "*the ultimate goal of the populist radical right is an* ethnocracy, *that is, democracy in which citizenship is based on ethnicity*" (Mudde, 2019: 28). Assimilation remains, then, the only viable option available to out-group aliens besides repatriation. References to assimilation go hand in hand with the rejection of the idea of a multicultural society. For example, VOX underlines that "*immigration will be addressed taking into account the needs of the Spanish economy and the immigrant's capacity for integration. Origin quotas will be established, privileging nationalities that share a language and important ties and culture with Spain"* (VOX manifesto: 6).

The messaging of this passage is noteworthy for two reasons. Firstly, it mirrors the strategy adopted by parties that promote nativist agendas by linking opposition to immigration to concerns over the economy. A wide body of work highlights the potential for electoral support for PRRPs amongst those fearful of the effects of immigration on the labour market. By "taking into account the needs of the Spanish economy" VOX is invoking the legitimizing effect of economic concerns to justify their nativist policies. Second, the party advocates for a preferential treatment mainly for those with cultural (read ethnic) ties with Spain and discriminatory rejection of those who are culturally dissimilar. In short, this signals that VOX does not oppose immigration per se but rather certain types of immigration, where only those from the ethnic out-group (those perceived threatening to the romanticized and homogenous people) are unwelcome.

On the other hand, VOX's electoral programme[10] also dedicates more than 4 per cent to negative statements on new immigrants. This is also hardly surprising considering that since 2015 Southern European countries have been harshly affected by the so-called migration crisis. Concerning the latter category, a qualitative analysis of the manifesto, which presents a whole section on immigration, shows a negative stance on immigration targeted mostly towards illegal (undocumented) migrants and NGOs that, as VOX alleges, profit from illegal immigration. This argument is increasingly recurrent in PRRPs' rhetoric in the last years (Pytlas et al., 2018).

To give an example, one of the proposals laid out in VOX's programme calls for reforms that stipulate that *"any immigrant who has entered Spain illegally will be unable, for life, to legalize their situation and therefore to receive any help from the administration"* (VOX, manifesto: 5). Also, concerning the role of the NGOs, the manifesto claims that there will be *"harsher sentences to combat the mafias of illegal immigration, as well as for those who collaborate with them, be it NGOs, companies or individuals"* (VOX manifesto: 5).

Combined, the two categories dedicated to immigration in VOX's electoral programme represent almost 9 per cent of the document. This proportion is far from trivial. As detailed above, manifesto documents have high thresholds when it comes to issue salience. Those issues that "make the cut" are those that the party deems to be those most likely to rally the troops and win votes on election day and are the issues that the party has decided to focus on *over others.* The sum of these two categories relative to immigration for the four main parties in the system from 2015 are below 1 per cent, except for the PP in 2019 which reached a percentage close to 2 (MARPOR data).

At this point it is crucial revealing that the issue of immigration – intended as both favourable and unfavourable mentions – has not been common in Spain. Indeed, immigration has never been a primary issue in the Spanish political debate Using an index that averages the sum of negative and positive stances towards

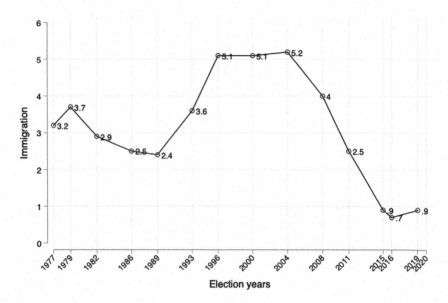

FIGURE 3.1 Evolution of immigration saliency in the Spanish party system

Source: (1977–2019) Elaboration of the authors based on Alonso and Rovira Kaltwasser (2015)

multiculturalism and the mentions of unprivileged minority groups, Alonso and Rovira Kaltwasser, (2015).were able to examine the salience of immigration.[11]

Observing the trend of this index for the electoral programmes of the Spanish parties over time (Figure 3.1), before the emergence of VOX we can observe that it is relatively low – the highest level achieved is 5 per cent – meaning that immigration has never been an issue much politicized in the Spanish party system (see Alonso and Rovira Kaltwasser, 2015).

Figure 3.1 shows that, between 1996 and 2004, when the conservative PP was in office, immigration salience reached its zenith, occupying more than 5 per cent of the party manifestos on average. This was because the party led by José María Aznar used nationalism and immigration as strongpoints in his strategy of electoral competition (Alonso and Rovira Kaltwasser, 2015: 37). From 2004, however, the salience of the issue started to fall after the decision adopted in 2005 by the former PSOE Spanish Prime Minister, José Luis Rodríguez Zapatero, to legalize the status of those illegal immigrants living and working in Spain for at least two consecutive years.[12]

Having updated Alonso and Rovira Kaltwasser's index with the data for the 2015, 2016, and 2019 elections, we can appreciate a further fall in 2015 and 2016, with a small upturn in 2019. It is quite evident that especially in the two elections before the entrance of VOX in the system, the parties in the system did not treat immigration as a primary issue, while the increase in 2019 is the product of the higher salience that VOX gave to this issue. Indeed, the value of the index for VOX is 4.74. It is essential to note that it was in July 2018 that immigration started to become a question that worried Spaniards, as the longitudinal series of the Sociological Centre of Investigations (CIS) underlined, and as we can see in the Figure A3.1 in the Appendix section.[13]

All in all, observing more in depth the MARPOR data, we can appreciate that the high percentage of the electoral programme dedicated to the assimilation of non-natives goes hand in hand with the almost as numerous references to the exaltation of the national way of life that we have mentioned above.

Traditional morality

The fourth most salient category in VOX electoral programme is traditional morality.[14] Following the MARPOR Handbook, this category contains the references to favourable mentions of traditional and/or religious, moral values. For example, these may include the "*maintenance and stability of the traditional family values and the support for the role of religious institutions in state and society*" (MARPOR Handbook: 23). While the other categories, i.e. immigration and security, are frequently found in the discourse of populist radical right political actors (Mudde, 2019), this is not the case for traditional values. However, in both VOX's electoral programme and speeches in parliament, constant references to the defence of moral values are patent. In the section dedicated to life and family, the party proposes the "*suppression of subsidized radical feminist organization*" and the "*effective prosecution of false allegations*" in case of domestic violence (VOX manifesto: 17). The attack against feminist organizations is perhaps one of VOX's more specific characteristics, even beyond its electoral programme. It suffices to think of the manifesto[15] written by the party on the occasion of the celebration of International Women's Day, with the title *Do not speak in my name.* On the occasion of the presentation of the manifesto, VOX's representatives mentioned that 8 March celebrations are an "*invention of the radical left*", which allegedly depicts women as "*victims*" and "*in contraposition to men*". In general terms, VOX's central claim is the alleged hypocrisy of "*those who have a way of understanding the world that speaks of 'us together' but condemns us for disagreeing with the dominant ideology*".

Again, the party proposes policies to defend "*life since conception to the natural death*" (VOX manifesto: 18). The party leaders advocate for the traditional values and morality also in parliamentary interventions. On 18 March 2020, Espinosa de Los Monteros, Abascal's number two, stressed that young people "*must learn from our elders the values of family, of unity, and the nation. Although they see a dark panorama today, they must be aware that they are part of something greater than what each one is individually, and it is not a community, it is much more than that*". Moreover, he finished with "*we [Spaniards] were, we are, and we will be a strong nation: the Spanish nation*" (Zanotti and Rama, 2020). In this last example, it is patent how in VOX's discourse, traditional values, and the exaltation of the national way of life go hand by hand. The latter is depicted as great because it allegedly relies on these values. In other words,

52 What does VOX want?

TABLE 3.5 Salience of traditional values: positive and negative mentions [a]

Election year	UP	PSOE	Cs	PP	VOX
2015	2.12	1.42	0.49	0.25	–
2016	2.12	1.32	0.24	0.25	–
2019	1.74	0.49	2.25	0.94	7.90

a: Per603 + per604.

Source: Elaboration of the authors, based on MARPOR data

TABLE 3.6 Traditional values: positive mentions [a]

Election year	UP	PSOE	Cs	PP	VOX
2015	0.00	0.00	0.08	0.25	–
2016	0.00	0.00	0.00	0.25	–
2019	0.00	0.00	0.75	0.85	7.90

a: Per603.

Source: Elaboration of the authors, based on MARPOR data

these (traditional) values, according to VOX, were the main element that made Spain great.

As we did for security issues, we create an index to observe the salience of traditional values in the Spanish party system from 2015 to 2019, considering both favourable and unfavourable assessments. Table 3.5 gives an overview of the salience of traditional values in Spain before and after VOX's entrance in the competition.

It is evident how the issue was not politicized by the main parties in the system in both the 2015 and 2016 elections. Also, VOX's entrance seems to have a different effect on this index for each party. While in Cs's and the PP's manifestos the quasi-sentences dedicated to the issue increased, in the PSOE's and UP's they went in the opposite direction.

Table 3.6 gives more insights into the percentage of the manifestos dedicated to support traditional values. While Table 3.5 shows the salience of the traditional values category summing up positive and negative stances, Table 3.6 focuses only on the positive ones. Thus, we can appreciate that the increment in the case of Cs observable in Table 3.5 is due to an increasing aversion to traditional values.[16] The only party that slightly increased the percentage of support for the traditional values category is the PP. However, the increment is not relevant, since the salience remains below 1 per cent.

Welfare state: expansion

Finally, 7.5 per cent of VOX's manifesto is composed by quasi-sentences that advocate for an expansion of the welfare state. At first sight, this is not uncommon, at least for populist radical right parties in Western Europe (Schumacher and van

Kersberger, 2016; Mudde and Rovira Kaltwasser, 2018). This may seem counterintuitive, since PRRPs are rightist parties. Conventional wisdom regarding the political cleavage between the left and right assumes that the parties on the left, as the primary defenders of labour, are more inclined towards welfare expansions, whereas those on the right, as the primary defenders of capital, are more likely to oppose welfare spending (Huber and Stephens, 2001).

However, the fact that VOX supports the expansion of the welfare state is in line with the primary characteristic of populist radical right parties: nativism. Welfare chauvinism can be thought of as a political view guided by nativism (Greve, 2019): it maintains that benefits and services should go only to natives since they are the only ones entitled to receive support from the welfare state (Ennser-Jedenastik, 2018; Rovira Kaltwasser and Zanotti, 2021). Conversely from some of the other issues politicized by VOX, the welfare state was not new in the Spanish political arena. The average level of salience of the welfare state among the main Spanish parties from 1977 until 2011 was 11.7 per cent (Alonso and Rovira Kaltwasser, 2015).

If we look at the value of the welfare state index from 2015, a further increase is noticeable, and in 2019 the mean of the welfare state mentions for all the parties in the system – i.e. the five main parties plus regional and minor parties – reached 11.8 per cent. Table 3.7 shows the value of the welfare index just for the main parties in the system from 2015. We can observe that the issue of the welfare state is highly politicized by all parties.

Moreover, looking at MARPOR data,[17] we can observe that all the parties in the system are supportive of a further expansion of the welfare state, since this category is much more relevant than the one measuring the quasi-sentences that advocate a limitation of the welfare state.

While adhering to welfare chauvinism is not new for populist radical right parties, VOX, in general, shows a much more libertarian discourse than other PRRPs. In several passages of the electoral programme, the party advocates for a smaller role of the state in citizens' life. To give an example, the manifesto introduction claims: "*Our project is summarized in defence of Spain, family and life; in reducing the size of the State, guaranteeing equality among Spaniards and expelling the Government from private life*". This being true, it is crucial to notice that populist radical right parties, in general terms, tend to be libertarian with respect to economic issues but conservative on cultural ones. The support for more welfare state

TABLE 3.7 Welfare state: positive and negative mentions [a]

Election year	UP	PSOE	Cs	PP	VOX
2015	11.20	14.50	8.90	11.40	–
2016	11.20	13.90	11.60	11.40	–
2019	15.50	18.60	9.60	14.10	9.10

a: Category 504 + 505.

Source: Elaboration of the authors based on Alonso and Rovira Kaltwasser (2015)

54 What does VOX want?

fits in the latter category, since the increased benefits will eventually be allocated just to natives.

To conclude, this section shows which issues are more salient in VOX's electoral programme and interprets them in light of the salience given to these very issues by the other main parties in the Spanish party system. In the next section, we assess the emergence of VOX based on a cleavage-based analysis. In other words, by examining the main cleavages that have structured the Spanish party system in a longitudinal perspective, we make inferences on the reasons that explain VOX's electoral breakthrough at this particular time.

The emergence of VOX: a cleavage-based analysis

This section envisages the analysis of the relevant dimensions of political competition in Spain. In recent years, attention has been focused on how the cleavage approach can be useful to analyse the electoral fortune of PRRPs in Western Europe, since the existing cleavage structure of a country can obstruct or facilitate the success of these parties (Alonso and Rovira Kaltwasser, 2015: 27).

A cleavage-based analysis of the Spain party system is useful, since assessing the dimensions in which parties compete can give us insights on the chances that any new party can have to enter the system and become electorally relevant. In this line, using MARPOR data, we calculate the evolution of left–right and centre–periphery levels of polarization from 1977 until 2019, mapping the salience and the position of parties along these two main lines of conflict.

Examining the levels of polarization along different axes is relevant since the literature has established that the growing programmatic convergence between mainstream parties in Western Europe had facilitated the rise of different types of niche parties. These parties opt to politicize sets of issues previously outside of the party competition (ecology, immigration, regionalism, etc.) and present themselves as the only ones capable of handling them (Madariaga and Rovira Kaltwasser, 2019).

Convergence tends to deepen mainly in situations of crisis. When mainstream parties converge on the same positions for prolonged periods, it results in a representation deficit. In other words, programmatic convergence of mainstream parties largely ceased to offer the electorate a meaningful range of policy alternatives (Roberts, 2017).

Convergence arguments, with some variations, have also been used by scholars to explain the emergence of the populist radical right (Ignazi,1992; Mudde, 2007:239). For example, some scholars argue that the centrist position of the largest mainstream right-wing competitor is crucial (Van der Brug, Fennema and Tillie, 2005; Norris, 2005). When mainstream parties programmatically converge on some issues, leaving aside policies that are important to voters, such as immigration and security, the latter may feel unrepresented and come to support other, more radical political options (Zanotti, 2019).

Various factors have contributed to high levels of programmatic convergence. The process of economic globalization, which translates in a widespread agreement on European integration, for instance, made the ideological positions of mainstream parties less easily differentiable for the voters (Kriesi et al., 2008).

One example is the so-called Third Way in Europe (Giddens, 2013), a position akin to centrism that tries to reconcile right-wing and left-wing politics by promoting different combinations of right-wing economic and left-wing social policies. This stance has been represented, for instance, by the premierships of Tony Blair in the United Kingdom and Gerhard Schröder in Germany (Giddens, 2013; Zanotti, 2019). Moreover, at the zenith of the Eurozone crisis, the convergence of mainstream parties on austerity measures, particularly in those states, like Spain, in receipt of financial rescue packages from the EU institutions, led to a rise in non-establishment parties (Alonso and Ruiz-Rufino, 2020).

To assess the role of convergence in explaining the emergence of new parties in the system, we analyse the level of polarization in the Spanish party system in those divides that previous studies have identified as structuring the Spanish system.

Polarization in the left–right divide

To measure polarization, we first assess the position on the left–right continuum using the RILE index developed by the Manifesto Project. This index is the result of the sum of 13 seen as being on the "left", 13 seen as being on the "right". These 26 categories are then compiled in an index that ranges from -100 (leftist) to +100 (rightist) (see Madariaga and Rovira Kaltwasser, 2019: 349).

The RILE scale is thought to be more reliable than any single coding category, since it is likely that most of the stochastic variation in text coding will result from different coders allocating the same text unit to different categories on the "left" or the "right" (Mikhaylov, Laver and Benoit, 2008: 9). The categories in question are part of the core of the dispute between right and left, such as economic redistribution versus free market or as expansion of the welfare state versus reduction of the welfare state (Rovira Kaltwasser, 2019).

Furthermore, to obtain an index of party system polarization we weighted these values by the vote share of each party for each national election,[18] using the following formula developed by Dalton (2008):

$$Polarization\ Index_{c,t} = \sqrt{\sum_{i=1}^{n} \left(\frac{PartyRILE - SystemRILE}{100} \right)^2 \star VoteShare_{i,t}}$$

Here, i represents individual parties. Following Dalton, "*this index is comparable to a measure of the standard deviation of a distribution and is similar to the statistic used by other scholars*" (: 906). Since Dalton uses CSES survey data for the L/R score, to employ this formula, we standardize the RILE, which originally ranges from -100 to 100, on a 0 to 10 scale. Doing this, the polarization index ranges from 0 to 10, where 0 is total convergence, and 10 is extreme polarization. Figure 3.2 displays the evolution of these levels of polarization since the first democratic elections in 1977, until the

56 What does VOX want?

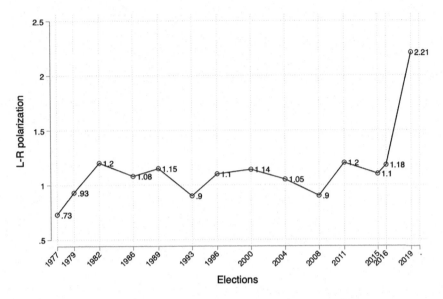

FIGURE 3.2 Trend of programmatic polarization in post-democratic Spain

Source: Elaboration of the authors based on MARPOR data and Dalton (2008)

April 2019 elections, the last ones that we have information on the manifestos of the different political parties in MARPOR.

It is quite patent in Figure 3.2 that the levels of programmatic polarization in the left–right axis in the Spanish party system have been stable and low since the return to democracy. Even in the 2015 national elections, with the entrance in the system of the radical left Podemos and the liberal Ciudadanos, programmatic polarization did not rise. This goes in the very same line of the findings of Linz and Montero (2001), which suggest that despite almost 40 years of dictatorship, partisan preferences in Spain have been mobilized mainly by moderate forces.

While the levels of ideological polarization during the Second Republic (1931–1939) were high, with the alternation in power of socialist and radical-conservative forces, after the proclamation of the 1978 constitution, the majority of political parties with political representation in Congress could be considered moderate forces.

If we take a look at the values of polarization for the April 2019 election, it reached 2.21 out of 10. This may seem a low value, but it is the highest value of polarization reached within the Spanish party system in more than 40 years, and it equates to more than a one-point increment since 2016 and is close to 1.5 points greater than that observed at the beginning of Spain's democratic restoration in 1977. Also, at least until April 2019, the low levels of polarization in the Spanish party system could be explained because – despite the ideological distance of those parties located at the extremes, UP and PP – in both the 2015 and 2016 general elections the political elites avoided embarking on strategies of tension or ideological clash (Llera et al., 2018).

What does VOX want? 57

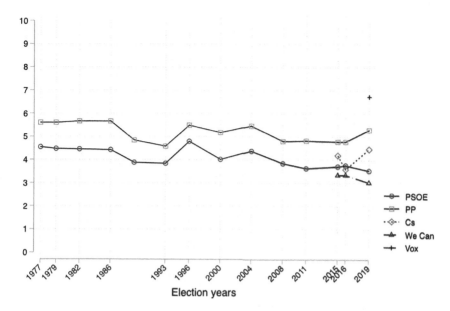

FIGURE 3.3 Trend of the RILE index for the five main parties in Spain, 1977–2019

Source: Elaboration of the authors, based on MARPOR data (1977–2019)

However, things changed with the emergence of VOX. This is due to the polarizing political strategies of VOX's party leaders, which affect the political debate, and which was closer to an antagonistic populist confrontation than a political consensus (Olivas Osuna, 2020). In general terms, left–right polarization within the system was a direct product of the emergence of VOX. As Figure 3.3. shows, there is a reaction of the main parties in the system to the emergence of this new party.

This is even more patent observing the evolution of the social-democratic PSOE and the conservative PP since 1977. Here we can appreciate that the trajectories of both parties have followed the same trend until 2016 despite the entrance of Cs and Podemos in the system. Nevertheless, the manifestos of the five main parties on the occasion of the April 2019 election showed a tendency towards a more radical discourse. The PSOE's left–right coefficient moved left from 3.77 to 3.54 while the PP's did the same towards the opposite pole: from 4.79 to 5.30 (to the right). Concerning the new parties in the system, the left–right index for Cs moved from 3.6 to 4.47, shifting almost one point to the right, while UP maintained the same position. This accommodation towards the right amongst Spain's existing right-wing parties, PP and Cs, is a typical example of the accommodating strategy adopted by the political mainstream in response to political challengers on the right (Abou-Chadi and Krause, 2018).

Even if the polarization on the left–right cleavage is relevant, we cannot forget that it is the sum of different issues. In this sense, following Alonso and Rovira Kaltwasser (2015), Table 3.8 summarizes the trend of the salience of two indexes

58 What does VOX want?

TABLE 3.8 Market liberalism, welfare state and centre–periphery indexes

Elections	Market Liberalism vs Market intervention	Welfare state	Centre–periphery
1977	6.9	13.5	9.0
1979	7.6	13.9	10.6
1982	8.7	14.2	9.3
1986	7.9	12.2	8.4
1989	6.6	13.5	10.9
1993	7.3	11.6	9.7
1996	4.6	8.5	11.7
2000	4.7	9.9	11.7
2004	2.8	10.7	13.3
2008	3.7	10.7	11.8
2011	7.4	11.9	12.3
2015	7.1	14.7	10.7
2016	7.6	15.1	9.4
2019	7.1	15.8	12.8
Simple mean	6.4	12.6	10.8

Notes: Market liberalism versus market intervention (issue categories: per401+per407 + per414 +per403+per404+per412). Welfare state pro and con (issue categories: per506+504+per507+per505).

Source: Elaboration of the authors based on Alonso and Rovira Kaltwasser (2015)

that refer to the socio-economic divide: market liberalism (right) vs market interventionism (left) and the defence of welfare state (left) vs a lesser expansion of this (right).

Regarding the socio-economic dimension, it is well known that there is an absolute consensus on the economic model: a developed welfare state characterized by a public health and education system, as well as a public pensions system. Differences among the major political options, PSOE and PP, are rather small, the former being more in favour of welfare state expansion, and the later more in favour of privatization (Montero and Lago, 2000; Montero, Lago and Torcal, 2007).

However, it is essential to underline that the conflicts that structure the competition within the Spanish party system go beyond the classic left–right divide. As Lipset and Rokkan (1967) pointed out in their classic work, the cleavages that can structure a party system are multiple (e.g. religious, social class, rural-urban, territorial). It would be therefore erroneous to conceptualize and measure polarization only on the left–right continuum. Indeed, if parties in a system compete alongside multiple axes, polarization needs to be assessed across each line of conflict.

States that host cultural minorities organized around nationalist parties that reinvigorate greater autonomy or an independent state are societies whose political spaces are crossed by at least two dimensions of competition. First, a left–right dimension, which can be exclusively socio-economic or also be accompanied by the cultural dimension, and second, a centre–periphery dimension. The centre–periphery axis accounts for the position of the parties concerning the territorial model of the state and the defence of the national identity of the majority cultural group with respect to the peripheral identity or vice versa (Alonso, Gómez and Cabeza, 2013).

Hence, it comes as no surprise that the literature on the cleavage structures shaping the Spanish party system has focused mainly on two of them: the socio-economic and the centre–periphery cleavage. For this reason, we also calculated the average of the salience for the centre–periphery divide.

Conflict over devolution, regional autonomy and state centralization are ultimately connected with ideology in Spain (Pérez-Nievas and Bonet, 2006). Thus, conservative national parties tend be more in favour of re-centralization and consolidated and centralized state control. In contrast, left-wing political parties have typically defended the current state of the autonomies (*Estado de las Autonomías*) or an increase in political decentralization or even a more widespread transformation toward federalism. However, at least referring to the electoral competition in the autonomous communities, recent data underlines that both PP and PSOE traditionally employed a moderation strategy in order to assess the centre–periphery question, given the secondary role this issue played in political competition (Gómez, Alonso and Cabeza, 2019: 421) and the need for both parties to rely on smaller (regional) parties with devolution-expanding preferences when it comes to government formation (Field, 2014; 2016).

The digits reported in Table 3.8 clearly show that socio-economic and centre–periphery issues have always been more critical for Spanish parties than immigration (see Figure 3.1). The centre–periphery dimension had even surpassed the welfare state dimension and the market-versus-state dimension in all elections since 1996, the year when the PP was elected to office for the first time, under the premiership of José María Aznar (Alonso and Rovira Kaltwasser, 2015: 17).

Figure 3.4 shows the evolution of the centre–periphery index from 1977 until 2019. Alonso and Rovira Kaltwasser (2015: 40) maintain that the existence of a centre–periphery cleavage acted as a barrier and prevented the emergence of a populist radical right party since, in general, both national and regional parties achieved to represent the ideas and interests of the electorate. In other words, there was not political space for another party to emerge since the interests of the citizens were well articulated by the parties in the system. It is clear that the barrier lost its efficacy.

In the last section, we analyse VOX's manifesto in comparative perspective, focusing on bearing in mind the proposals of other populist radical right parties, both in Europe and beyond. This is relevant to examine whether VOX's discourse is in line with the others belonging to the populist radical right.

VOX in comparative perspective

As we mentioned above, one of the advantages of using the MARPOR database is that we can compare the manifestos of different parties in a longitudinal perspective. In fact, currently it contains information for more than 50 countries covering

60 What does VOX want?

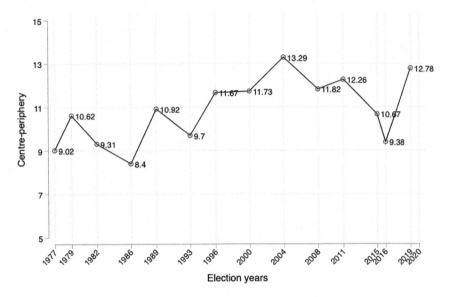

FIGURE 3.4 Centre–periphery index [a]

a: Per301 + per302.

Source: Elaboration of the authors, based on MARPOR data (1977–2019)

free, democratic elections since 1945.[19] In recent years, the project includes data for non-Western European countries. This allows us to compare VOX's manifesto with those of other populist radical right parties in Western Europe and beyond.

Table 3.9 summarizes the more salient categories for VOX and five other populist radical right parties and leaders. We analyse, in further detail, two of the most established populist radical right parties in Western Europe, the Freedom Party of Austria [*Freiheitliche Partei Österreichs*] (FPÖ), in Austria and the National Rally [*Rassemblement national*] (RN), formerly National Front [*Front national*] (FN) in France. Moreover, we analyse the most salient categories of three populist radical right parties and actors outside Western Europe: namely the United States's Republican Party (RP) under Donald Trump, Jair Bolsonaro in Brazil (JB), and José Antonio Kast in Chile (JAK). The rationale for comparing these cases is that they represent a broad universe of populist radical right parties and leaders in different regions of the world. Selecting cases that are different from each other, but still belonging to the populist radical right family, allows us to highlight both the core similarities among them as well as VOX's particularities.

Table 3.9 shows which categories VOX shared with the other populist radical right parties. On the one hand, the results of our comparative analysis show that VOX shares some of the classic programmatic features of Western European populist radical right parties, namely the emphasis on immigration, law and order, and welfare expansion which, for most of the parties and leaders analysed, is closely linked with welfare chauvinism. On the other hand, however, it has concrete

What does VOX want? 61

TABLE 3.9 Salient categories for the populist radical right

Issues	Parties / leaders and years					
	Europe			Americas		
	VOX[a]	FN	FPÖ	RP	JB	JAK
	2019	2017	2017	2016	2018	2017
National way of life positive (per601.1)	10.3	5.4				
Law and order positive (per605.1)	9.5	12.9	6.4		13.2	8.3
Traditional morality positive (per603)	7.9			8.5		
Welfare state expansion (per504)	7.5	6.3	5.5			10.9
Equality positive (per503)		5.9	5.8	5.7		
Free market economy (per401)				9.7	14.7	
Technology and infrastructure (per401)					7.7	11.9
Governmental and administrative efficiency (per303)						6.3
Economic orthodoxy (per414)					8.4	
Political corruption (per304)					5.3	
Education expansion (per506)					5.5	
Protectionism positive (per406)		5.4				
Labour groups positive (per701)		6.3				
Democracy positive (per202.1)						9.8
Environmental protection positive (per501)			5.9			
Freedom (per201)				6.5		
Military positive (per104)				6.7		

a: Differently from Table 3.1, immigration is not mentioned here because we are comparing single categories.

Notes: FN: Front National (National Front, currently National Rally), FPÖ: Freiheitliche Partei Österreichs (Freedom Party of Austria), RP: United States's Republican Party under Donald Trump, JB: Jair Bolsonaro in Brazil, JAK: José Antonio Kast in Chile.

Source: Elaboration of the authors, based on MARPOR data

particularities which reflect characteristics of the radical right *outside* of Europe, such as issues of defence of traditional morality. As mentioned previously in this chapter, it is essential to underline that some issues can be considered as "classic" for the populist radical right. This is, for example, the case of "law and order positive", which represents one of the most salient categories for all the parties and leaders in Table 3.9, with the exception of Trump's Republican Party. The fact that, under Trump, Republicans do not emphasize the law and order dimension does not mean that security, in general, is not a relevant issue in Trump's discourse. Concerning this, two considerations are in order. First, in the Republican manifesto, the emphasis on

62 What does VOX want?

security focuses more on the protection of the external border. Indeed, the quasi-sentences dedicated to the military: positive category represent almost 7 per cent of the whole manifesto. This category stresses the importance of external security and defence, for example, reflecting all the mentions in favour of increasing military expenses. The second consideration is linked to the current situation in the U.S. While during the election internal security was not a relevant issue in the country, the recent (2020) wave of protests has put law and order in the forefront of political debate.[20] In a speech held while the country was shaken by the protests brought about by the police's murder of George Floyd in Minneapolis, in the White House Rose Garden, Trump depicted himself as "your president of law and order".[21]

Another relevant factor that the populist radical right in Western Europe has in common is the defence of the welfare state. This can seem counter-intuitive, but the so-called welfare chauvinism is a feature that PRRPs often display, mostly in Western Europe. The rationale behind welfare chauvinism is the idea that social benefits should be provided only to the natives. Because most of those voters who support populist radical right parties are labour market insiders (Roberts, 2019), it is not surprising that populist radical right parties increasingly adopt welfare-chauvinist stances (Akkerman, de Lange and Rooduijn, 2016). Indeed, welfare chauvinism is a political view guided by nativism, since it holds that benefits and services should go only to natives. In this view, natives are, in fact, the only ones entitled to receive benefits from the welfare state (Ennser-Jedenastik, 2018; Rovira Kaltwasser and Zanotti, 2021). VOX is not an exception to this pattern, scoring 7.5 in the welfare state: positive category. If we look at the manifesto, the nativist approach to the welfare state is evident mostly with regards to the health system. One of the key proposals in this section, the party advocates for the *"elimination of free access to healthcare for illegal immigrants as well as co-payment for all legal residents who do not have a minimum of 10 years of residence on our land. [In these cases] only emergency services will be covered"* (VOX manifesto: 14).

The last point that seems relevant has to do with one feature that *differentiates* VOX from the other populist radical right parties in Western Europe but which the party shares with Trump's programme. As we mentioned before in this chapter, the emphasis on the defence of traditional morality is one of the particularities of VOX. This is patent in Table 3.9, since this category is salient only for two actors: VOX and the Republican Party in the U.S. On this topic, the two platforms are similar with respect to the salience, but when it comes to the parties' spatial position, the Republican party programme is much more conservative. It underlines that *"[t]he lawmakers use religion as a guide when legislating [stipulating that] man-made law must be consistent with God-given, natural rights"*. Also, it encourages *"the teaching of the Bible in public schools because a good understanding of its contents is indispensable of an educated citizenry"*.[22]

One final mention needs to be done regarding immigration. As we mentioned above, in most cases populist radical right parties show strongly anti-immigration stances. However, this is not reflected if we consider their party manifesto, at least with respect to single categories. At the beginning of this chapter, we observed that in the case of VOX the two categories that represent respectively unfavourable or assimilationist stances toward immigrants reached almost 9 per cent of the electoral programme. However, this does not stand for the other parties examined in Table 3.9.[23] This counter-intuitive aspect can be explained taking into account the coding categories of the MARPOR project. As we have mentioned above, there is not a single category that somehow sum up all the negative references to immigrants. Those categories that refer more generally to multiculturalism and minorities are somehow linked to anti-immigration stances. In this case, a qualitative analysis of the manifestos will for sure be useful to clarify this issue.

This comparison presents somewhat of a mixed bag of evidence. On the one hand, we see clear indications of programmatic congruence between the issues of salience for VOX and those that constitute common concerns for the populist radical right in Western Europe, such as concern over immigration, law and order, or issues related to welfare chauvinism. At the same time, however, our analysis points towards a focus on issues of traditional morality, which have softened among the populist radical right in Europe (Akkerman, 2005; Lancaster, 2019) but remains important and salient for populists on the ride outside of the European context (Mudde and Rovira Kaltwasser, 2018).

Conclusion

In this chapter, we analysed the characteristics of VOX's April 2019 electoral programme using the MARPOR database. In the first section, we analysed the five most salient issues: national way of life, law and order, immigration, traditional values, and welfare state expansion. We examined these issues in light of their salience in the Spanish party system in a longitudinal fashion. We found evidence that VOX has contributed to the politization of these issues, and VOX's arrival within the party system has represented a significant break-up of the status quo.

The second section builds on the analysis of the cleavage structure of the Spanish party system. First, in general, we observed that on the left–right dimension, the Spanish two-party system has been historically convergent until 2015, before the entrance of Podemos and Ciudadanos. Polarization in the system rose in 2019 with the entrance of VOX. Relying on Dalton's (2008) polarization index, we show that VOX's ascendency is associated with levels of polarization not yet observed in Spain's recent democratic history. In addition to the conflict over the conventional left–right (labour–capital) dimension, we also analysed polarization along another important dimension of competition that the literature has considered as relevant: namely market liberalism vs market intervention, the welfare state, the centre–periphery cleavage. Our most revealing results are concerned with the centre–periphery cleavage, which has been historically one of the most salient cleavages that structured the Spanish party system (Gray, 2020; Pardos-Prado and Sagarzazu, 2019). Here we find that, even though this cleavage has always been salient in the political debate, the

64 What does VOX want?

entrance of VOX has further exacerbated its politicization. This was mainly a consequence of the so-called *Procès* (see Chapter 2), which culminated in the unauthorized independence referendum in Catalonia in 2017.

Finally, the last section compared VOX with other populist radical right parties or actors in Western Europe, the United States and Latin America in terms of issue salience. Here we found that even if VOX shares many of the classical traits of the populist radical right, the extreme emphasis that VOX's leaders put on traditional values and the primacy of the national way of life seem a peculiar characteristic of VOX.

After having analysed the discourse of VOX, Chapter 4 focuses on VOX's voters both in terms of their characteristics with respect to the voters of the other Spanish political parties *and* examining their similitudes and differences with the voters of other populist radical right parties in Western Europe.

Notes

1 See: www.VOXespana.es/espana/programa-electoral-VOX.
2 See: www.manifesto-project.wzb.eu/.
3 The MARPOR project continues the work of the Manifesto Research Group (MRG) and the Comparative Manifesto Project (CMP).
4 Per 601.1.
5 For instance, according to the Linguistic Policy Directorate [*Direcció General de Política Lingüística*] (DGPL) of the Catalan Government [*Generalitat de Catalunya*], in 2018, the most usual language of communication among the Catalan population was Spanish for 48.6 per cent, Catalan, for 36.1, and both Spanish and Catalan, for 7.4 per cent (the remaining 7.4 per cent corresponds to people indicating other languages or combinations of languages). See: https://llengua.gencat.cat/web/.content/documents/dadesestudis/altres/arxius/presentacio-resultats-eulp-2018.pdf (page 16).
6 España, Unidad y Soberanía.
7 Per 605.1.
8 The salience of the "law and order" index (605.1+605.2) and the "law and order" positive (per605.1) is the same because per 605.2 equals zero.
9 We are aware that the argument of Meguid (2005) refers to position, not to salience. However, here we refer to "favourable mentions of strict law enforcement", which can be interpreted as a position on the matter of security.
10 See category 601.2.
11 Per 607+per608+per705
12 See: www.20minutos.es/noticia/42284/0/regularizacion/inmigrantes/inmigracion/.
13 For further details of the evolution of the trend on the mains problems for Spaniards, see: www.cis.es/cis/export/sites/default/-archivos/Indicadores/documentos_html/TresProblemas.html.
14 Per603.
15 See: www.europapress.es/nacional/noticia-VOX-lanza-manifiesto-8m-dia-pensado-extrema-izquierda-no-hables-nombre-20200307211615.html.
16 While the salience of the per603+per604 rose from 0.24 in 2016 to 2.25 in 2019, the salience of per603 is responsible just for the 0.75 of the total increment.
17 Just the category "welfare state expansion" (504).

18 This formula has been used by Dalton (2008) to measure polarization using CSES survey data.
19 See: www.manifesto-project.wzb.eu.
20 President Trump's Twitter status features "LAW AND ORDER" many times in the last months.
21 See: www.youtube.com/watch?v=1V46JPtj31s.
22 See: www.nytimes.com/2016/07/13/us/politics/republican-convention-issues.html?_r=0
23 Values: RP 2016 (1.413); JAK 2017 (0,875); JB (2018) 0; FPO 2017 (6.95); FN 2017 (4, 603)

References

Abou-Chadi, Tarik, and Werner Krause (2018) The Causal Effect of Radical Right Success on Mainstream Parties' Policy Positions: A Regression Discontinuity Approach. *British Journal of Political Science*, 1–19.

Adams JF, Merrill, S and Grofman B (2005) *A Unified Theory of Party Competition. A Cross-National Analysis Integrating Spatial and Behavioral Factors.* Cambridge: Cambridge University Press.

Akkerman T (2005) Anti-immigration parties and the defence of liberal values: The exceptional case of the List Pim Fortuyn. *Journal of Political Ideologies*, 10:3: 337–354, DOI: 10.1080/13569310500244354

Akkerman T, De Lange SL and Rooduijn M (eds) (2016) *Radical Right-Wing Populist Parties in Western Europe: Into the Mainstream?* London: Routledge.

Alonso S., Volkens A and Gómez B (2012) *Análisis de contenido de textos políticos. Un enfoque cualitativo.* Madrid: Centro de Investigaciones Sociológicas.

Alonso S, Gómez B and Cabeza L (2013) Measuring Centre–Periphery Preferences: The Regional Manifestos Project. *Regional & Federal Studies* 23(2): 189–211. DOI: 10.1080/13597566.2012.754351.

Alonso S and Rovira Kaltwasser C (2015) Spain: No Country for the Populist Radical Right? *South European Society and Politics* 20 (1): 21–45. DOI: 10.1080/13608746.2014.985448.

Dalton RJ (2008) The Quantity and the Quality of Party Systems: Party System Polarization, Its Measurement, and Its Consequences. *Comparative Political Studies.* 41(7): 899–920. DOI 10.1177/0010414008315860.

Debus M (2009) Analysing Party Politics in Germany with New Approaches for Estimating Policy Preferences of Political Actors. *German Politics* 18(3): 281–300. DOI: 10.1080/09644000903055773.

De Vries C and Hobolt S (2020) *Political Entrepreneurs. The Rise of Challenger Parties in Europe.* Princeton – New Jersey: Princeton University Press.

Dinas E and Gemenis K (2010) Measuring Parties' Ideological Positions with Manifesto Data: A Critical Evaluation of the Competing Methods. *Party Politics* 16(4): 427–450. DOI: 10.1177/1354068809343107.

Downs A (1957) *An Economic Theory of Democracy.* New York: Harper and Row.

Ennser-Jedenastik L (2018). Welfare Chauvinism in Populist Radical Right Platforms: The Role of Redistributive Justice Principles. *Social Policy & Administration* 52 (1): 293–314. DOI: 10.1111/spol.12325.

Ferreira C (2019) VOX como representante de la derecha radical en España: un estudio sobre su ideología. *Revista Española de Ciencia Política* 0 (51): 73–98. DOI: 10.21308/recp.51.03.

Field BN (2014) Minority parliamentary government and multilevel politics: Spain's system of mutual back scratching. *Comparative Politics* 46(3): 293–312.

Field BN (2016) *Why Minority Governments Work: Multilevel Territorial Politics in Spain*. Basingstoke: Palgrave MacMillan.

Giddens A (2013) *The Third Way: The Renewal of Social Democracy*. United States: John Wiley & Sons.

Gómez B, Alonso S and Cabeza L (2019) *En busca del poder territorial: cuatro décadas de elecciones autonómicas en España*. Madrid: Serie Academia, 42, Centro de Investigaciones Sociológicas.

Gould R (2019) VOX España and Alternative für Deutschland: Propagating the Crisis of National Identity. *Genealogy* 3(4): 1–24. DOI: 10.3390/genealogy3040064.

Gray C (2020) *Territorial Politics and the Party System in Spain: Continuity and change since the financial crisis*. Routledge

Greve B (2019) *Welfare, Populism and Welfare Chauvinism*. Bristol: Palgrave.

Huber E and Stephens J (2001) *Development and Crisis of the Welfare State: Parties and Policies in Global Markets*. Chicago: University of Chicago Press.

Hutter S, and Kriesi H (2019) *European Party Politics in Times of Crises*. Cambridge: Cambridge University Press.

Ignazi P (1992) The silent counter-revolution. *European Journal of Political Research* 22(1): 3–34. DOI: 10.1111/j.1475-6765.1992.tb00303.x.

Krause W, Cohen D and Abou-Chadi T (2019) Does Accommodation Work? Mainstream Party Strategies and the Success of Radical Right Parties. The WAB Berlin Social Science Center, unpublished manuscript.

Körösényi A and Sebók M (2013) The Realistic Version of Positive Mandate Theory. A Political Theory of Pledge-Fulfillment. MTA TK Politikatudományi Intézet Working Papers in Political Science 2013/14: 1–21.

Linz JJ (1973) Early State-Building in the Late Peripheral Nationalisms against the State: the case of Spain. Eisenstadt SN and Rokkan S (eds) *Building States and Nations: Models, Analysis and Data across Three Worlds*. Beverly Hills, CA: Sage, pp. 32–116.

Linz JJ and Montero JR (2001) The Party Systems of Spain: Old Cleavages and New Challenges. Karvonen L and Kuhnle S (eds.) *Party Systems and Voter Alignments Revisited*. London: Routledge, pp. 150–196.

Lipset SM and Rokkan S (1967) *Party Systems and voter alignments: Cross national perspectives*. New York: Free Press.

Llera Ramo F, Baras MJ and Montabes Pereira J (2018) *Las elecciones generales de 2015 y 2016*. Madrid: Centro de Investigaciones Sociológicas.

Madariaga A and Rovira Kaltwasser C. (2020) Right-Wing Moderation, Left-Wing Inertia and Political Cartelization in Post-Transition Chile. *Journal of Latin American Studies* 52(2): 343–371. DOI: 10.1017/S0022216X19000932.

Manin B, Przeworski A and Stokes S (2001) *Democracy, Accountability, and Representation*. Cambridge: Cambridge University Press.

Meguid B (2005) Competition Between Unequals: The Role of Mainstream Party Strategy in Niche Party Success. *The American Political Science Review* 99(3): 347–359. DOI: 10.1017/S0003055405051701.

Mikhaylov S, Laver M and Benoit K (2008) Coder Reliability and Misclassification in Comparative Manifesto Project Codings, Prepared for presentation at the 66th MPSA Annual National Conference, Palmer House Hilton Hotel and Towers, April 3–6, 2008.

Montero JR, Lago I and Torcal M (eds.) (2007) *Elecciones generales 2004*. Madrid: Centro de Investigaciones Sociológicas.

Montero JR and Lago I (eds.) (2010) *Elecciones generales 2008*. Madrid: Centro de Investigaciones Sociológicas.

Mudde C (2007) *Populist Radical Right Parties in Europe*. Cambridge: Cambridge University Press.

Mudde C (2019) *The Far Right Today*. Cambridge: Polity Press.

Mudde C and Rovira Kaltwasser C (2018) Studying populism in comparative perspective: Reflections on the contemporary and future research agenda. *Comparative Political Studies* 51(13): 1667–1693. DOI: 10.1177/0010414018789490.

Norris P (2005) *Radical Right. Voters and Parties in the Electoral Market*. Cambridge: Cambridge University Press.

Olivas Osuna JJ (2020). From chasing populists to deconstructing populism: a new multidimensional approach to understanding and comparing populism. *European Journal of Political Research*. https://doi.org/10.1111/1475-6765.12428

Pardos-Prado S and Sagarzazu I (2019) Economic performance and center-periphery conflicts in party competition. *Party Politics* 25(1) 50–62.

Pérez Nievas S and Rama J (2018) Las bases sociales y actitudinales del nacionalismo: Cataluña, Galicia y País Vasco. Blanco Martín A, Chueca Sánchez AM, López Ruiz JA, Mora Rosado S (eds.) *Informe España 2018*. Cátedra Martín Patino. Madrid: Universidad de Comillas, pp. 301–364.

Pérez-Nievas S and Bonet E (2006) Identidades regionales y reivindicación de autogobierno. El etnorregionalismo en el voto a partidos nacionalistas de Bélgica, España y Reino Unido. *Revista Española de Ciencia Política* 15: 123–161. Available at: https://recyt.fecyt.es/index.php/recp/article/view/37433 (accessed 16 October 2020).

Kriesi HP, Grande E, Lachat R, Dolezal M, Bornschier S and Frey T (2008) *West European politics in the age of globalization*. Cambridge: Cambridge University Press.

Lancaster CM (2019) Not So Radical After All: Ideological Diversity Among Radical Right Supporters and Its Implications. *Political Studies*. Online First. DOI:10.1177/0032321719870468.

Pytlas B, Herman LE and Muldoon J (2018) Populist radical right mainstreaming and challenges to democracy in an enlarged Europe. Herman LE and Muldoon J *Trumping the Mainstream: The Conquest of Democratic Politics by the Populist Radical Right*. Abingdon: Routledge.

Roberts KM (2017) State of the Field: Party Politics in Hard Times: Comparative Perspectives on the European and Latin American Economic Crises. *European Journal of Political Research* 56(2): 218–233. DOI: 10.1111/1475-6765.12191.

Roberts KM (2019). Bipolar disorders: Varieties of capitalism and populist out-flanking on the left and right. *Polity 51*(4): 641–653.

Rovira Kaltwasser C (2019) La (sobre)adaptación programática de la derecha chilena y la irrupción de la derecha populista radical. *Colombia Internacional* 99: 29–61. DOI: 10.7440/colombiaint99.2019.02.

Rovira Kaltwasser C and Zanotti L (2021). Populism and the Welfare State. Greve B (ed) *Handbook on Austerity, Populism and the Welfare State*. Cheltenham, UK: Edward Elgar Publishing.

Schumacher G and van Kersbergen K (2016) Do mainstream parties adapt to the welfare chauvinism of populist parties? *Party Politics* 22(3): 300–312. DOI: 10.1177/1354068814549345.

Van der Brug W, Fennema M and Tillie J. (2005). Why Some Anti-Immigrant Parties Fail and Others Succeed? *Comparative Political Studies* 38(5): 537–573. DOI: 10.1177/0010414004273928.

VOX España (2018) 100 medidas para la España Viva. Available at: www.VOXespana.es/biblioteca/espana/2018m/gal_c2d72e181103013447.pdf (accessed 17 October 2020).

Zanotti L (2019). *Populist polarization in Italian politics, 1994–2016: an assessment from a Latin American analytical perspective* (Doctoral dissertation). Leiden University.

Zanotti L and Rama J (2020). VOX: Nativismo y tradicionalismo en tiempos de Coronavirus. The Conversation España. Avaliable at https://theconversation.com/vox-nativismo-y-tradicionalismo-en-tiempos-de-coronavirus-134920 (accessed 20 October 2020).

Appendix

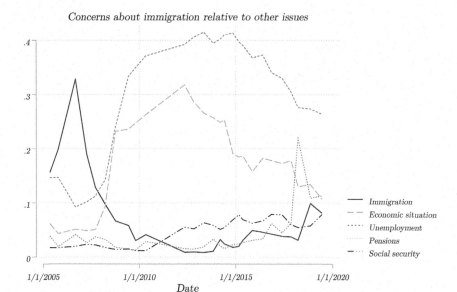

FIGURE A3.1 Concerns about immigration compared with other issues in Spain

Source: Elaboration of the authors, based on data from Eurobarometer

4

A QUESTION OF DEMAND

Who votes for VOX?

"SPAIN, UNITED, WILL NEVER BE DEFEATED!"
(VOX party supporters on the night of 10 November 2019)

2,677,173 people carried a ballot with VOX's name on it to the polling booth in April 2019. Just seven months later, in November, that number increased to 3,640,063, placing VOX as the third largest party in Spain in terms of both seats (52 out of 350) and votes (15.21 per cent). Three and a half million people is no small number, so who are these people? The chapters up until now have painted a picture of how VOX came to be the third largest political party in Spain and what the party advocates in its platform.

In this chapter we turn our attention away from what VOX wants and ask: who votes for VOX? And, additionally, to what extent are VOX's supporters different from their West European contemporaries? We provide an answer to these questions by pulling on a cross-section of different survey data sources including national election study data provided by the CIS in Spain as well as comparative surveys with cross-national data on the voter profiles of populist radical right-wing parties from across Western Europe, such as the European Social Survey (ESS round 9).

Who votes for VOX?

We begin our analysis of VOX's electorate by focusing on their socio-demographic profile. What do VOX's supporters look like? Are they different in substantive ways from the average Spaniard? What makes them distinct from the supporters of Spain's established right-wing parties? Are there clear differences in who supports the populist and radical offering? We answer these questions and consider how class, education, age, gender, and geography are linked to the support for the populist radical right-wing challenger.

70 Who votes for VOX?

Gender

Whilst there may be some debate on the demographic determinants of support for populist radical right-wing parties (Rooduijn, 2018), where there is a strong empirical and persistently replicated finding is on the issue of gender (Stockemer et al., 2018). In his 1994 monograph *Radical Right-Wing Populism in Western Europe*, Betz argued that "*[a]s if following some unwritten law, radical right-wing populist parties have consistently attracted a considerably higher number of male than female voters*" (Betz, 1994: 142). Almost 30 years later, this observation still rings true (Immerzeel et al., 2015): men are significantly more likely to support populist parties on the radical right than women (for a summary, see Spierings et al., 2015).

The reasons behind the gender gap are numerous. First, it is argued that the increased support among men is driven by the fact that they are more susceptible to the negative economic consequences of the processes of deindustrialization and automation that disproportionately impacts those working in labour-intensive industries (Im et al., 2019; Oesch, 2008a). Second, women are assumed to hold more tolerant and less hostile attitudes towards immigration, reducing the appeal of radical right-wing politicization of this issue (Givens, 2004; Spierings et al., 2015). Third, populist radical right parties (PRRPs) and other radical right parties sustain more traditional principles as regard gender, and this has electoral consequences (Campbell and Erzeel, 2018). Fourth, Spierings and Zaslove (2017) argue that independently of these two mechanisms, women are less likely to hold populist preferences[1] and this reduced sympathy with populism is what drives the lower level of support for these parties, regardless of their ideological colour on left–right spectrum, among women. Finally, Harteveld et al. (2015) show that women do not differ much from men in their level of nativism, authoritarianism or discontent with democracy, but these attitudes translate more strongly into votes for the radical right among men, possibly because they find these issues more salient.

Table 4.1 reports the gender breakdown of VOX's electoral constituents and that of Spain's other four main nationwide parties: the populist radical left Together We Can [*Unidas Podemos*] (UP), the centre-left Spanish Socialist Workers' Party [*Partido Socialista Obrero Español*] (PSOE), the centre-right Citizens [*Ciudadanos*] (Cs), and the conservative People's Party [*Partido Popular*] (PP).

TABLE 4.1 Gender gap in support for VOX

Sex	Party voters					
	UP	PSOE	Cs	PP	VOX	Total
Man	55.34	46.43	42.34	43.52	61.60	48.74
Woman	44.66	53.57	57.66	56.48	38.40	51.26
Total	100.00	100.00	100.00	100.00	100.00	100.00

Source: elaboration of the authors based on CIS (2019b)

As expected by the extensive empirical work presented across other countries, it comes as no surprise to see that the gender gap between party voters is the largest within VOX. 61.6 per cent of VOX voters are men whereas only 38.4 per cent of the party's supporters are women. This gender gap is significant at 23.2 percentage points and dwarfs the gaps observed across all other parties. Interestingly, the only other party to be significantly "over supported" by men is UP, although the gap is half of that observed in the case of VOX (10.7 percentage points).

Female Spanish voters appear to favour parties that are more moderate in comparison to men as the increased proportion of men to women in electoral support is only observed amongst those parties on the extreme ends of the ideological space. This is consistent with Spierings and Zaslove's (2017) thesis that a rejection of populism (which is articulated on both sides of the traditional left–right space) is what engenders the lack of support for these parties.

In the case of VOX, part of the lower electoral support among women may be a function of i) their treatment of feminism and gender equality in their political programmes and ii) the party's reliance on traditional masculinity in the imagery and rhetoric of their campaign material. VOX positioned itself as a clear defender of traditional gender roles and was explicitly opposed to any public policy proposals focused, specifically, on the expansion of women's socio-economic welfare. Concretely, the party is critical of the expansion of what it pens "gender ideology" and has sought the repeal of gender violence laws (introduced in Spain because of the high level of domestic abuse cases), which it views as discriminatory against men (Turnbull-Dugarte, 2019). There is, as a result, a specific and strong anti-feminist streak within the party who have a penchant of referring to feminist activists as "*Feminazis*", the "*Feminist Jihad*", and part of the "*progressive dictatorship*" they portray as a threat to Spain and traditional (read Catholic) Spanish values.

In addition to this anti-feminist messaging, is also the reliance of masculine imagery. Ralph-Morrow (2020) argues the radical right leans heavily on a masculine-orientated discourse in order to appeal to individuals who wish to feel like "real" men. Relying on evidence from the case of the English Defence League (EDL), she shows that radical right parties leverage militaristic messages with violent and dominating imagery throughout their campaigns in order to mobilize supporters.

Appeals to the masculine are abundant in VOX's political communication. The party's, now infamous, "Make Spain Great Again" campaign video[2] provides just but one example in which the party leader, Abascal, is presented in a number of masculine settings in the rural countryside, in hunting gear, horse-riding, or mountain hiking. Abascal's social media profiles are full of images of the leader engaged in sports and strenuous exercise, signalling his strong *macho* image, or presenting him attending both military gatherings and bull-fighting events (Sampietro and Sánchez-Castillo, 2020). VOX has positioned itself as an advocate of Spain's armed forces, in line with the far-right's traditional fetishization of the military (Heinisch and Werner, 2019) and is also a keen defender of Spain's tradition of slaughtering

72 Who votes for VOX?

bulls for sport. Note that both of these positions, which are closely associated with the party, tend to find their majority support amongst men.

Age

In general, older voters are far less likely to vote for new candidates and entrepreneurial challenger parties. Partisanship, emotive attachment to a particular party, tends to form during an individual's formative years and, over time, individuals tend to become socialized into identifying with and voting for the same party (Dalton and Wattenberg, 2002). Voters who have been around the block a few times are therefore more likely to stick to what they know and vote for electoral options that they already tend to support or are more familiar with (Lupu, 2015). The (historical) dominance of two-party politics in Spain is also likely to steer older voters away from political challengers. When We Can (*Podemos*, the initial brand of UP) and Cs emerged onto the national political arena for the first time in 2015, the vast majority of their voters were sourced from younger members of the electorate (Cordero and Montero, 2015; Orriols and Cordero, 2016) who had lower levels of partisan attachment to the PP and PSOE and were far more disenchanted with the functioning of democratic governance under the repetitive alternation in power between PSOE- and PP-led governments. In short, this meant that, as Spain's two-party system came under threat, party virginity and entrepreneurial "newness" was a vote-winner amongst the Spanish youth.

Of course, VOX is not just any political challenger but one that has broken with Spain's clean record as a young democracy that had (until now) remained free of the radical right (Alonso and Rovira Kaltwasser, 2015). Younger voters tend to be socially liberal and the new parties that banked Spain's young vote emerged on the political scene promoting socially liberal policies. Young voters are more likely to support international integration (Lauterbach and DeVries, 2020), endorse sexually modern values such as gender equality measures and LGBT+ rights (Dotti Sani and Quaranta, 2020), and are also more prone to endorse liberal policies towards immigration (McLaren and Paterson, 2020). As shown in Chapter 3, the political platform advocated by VOX is the antithesis of what we would expect young voters to support.

To further complicate the age–PRRP relationship, it has been shown that, under certain conditions, there are also groups of young people who tend to vote for these parties. Young people have been adversely affected by soft economic growth and tough labour market conditions to the point that, in many developed countries, they are the age group facing the highest unemployment and poverty rates, and high levels of part-time unemployment and job insecurity (Pitt et al., 2018). Many young people constitute part of the new "precariat" (Bessant, 2018) that are deprived of the socio-economic security designed by social democrats, labour parties, and trades unions for the traditional working class (Standing, 2013). For instance, Siedler (2011) has shown that economic insecurity predicts youth far right party identification in Germany.

Who votes for VOX? **73**

TABLE 4.2 Age distribution of Spanish party voters

Age group	Party voters					
	UP	PSOE	Cs	PP	VOX	Total
18–24	14.10	6.88	11.29	3.31	12.98	8.36
25–34	19.44	7.82	15.32	8.58	19.89	12.01
35–44	**25.00**	16.08	19.35	13.10	20.17	17.62
45–54	20.09	18.92	**24.19**	18.52	**20.72**	19.69
55–64	13.68	19.00	15.32	17.32	14.64	16.90
>64	7.69	**31.30**	14.52	**39.16**	11.60	**25.40**
Total	100.00	100.00	100.00	100.00	100.00	100.00

Notes: The largest age group of voters of each party is highlighted in bold.

Source: elaboration of the authors based on CIS (2019b)

There are, therefore, competing expectations about where we might expect the young to fall when it comes to voting for VOX. Table 4.4 reports the percentage of each party's voter population that belongs to different age categories. Looking at the distribution of VOX's support across different cohorts, we see that the attractive pool of partisan novelty wins out.

Let's compare VOX with the PP. In the case of the new populist challenger, more than half (53 per cent) of their support came from those aged under 44. Only one in four of the PP's supporters came from the same age bracket. Looking at the youngest cohort of voters (those aged 18–24) there is close to a ten percentage-point gap between the two right-wing parties. The young may not like the traditional right-wing option on the party menu, but the new and radical alternative enjoys more success amongst Spain's newest voters. The reverse relationship is seen amongst those who have been in the electorate the longest. Some 40 per cent of the PP's voters were aged 64 or older whilst under 12 per cent of VOX's voters come from the same category. Note that similar patterns are observed in the gap between the PSOE and Podemos.

The age distribution of the party's supporters should be worrying for the PP. Assuming VOX's fixture as part of Spain's party system and the establishment of a "new normal" multiparty space (Zanotti and Rama, 2020), VOX represents an important threat to the PP's future vote revenue. Whilst the PP's support amongst the elderly is strong, the natural laws of the biological world dictate that these voters may not be around to participate in many future elections, whereas VOX's support is heavily concentrated amongst those who are being socialized to become partisans and more likely be around to vote in future electoral competitions. The strong relationship between age and support for VOX is demonstrated in Figure 4.2. What this figure shows is the effect of age on the probability of an individual voting for VOX over either of the two other right-wing parties (PP and Cs).[3] The visualization shows a significant negative slope, indicating that there is a strong

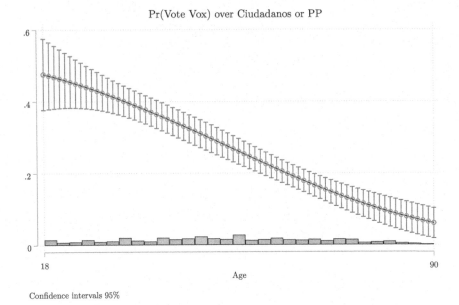

FIGURE 4.1 Marginal effect of age and electoral support for VOX

Source: elaboration of the authors based on CIS (2019b)

negative relationship between age and voting for VOX over the other right-wing alternatives. The younger (older) you are, the more (less) probable it is that you will vote for VOX.

Class

Political conflict has traditionally been shaped by sociological cleavages. One of these cleavages is constructed by social class, which involves an antagonistic relationship between capital and labour, the haves and have-nots, or aristocratic landowners and the working-class proletariat (Lijphart, 1984; Lipset and Rokkan, 1967). Spain is no different. One of the main divisions between the country's hegemonic left-wing and right-wing parties, class conflict, has persisted over the period since the country's transition to democracy and pre-dates Spain's democratic collapse during the civil war that led to the establishment of the Francoist regime (Payne, 1993).

We know from a wide catalogue of studies in political science, economics, and sociology that class matters. Those who are better off are far more likely to take an interest in politics, participate in the electoral process, have higher political efficacy, and feel that their vote allows them to have a say in what the government does. Even if the effects of social class divisions may be becoming diluted (see, for example, Oesch (2008b) and Oesch and Rennwald (2018)), class still remains an important determinant when it comes to understanding political behaviour and partisan preferences.

Who votes for VOX? **75**

TABLE 4.3 Subjective class identities

Social class	Party voters					
	UP	PSOE	Cs	PP	VOX	Total
Upper-middle class	3.42	3.96	6.05	7.38	5.25	4.99
Middle class	44.66	42.22	60.48	54.67	55.25	48.64
Lower-middle class	20.51	22.44	15.73	15.81	17.96	19.48
Working class	25.43	23.39	12.10	14.01	16.85	19.79
Poor	1.71	3.35	1.61	2.26	1.10	2.41
Other/Don't Know	4.27	4.64	4.03	5.87	3.59	4.68
Total	100.00	100.00	100.00	100.00	100.00	100.00

Source: elaboration of the authors based on CIS (2019b)

To gain an insight in the class constitution of VOX's electoral base, we first seek to compare the class labels that the party's supporters self-identify with. Table 4.3 compares the self-reported subjective class of Spanish voters for each of the five main political parties. Values in each column indicate the percentage of each party's voter population that self-identify with each class bracket.

Across the board, the largest proportion of party voters identify as being middle class. There is a significant difference, however, between right-leaning and left-leaning parties' subjective class identities. Left-leaning voters identify as middle class significantly less than their right-leaning peers. Whilst only 42 per cent of the PSOE's and 45 per cent of the UP's voters identify as middle class, the proportions observed amongst the supporters of the PP (55 per cent), Cs (60.5 per cent), and VOX (55 per cent) are notably larger. Congruently, the relationship is reversed in the case of the working-class proportions of each party's voting base. Comparing the percentage of voters who identify as working class between the PP and the PSOE, the latter is 10 percentage-points larger.

Comparing the subjective class divisions confirms our expectations regarding the marked class distinction between voters on the left on the right. It does not, however, display any differences of note *within* the ideological camps. In other words, between right-leaning parties, there is no significant divergence between the proportion of voters' class-based identities between the different parties (VOX, PP or Cs). In terms of class, VOX's electoral support is then not descriptively distinct from that of the party's right-wing colleagues but is illustrative of the traditional left–right dichotomous cleavage between lower-class supporters of the left and higher-class supporters of the right.

We now turn to see how the class-based distinction between party support is represented in terms of income. Whilst self-reported class is an important indicator of where an individual falls in the socio-economic distribution as it captures the measurement of identification with the class-group, citizens' perceptions of their class may not necessarily correlate with where their economic status lies within the range of income groups in the population.

76 Who votes for VOX?

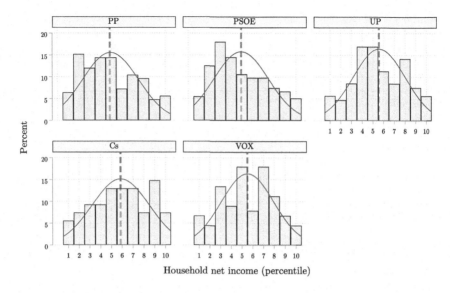

FIGURE 4.2 Income distribution of voters

Source: elaboration of the authors based on ESS (2020)

Taking a closer look at income as a measure of class, we observe some important divergences between the different party supporters including those who voted for Spain's new populist right-wing challenger. Figure 4.2 visualizes the distribution of each party's supporters across the different income percentiles in Spain. Voters with income value 1 belong to the bottom percentile whilst individuals with income value 10 belong to the top percentile. The vertical dashed line signals the mean income level for each party's supporters.

The highest (mean) level of income is reported among the voters of Cs, whose mean level is 5.9 on a ten-point scale. This is followed by VOX and UP, whose voters both have mean income values of 5.6. In the case of the data from the European Social Survey (ESS), the dividing line between income and party choice is not ideological but rather based on party novelty. The voters of all three "new" parties have a mean *self-reported* income that is significantly higher than that of the traditional parties.

As a final measure of economic status and social class, we explore the extent to which social status and economic wealth matter to the voters of the different parties. The ESS includes a battery of different survey items that are included to aid the identification of concrete psychological traits and latent values of respondents across different measures. These questions present respondents with a statement such as "It's important to seek fun and things that give you pleasure" and individuals are required to report the extent to which they believe that the same statement is something that they believe characterizes themself. We rely on responses to one of these questions in an attempt to explore to what extent social status matters for

TABLE 4.4 Importance of being rich, having money and owning expensive things

"Wealth matters"	Party voters					
	UP	PSOE	Cs	PP	VOX	Total
Like me	8.15	8.94	8.82	4.30	16.67	8.70
Somewhat like me	28.15	24.50	29.41	33.33	24.51	27.62
Not like me	63.70	66.56	61.76	62.37	58.82	63.68
Total	100.00	100.00	100.00	100.00	100.00	100.00

Source: elaboration of the authors based on ESS (2020)

those who sympathize with VOX. Table 4.4 reports the proportion of each party's supporters who think the statement "It's important to be rich, have money and expensive things" sounds i) like them, ii) somewhat like them, or iii) not like them. The results indicate that being rich matters for VOX's voting constituents.

The proportion of VOX supporters who confirmed that they viewed being rich and having status as something that was important to them was twice as large as that observed in the case of the PSOE, UP or Cs and four times that of PP voters. The gap in the importance of being wealthy between VOX and the mainstream right is significant. Modelling the probability of identifying with the statement ("like me") reports that VOX voters are 12 percentage points (p<0.01) more likely to identify with the statement relative to PP voters. Status and aspiration are, therefore, an important aspect of the identity of VOX's voters.

Education

If social class-based distinctions only partially explain the electoral divisions between VOX and Spain's established parties, perhaps education can. A growing body of literature points towards the increasing cleavage-structuring role of education in post-industrial societies (Stubager, 2009: 2013) given the effect of education in shaping distinct social identities and ideological preferences. Levels of education have never been higher. Across Europe, there is an increasing number of university graduates and subsequent generations of voters tend to receive more years of education and host a higher proportion of graduates than those that came before.

We can see this also in the case of Spain. In the first wave of the ESS (2002–2003), only 15.21 per cent of the population were degree-holders. In wave nine (2019–2020), this figure had risen to 29.2 per cent. The change is even more drastic amongst those under 35: increasing from 18.39 to 63.55 per cent. Of course, levels of education cannot be taken as wholly independent of social class (nor of income), as those with higher social standing also tend to be those most likely to earn a university education, but the role of education is important in establishing and shaping political preferences.

78 Who votes for VOX?

TABLE 4.5 Educational profiles of Spanish party support

Education	Party voters					
	UP	PSOE	Cs	PP	VOX	Total
Primary or less	6.64	26.72	11.29	27.38	6.37	19.78
Secondary	62.74	54.31	54.44	48.71	77.84	57.34
University	30.62	18.97	34.27	23.90	15.79	22.89
Total	100.00	100.00	100.00	100.00	100.00	100.00

Source: elaboration of the authors based on CIS (2019b)

A catalogue of research in political science shows that increased exposure to education can increase support for social liberalism and engender more tolerant attitudes towards LGBT+ rights (Dotti Sani and Quaranta, 2020), tolerance of ethnic minorities, and acceptance of immigration (Cavaille and Marshall, 2019; Hainmueller and Hiscox, 2007), as well as increased support for the EU (Hakhverdian et al., 2013; Kunst et al., 2020) and globalization (Hainmueller and Hiscox, 2006). Given the salient role of these different issues when it comes to electing parties at the ballot box, particularly in Spain, assessing the educational profile of partisan support for VOX in comparison to Spain's established parties is important.

Table 4.3 focuses on the proportion of each party's electoral support that has a primary, secondary or university-level education. Compared to all other parties, VOX's voters have the lowest proportion of university graduates with only 15.79 per cent holding a degree. This stands out significantly across two paired comparisons. Firstly, compared to the other parties that belong within the same (right-wing) dichotomy of the ideological space, 24 per cent of the PP's voter population are degree-holders whilst the university-educated population of Cs's constituents is more than double that of VOX, with close to 35 per cent having attended university.

VOX also breaks the mould in comparison to the other "new" parties.[4] Both Cs and UP boast voting populations with large support from university-educated individuals. Previous research has argued that the more educated voters in Spain have been drawn towards the entrepreneurial status of new parties because they break with the status quo (Orriols and Cordero, 2016), but this conclusion doesn't bear out in the case of VOX.

Although the share of university-degree-holders is comparatively small in VOX, this does not mean that the share of those with primary education is high: indeed, as it was the case for UP, it is very low (6.4 per cent). A final point of interest is then the *very* large proportion of those with mid-level qualifications amongst the bank of the party's vote. Close to four in five (77.84 per cent) of the party's support is sourced from those with secondary level education. These voters likely make up the skilled vocational class or "the Spain that wakes up early" ["*la España que madruga*"] that VOX has sought to target in their election campaigns (Portillo and Bracero,

2020). This focus on banking votes from the median, humble and everyday trades-people is something that the party has leaned into heavily in an attempt to expand their electoral support, and judging by the educational distribution of their voters, the strategy appears to have been fruitful.

The underperformance of VOX amongst Spain's educated class may prove problematic for the party's electoral longevity. As discussed above, the advancement of educational attainment is progressing rapidly across subsequent electoral cohorts. If the low level of support for VOX is the result of the value-shaping role of education on individual preferences, a highly educated population may not prove to be a fruitful revenue of support for the radical right-wing party.

Modelling socio-demographic support for VOX

To take stock of the socio-demographic determinants that define VOX's electoral supporters, we carry out a multivariate logistic regression analysis using data from the November 2019 post-electoral survey data provided by the CIS. Our dependent variable indicates those who voted for VOX (1) in the November general election and those who voted for any other party (0). We include a battery of different socio-demographic variables from our discussion above.

The coefficients visualized in Figure 4.3 report the average marginal effect (AME) of each socio-demographic variable on the probability of voting for VOX holding all other variables constant. Each coefficient value can be interpreted as the percentage-point change in the probability of voting for VOX relative to the baseline category. The confidence interval (horizontal line) of any variable that crosses the dashed vertical line should be interpreted as being insignificant. This indicates that, statistically, we cannot distinguish any difference that is significantly distinct from zero. Wherever the confidence intervals do *not* cross the zero vertical line, we can conclude, with 95 per cent certainty, that the effect we observe is a real measure of the average association between the variable and the probability of voting for VOX, taking into account the explanatory association of all other considered variables.

Let's take a first look at gender. Our coefficient for women is -2.6 (for men it is zero as this is the baseline category against which being a woman is compared). This indicates that women are less likely to vote for VOX controlling for other covariates. The confidence intervals do not cross zero so we can conclude that being a woman significantly reduces the probability of voting for VOX by 2.6 percentage points.

The effect of age is consistent with the descriptive data we reported above, and the binary relationship displayed in Figure 4.2. Increments in the age category to which voters belong significantly decreases the probability of voting for the new right-wing party. Voters aged 45–54 are 4.2 percentage points less likely to vote for VOX vis à vis those aged 18–24, and this age-induced probability gap increases to 5.3 percentage points amongst those over 64 years of age. When it comes to voting for VOX, age matters. Contrary to popular assumptions, however, regarding the social liberalism of the youthful voter, the younger members of Spain's electorate

80 Who votes for VOX?

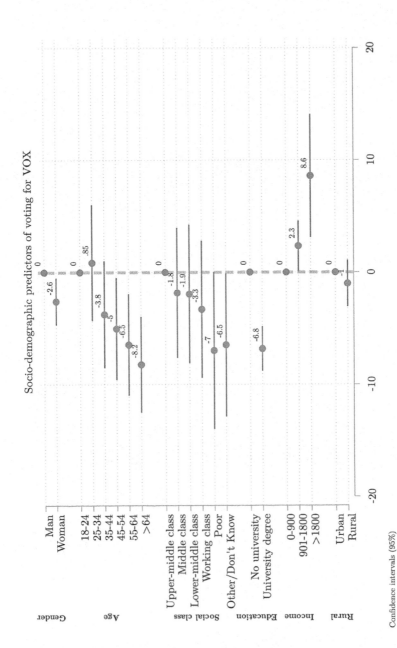

FIGURE 4.3 Average marginal effects on the probability of voting for VOX
Source: elaboration of the authors based on CIS (2019b)

are significantly *more* likely to support VOX than their (older) peers when they head to the polling booth.

Turning towards individual's (self-)identification with different social classes, the results in Figure 4.3 reveal that there is no difference of significance amongst the upper and middle classes. What we do find, however, is that those who identify on the lowest end of the social class ladder, as well as those who prefer not to report a class identity, are significantly less prone to vote for VOX. Comparing those who identify as upper class and those who identify as "poor", for example, shows that the latter observe a probability of voting for VOX that is seven percentage points lower.

Controlling for other socio-demographics, we observe a substantive education gap when it comes to electing VOX. University-degree-holders are significantly less likely to support the Spanish radical right compared to those with a high school education. Having a degree is associated with a significantly lower probability of voting for VOX equating to a 7.5 percentage-point degree-holder gap.

In line with preliminary assessments of the economic profile of VOX's electoral support provided elsewhere (Turnbull-Dugarte et al., 2020), we find evidence of a strong relationship between income and voting for the new radical-right new-comer. Comparing those with a monthly income in surplus of €1,800 with those who earn less than €900, we see that the former are 7.6 percentage points more likely to vote for VOX that the latter. In other words, those who fall on the higher end of the income distribution are significantly more likely to cast their ballot for VOX than those with the lowest incomes. VOX, then, is a party of the bourgeoisie rather than the economically "left behind".

Finally, we test for the role of geographic concentration. Although we do not show this comparison here, controlling for the considered socio-demographic covariates, we find that there is no significant or independent urban–rural divide in VOX's electoral support. This is consistent with earlier empirical assessments that show no relationship of note between the rural–urban divide and VOX's electoral success (Turnbull-Dugarte et al., 2020).

What do VOX's voters want?

We now know that those who pick up a ballot for VOX on the way to the polling booth are likely to be male, young, with above-average income but medium-level education, but we still do not yet have a full picture of what motivates VOX's supporters politically. It is to this question that the remaining part of this chapter will turn. First, we take a broad look at the ideological preference of the party's supporters within the traditional left–right (labour–capital) super-issue of political competition as well as voters' attitudes towards so-called "second dimension" issues. We then take a closer look at, what we argue, are two of the fundamental drivers of support for the right-wing challenger (immigration and nationalist separatism), before providing a comparative overview of how VOX's voters compare to those of their populist and radical right-wing contemporaries in other Western European states.

82 Who votes for VOX?

Ideology

We start by looking at where the different parties' supporters stand on the general left–right axis. The utility of concepts such as left and right is not without critique and some scholars highlight the redundant nature of the left–right typology in political systems where preferences need not be absorbed within a unidimensional space (Bakker et al., 2012) and where dynamics of political conflict have been reshaped over time (Caughey et al., 2019).

That being said, the left–right typology serves a number of important uses, not only for those of us interested in analysing where voters fall within an ideological space, but also for individual voters. Politics is a complex and confusing place. If you were to stop an average voter on the street and ask their view on a certain policy proposal, they are unlikely to be able to respond with a clear answer (Converse, 2006). But if you were to ask them what party they support or if they identify with the left or the right, they're far more likely to be able to give you a clear response. This is because voters like shortcuts (Arian and Shamir, 1983) and falling onto one side of the left–right "super-issue" (Inglehart and Klingemann, 1976) is helpful for them to organize their political preferences.

Table 4.6 focuses on voters' self-reported placement on the left–right space (scaled 0–10) for all nine waves of the ESS (2003–2019). This provides us with a snapshot of voters' ideological preferences both before and after VOX's maiden electoral success in 2018 (Andalusian regional elections). First of all, looking at the mean position of the population in both years, we observe that Spain's electorate leans slightly to the left. There is little change over time in the electorate as a whole, the mean position ranging from a minimum (or most leftist) of 4.40 in 2005 to a maximum (or most rightist) of 4.64 in 2011.

Notice that the stability of the Spanish electorate's mean position is not even altered by the entrance of new competitors: for instance, in 2015, year of the entrance of Cs and We Can,[5] the mean in the Spanish electorate fell by 0.12 percentage points, and in 2019, year of the transformation of VOX into a major player, the mean only fell 0.01 percentage point.

The data from 2019, which includes the mean left–right spatial position of VOX, shows that the populist radical right-wing party's voters are the most right-leaning within the electorate and by a substantive amount.

Important also is that the mean party voter positions we report in Table 4.6 mask the within-party distribution of voters along the ideological space. Table 4.7 provides that information for the 2019 ESS wave. For example, comparing the proportion of party voters that place themselves on each of the 11-point (0–10) values of the left–right axis, the 4.52 per cent of the PP's voters with an ideological position of 10 is dwarfed by the 17.02 per cent of VOX supporters. In other words, not only is the collective position of VOX's support significantly further to the right than that of the established right-wing parties, but also the proportion of VOX's voters who identify with the polar extreme of the ideological space is also notably

Who votes for VOX?   **83**

TABLE 4.6 Partisan supporters' ideological position

Year	Party voters					
	UP	PSOE	Cs	PP	VOX	Population
2003	–	**3.12**	–	**6.32**	–	**4.42**
		[2.95–3.29]		[6.15–6.49]		[4.32–4.53]
2005	–	**3.26**	–	**6.48**		**4.40**
		[3.11–3.41]		[6.29–6.67]		[4.28–4.51]
2007	–	**3.54**	–	**6.28**	–	**4.50**
		[3.41–3.67]		[6.12–6.44]		[4.41–4.60]
2009	–	**3.42**	–	**6.74**	–	**4.54**
		[3.32–3.52]		[6.60–6.87]		[4.46–4.62]
2011	–	**3.50**	–	**6.59**	–	**4.64**
		[3.37–3.63]		[6.43–6.75]		[4.55–4.73]
2013	–	**3.17**	–	**6.32**	–	**4.54**
		[2.95–3.38]		[6.15–6.50]		[4.43–4.65]
2015	n.a.	**3.17**	n.a.	**6.32**	n.a.	**4.42**
		[2.99–3.33]		[6.18–6.47]		[4.31–4.52]
2017	**2.45**	**3.29**	**5.08**	**6.47**	n.a.	**4.46**
	[2.25–2.65]	[3.12–3.47]	[4.87–5.30]	[6.30–6.64]		[4.37–4.57]
2019	**2.24**	**3.43**	**5.52**	**6.58**	**7.15**	**4.45**
	[1.99–2.50]	[3.27–3.59]	[5.21–5.83]	[6.37–6.81]	[6.73–7.56]	[4.33–4.56]

Notes: Square brackets indicate 95 per cent confidence intervals. Key: n.a. = not available (although in those dates the party existed and competed, the ESS did not consider a response option for the party, because it was not yet considered a relevant player in the Spanish electoral arena).

Source: elaboration of the authors based on ESS (2002–2020)

greater. This suggests that, at least in the case of VOX, the ideological element of their preferences is not "thin" (Stanley, 2008) but rather deeply rooted within the polar extreme of the right.

The temporal comparison amongst the established right-wing parties is also important. We know that a large proportion of VOX voters came from past supporters of the PP and Cs (Turnbull-Dugarte, 2019; Turnbull-Dugarte et al., 2020). In the case of VOX's initial success in Andalucía in 2018, this amounted to 69.6 per cent of the party's voters, and in the first general election in April 2019, it was 72.4 per cent.

What is noteworthy is that even though those with the most ideologically conservative right-wing preferences abandoned the PP and Cs in favour of VOX in 2019, both parties *still* retained the same ideological position (i.e. there was no right-wing ideological dilution as a result of the haemorrhaging of electoral support).[6] Given that it is likely that the PP (and Cs) had lost their most right-wing voters to VOX, the fact that we do not observe a lower (more leftist) mean for PP and Cs in

84 Who votes for VOX?

TABLE 4.7 Distribution of ideological placement by parties

Left–Right position	Party voters					
	UP	*PSOE*	*Cs*	*PP*	*VOX*	*Population*
Left (0)	14.07	5.07	0.00	0.00	1.06	4.84
1	20.00	4.05	0.00	0.00	0.00	5.33
2	21.48	10.47	0.00	0.00	0.00	8.65
3	25.93	30.74	3.08	0.56	2.13	16.40
4	9.63	28.38	9.23	0.56	3.19	13.36
5	7.41	17.57	50.77	25.42	17.02	24.50
6	1.48	2.70	15.38	26.55	17.02	9.76
7	0.00	0.68	16.92	21.47	13.83	7.47
8	0.00	0.34	3.08	15.82	18.09	5.26
9	0.00	0.00	0.00	5.08	10.64	1.80
Right (10)	0.00	0.00	1.54	4.52	17.02	2.63
Total	100.00	100.00	100.00	100.00	100.00	100.00

Source: elaboration of the authors based on ESS (2020)

2019 suggests that the ideological preferences of those who remained moved more to the right over the same period.

It's (not) the economy, stupid!

Breaking down the preferences with the left–right (labour–capital) cleavage, we turn to focus on individual preferences regarding the economy and welfare. The Spanish electorate has long boasted a higher amount of support for welfare spending and economic distribution. Following the country's transition to democracy, political parties on the left and the right adopted a centripetal approach to the welfare state and state intervention in the economy (Royo, 2000). Essentially, the voters of both ideological camps, at least of the PSOE and the PP, maintained a consensual appreciation for welfare state spending and the provision of public health, and recognized the collective benefit of the state's role in establishing a social safety net (Fernández-Albertos and Manzano, 2012).

In Figure 4.4 we report partisan preferences relating to the state's role in the economy. Across the board, voters are supportive of redistribution. Figure 4.5 models the probability of agreeing with the proposition that governments should take measures to reduce income inequality (left-hand panel) or that society is fairer when wealth is distributed equally (right-hand panel). Whilst, across both of these measures of latent support for economic redistribution, we see an increased probability of agreement amongst left-wing party supporters vis-à-vis right-wing party supporters, it is worth noting that the probability (across ideological camps) leans towards agreement (it is always higher than 0.5, or 50 per cent). Notably, the

Who votes for VOX? 85

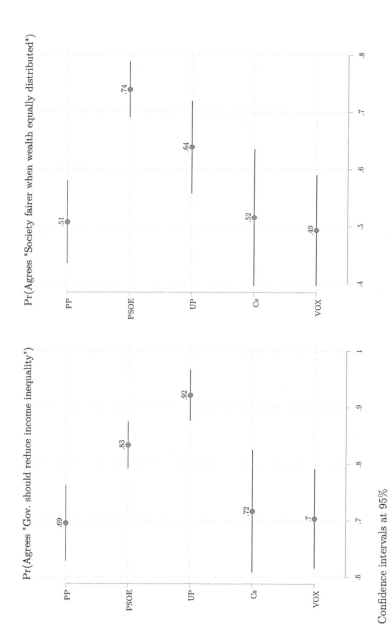

FIGURE 4.4 Support for state intervention

Source: elaboration of the authors based on ESS (2020)

86 Who votes for VOX?

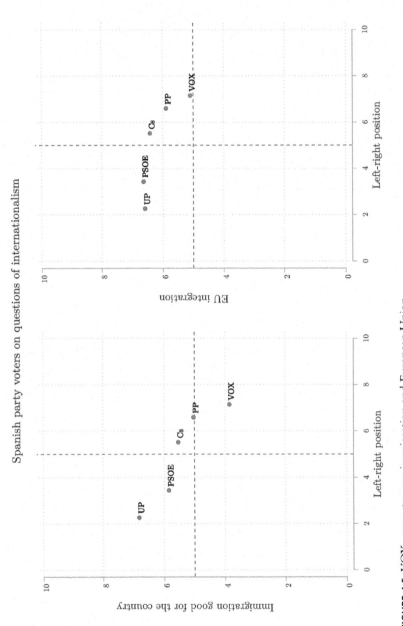

FIGURE 4.5 VOX supporters on immigration and European Union

Source: elaboration of the authors based on ESS (2020)

probability of agreeing with these pro-redistribution statements is the same for the voters of the PP, Cs, and VOX.

The lack of variation in voter preferences for these issues does not break away from our existing understanding of economic preferences of Spain's voters (Fernández-Albertos and Manzano, 2012). This lack of divergent preferences regarding the interventionist role of the state in the economy shows that demand-side preferences on economic issues do little to help us understand VOX's success. Where party supporters are likely to diverge is on the so-called "second dimension" issues.

Socio-cultural preferences: Europe, gays, and green politics

Scholars are generally in agreement that a coalesced unidimensional left–right "super issue" fails to encompass the multidimensional nature of both electoral and party competition in European states (Bakker et al., 2012; Caughey et al., 2019; Lefkofridi et al., 2014; Van der Brug and Van Spanje, 2009). Rising socio-economic conditions experienced through the post-war period in Europe gave rise to political conflict over post-materialist issues such as environmental concerns, social values related to individual liberty (e.g. abortion and LGBT+ rights), as well as cultural issues particularly over European integration and immigration (Kitschelt, 1995). The increasing saliency of cultural questions has been cemented in an independent second dimension cleavage between green/alternative/liberals and traditionalist/ authoritarian/nationalists (GAL-TAN) (Hooghe et al., 2002; Inglehart, 2008).

These second dimension issues, of which concerns over immigration and processes of globalization or international integration form a core part, are commonly signalled as the wedge issues that political entrepreneurs, particularly those on the populist radical right, leverage to their electoral advantage in order to disrupt the political system (De Vries and Hobolt, 2020; Van de Wardt et al., 2014). Do cultural (liberal-conservative) positions therefore explain VOX's success?

Figure 4.5 visualizes the spatial location of the voters from each of Spain's five main parties across the two dimensions. A coalesced liberal-left vs conservative-right dimension would visualize voters in diagonal, opposed quadrants across the different panels. As shown, however, this is not necessarily the case for the supporters of the main parties in Spain. Let us first consider the spatial preferences of VOX and the different Spanish parties' voters on the issue of immigration. As well established in the literature and shown in earlier chapters in the case of VOX, radical right-wing parties of the populist and non-populist varieties, tend to attract the bulk of their support from citizens who adopt negative opinions on the issue of immigration. What does this look like in the case of Spain? The left-hand panel of Figure 4.7 plots the mean ideological position of the different party supporters on the traditional left–right cleavage (horizontal axis) against voters' preferences towards immigration (vertical axis) using ESS data. The first thing we observe is that there is a clear demarcation on the issue of immigration between voters on the left and those on the right. The voters of Spain's two left-wing parties, UP and

88 Who votes for VOX?

the PSOE, tend towards a more liberal stance on the immigration question, whilst the voters of the three right-leaning parties, Cs, PP, and VOX, are all more prone to oppose immigration. In the case of Cs, however, the party's supporters remain on the liberal side of this divide. Not surprisingly, VOX's voters display the highest level of anti-immigration preferences.

What *is* surprising, however, is the extent of opposition to immigration with the traditionally right-wing hegemony of the PP. Whilst the new radical right-wing party in Spain has an electoral base that is spatially far from a moderate position on the question of immigration, the same can be said for the supporters of the traditional hegemon of the Spanish right. The PP's voters have a mean immigration position of 6.6 (10 indicates absolute opposition to immigration) which is only one point away from the mean position of VOX's voters (7.7). Given the large importance of the immigration concerns in understanding support for populist radical right-wing parties, we will return to revisit this question again in a later section.

On the question of European integration, there is very little variation between the electoral supporters of the different parties. This is not surprising. Spain has historically been one of the most Europhile nations in the EU. This Europhilia has come about for a number of reasons much of which stems from the country's "return to Europe" after transitioning to a democracy in the wake of Franco's death (Díez Medrano, 2003), the concrete economic benefits received by Spain via years of structural cohesion funds, as well as the relative disdain for domestic institutions which have been tainted with subsequent bouts of corruption scandals (De Vries, 2018; Sánchez-Cuenca, 2000). Of interest to us in the case of the new radical right-wing party, is that there *appears* to be little hint of Euroscepticism within the party's voter pool and this is reflected in the electoral revenue of the other parties in Spain (right-hand panel for Figure 4.7). On closer inspection, however, evidence points towards VOX's supporters being distinct from those of the other parties on the question of Europe.

As part of the recent iteration of the ESS, which took place in the wake of the UK's Brexit vote in 2016, voters across EU members states were asked how they would vote in a hypothetical referendum on their country's membership in the EU. In Spain, the results reveal, unsurprisingly, that the vast majority support their country's continued membership of the supranational polity. There is some significant cross-party variation, however, with the voters of the parties on the extreme ends of Spain's left–right divide being significantly more inclined to support *Spexit* (the exit of Spain of the European Union). Consistently with existing assessments of the radical left in Spain (Fernández-Albertos, 2015), close to 10 per cent of Podemos' voters would have supported Spain's exit from the EU. Looking at VOX's voters, we see a similar pattern: 15 per cent of VOX voters would vote for Spain to leave the EU.

The support for Spexit on the extremes of the left–right divide are consistent with existing understandings of Eurosceptic preferences being curvilinear to left–right positions (Hooghe et al., 2002). Both left- and right-wing ideologues have independent motivations to be critical of the European project whereas those who

TABLE 4.8 Support for Spain's exit from the European Union

Partisan voters	Support for Spexit (percentages)		
	Remain	Leave	Total
UP	90.24	9.76	100
PSOE	96.88	3.12	100
Cs	98.44	1.56	100
PP	96.45	3.55	100
VOX	85.42	14.58	100
Total	94.32	5.68	100

Source: elaboration of the authors based on ESS (2020)

place themselves in the centre tend to be more euro-pragmatist. Those on the left are theorized to be sceptical of the EU as they view the supranational institution as vehicle for increased market liberalization (Keith, 2017), the retrenchment of the welfare state and, particularly in the case of Spain, as the architect and enforcer of austerity measures associated with the *Troika* (della Porta et al., 2017). For those on the right, like those supporting VOX, Euroscepticism is motivated by different concerns, but these are primarily twofold. Firstly, there is the very strong link between the idea of EU integration and immigration. In the eyes of many voters, likely the result of successful attempts by entrepreneurial political parties to politicize and link immigration to European integration (De Vries and Hobolt, 2020), these two concerns are considered "twin issues" (Brinkmann and Panreck, 2019). Voters on the right tend to be less sympathetic towards immigration (Mudde, 2007) and, viewing the EU as a facilitator of increased migration and reduced border security (Goodwin and Milazzo, 2017), those on the right become less supportive of the EU. Second, yet of equal importance, are concerns over state sovereignty (Halikiopoulou et al., 2012). EU integration is viewed to be incompatible with national sovereignty in that it is *perceived* to result in the dilution of autonomous decision-making power and the state's capacity to make their own laws (Konstantinidis et al., 2019) .

Figure 4.6 illustrates the relationship between individual identification in the left–right space and support for Spexit. Consistent with both the asymmetrical distribution in support for leave between parties shown above and the curvilinear relationship between the left–right space and Euroscepticism observed elsewhere (Hooghe et al., 2004), we find significantly higher levels of support for leave on either end of the ideological distribution. Whilst those with an ideological value on the far-left (ideology value equal to 0) have a probability of .20 of voting leave, the probability amongst those on the far-right (ideology value equal to 10) is eight percentage points lower at .12. Whilst the overall probability of voters supporting Spain's exit from the EU is very low, as is too the probability that any of the mainstream parties would propose such a referendum, it is notable that the Spanish far-right and far-left are the largest opponents of Spain's membership of the EU.

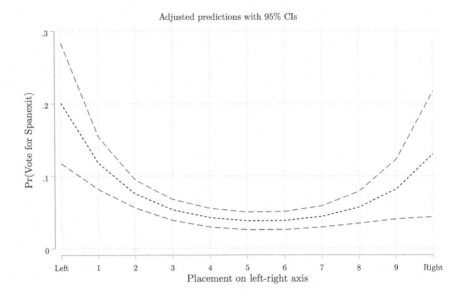

FIGURE 4.6 Left–right ideological values and support for Spexit

Source: elaboration of the authors based on ESS (2020)

Within the GAL-TAN dimension, concerns over immigration and the EU tend to dominate, but these are, of course, not the only second dimension issues that voters care about. Concerns over issues relating to sexual and individual liberty (such as abortion rights or LGBT+ issues) and environmental concerns often play an increasing role in the partisan and electoral spaces of Western Europe. Beyond the issues of the transnational cleavage between pro-immigration Europhiles and anti-immigration Eurosceptics, how do VOX's voters compare to others on non-globalization issues within the second dimensions?[7]

Let us consider voter attitudes towards the environment and LGBT+ politics, two core issues within the second dimensions of the GAL-TAN space. The left-hand panel of Figure 4.8 shows the position of party supporters in relation to economic growth and the environment (vertical axis) in relation to the left–right space: higher values indicate that greater prioritization of growth over environmental protections and lower values signal a prioritization of environmental protections over growth. This data comes from the European Election Study (EES), as neither the ESS nor the national election data provided by the CIS has spatial indicators of environmental preferences.

Traditional gender and sexual values have long been the bread and butter of populist radical right-wing parties. The populist radical right has tended to be characterized, in addition to their infamous nativism, by a penchant for conservatism when it comes to gender in that they portray women as a central part of the heteronormative family structure and are opposed to institutions at odds with these values, like same-sex marriage (Betz, 1994; Kitschelt, 1995). As Akkerman points out, however, there is a substantial amount of variation as regards gender issues within the populist radical-right party family (Akkerman, 2015). Salient opposition to liberal sexual values is not necessarily universal amongst the (populist) radical right-wing party family in Western Europe. Some radical right-wing parties have sought to harness the tolerance of LGBT+ issues to i) signal they have liberalized and ii) weaponize it as a means of rationalizing their nativist and xenophobic positions against ethnic outgroups, typically Muslims (Akkerman, 2005; Siegel, n.d.; Turnbull-Dugarte, 2020). The mutually supportive relationship between LGBT+ groups and radical right-wing parties has become less of an anomaly and there are increasingly a larger amount of "sexually modern nativist" constituents among these parties' supporters (Lancaster, 2019).

As discussed in Chapter 3, however, VOX's stance on questions of gender and sexuality do not engage with the promotion of sexual modernity and their political rhetoric is often tied to invoking a traditional (Catholic) view of a heteronormative society and gender roles.[8] In Figure 4.7 we consider the same issues among the party's voters. The right-hand panel of Figure 4.7 maps party voters' positions on the question of same-sex marriage, which we take as an illustrative indicator of individuals' preferences on LGBT+ rights issues. Note that, as in the case of immigration, there appears to be a linear relationship between voters' left–right positions and attitudes related to same-sex marriage. Whilst the voters of UP are the most supportive of LGBT+ rights, VOX and PP voters are the least supportive. Note, however, that whilst these right-wing parties' voters are the least supportive, their mean position does not cross the mid-point value on the 0–10 scale. This suggests that whilst they are less supportive, they are not, on average, opposed to same-sex marriage.

The voters of the PP are the most likely to oppose LGBT+ rights in Spain according to the data presented here. Given that the bulk of the PP's supporters are sourced from older sections of the electorate, as discussed above, and that the PP has close institutional ties with the Catholic Church, which leads to the strong prevalence of religious voting in Spain (Cordero, 2017), we expect that a large part of the attitudes related to LGBT+ issues, like same-sex marriage rights, may be a function of religiosity. We assess the divergent levels of religiosity between the parties' supporters in Table 4.9.

VOX's voters are *not* the most religious in Spain – in this horserace the PP's constituents take the crown. Around 45 per cent of the PP's voters report to pray on a weekly basis or more, which is significantly greater than the proportion observed amongst VOX's sympathizers (38 per cent). Of course, the PP has a long pedigree within the Spanish party system, whose roots go back to before the country's transition to democracy (Montero, 1987). Religious voters are more likely to feel strong partisan attachment to the PP and will not be inclined to abandon their electoral loyalties easily. Of significance is that VOX as a challenger to the right of the PP on socio-cultural questions (where religiously motivated concerns like attitudes towards LGBT+ rights, gender issues and abortion are likely to be most salient) has led to a strong religious break away from the hegemonic PP that was not observed in the case of Cs's emergence.

92 Who votes for VOX?

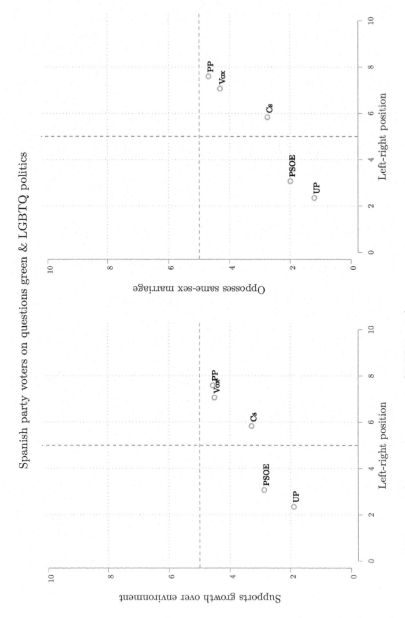

FIGURE 4.7 VOX supporters on environment and LGBT+ rights

Source: elaboration of the authors based on ESS (2020)

TABLE 4.9 Religious profile of party supporters

Religious practice	Partisan voter					
	UP	PSOE	Cs	PP	VOX	Total
Daily	5.15	16.72	11.76	26.88	25.00	17.76
>Weekly	2.21	4.82	5.88	8.06	8.65	5.71
Weekly	1.47	2.89	7.35	10.22	4.81	4.97
Monthly	6.62	8.36	8.82	8.06	3.85	7.45
Religious holidays	0.00	3.22	5.88	3.76	1.92	2.86
Less often	9.56	17.68	13.24	17.20	18.27	15.90
Never	75.00	46.30	47.06	25.81	37.50	45.34
Total	100	100	100	100	100	100

Notes: Question: "How often pray apart from at religious services (percentages)?"

Source: elaboration of the authors based on ESS (2020)

Voting for VOX: nativism vs nationalism

As detailed in Chapter 2, VOX's rise as a *viable* electoral option on the radical right began to emerge in 2018 in the lead-up to the first electoral contest to take place in the aftermath of the disputed separatist unauthorized referendum in Catalonia.[9]

We argue that VOX's success can be attributed to the entrepreneurial politicization by the party in response to, what it views as, two important threats facing Spain. The strategic presentation by populist and radical right-wing parties of a nation "under attack" from external threats has increasingly become a staple within the rhetorical toolkit of xenophobic actors seeking to mobilize support for their exclusionary policies by invoking fears within the wider population (Wodak, 2015).

The "threats" that VOX politicizes in the case of Spain are twofold: one internal and one external. The internal threat is manifested by the electoral success of pro-separatist parties and the subsequent attempts by these parties in power at the regional level to gain independence from Spain and dismantle the "unity" of the country. The second threat is external and comes in the form of (non-European) immigration.

In a preliminary assessment of the electoral determinants of VOX during the Andalusian elections, in which the party enjoyed its maiden electoral success, one of us made the case that concerns over nationalism were the driving force behind VOX's victory at the polls (Turnbull-Dugarte, 2019).

One of the core policy proposals put forward by VOX that differentiates the party from the more mainstream right-wing alternatives is its position regarding Spain's territorial structure. Essentially, the party advocates for the permanent dissolution of Spain's devolved communities and the consolidation of state power within a central (national) layer of government. The extremity of this position should not be overlooked. The PP's response to Catalan separatists' unilateral declaration of independence in October 2017 was to invoke Article 155 of the constitution,

94 Who votes for VOX?

which facilitated the dissolution of the regional government and the *temporary* rule over the region from Madrid. VOX's proposal is to make the dissolution of regional power a permanent feature of Spain's constitution. Carrying out the policy is something far beyond VOX's reach given that it would require substantial constitutional reform and would need to be ratified via a referendum – something which the other parties are keen to avoid, given the potential number of issues that could emerge if the pandora's box of constitutional reform was to be opened.

VOX's pledge to centralize power is, therefore, a pledge that the party is likely aware of being unable to fill. It is, however, an attention-seeking proposal that appears to have captured the attention of those Spaniards, particularly outside of Catalonia, that seek to suppress and punish separatists for challenging the integrity of the Spanish state.

Whilst preliminary evidence suggests that support for the centralization of autonomous government played a significant role in explaining VOX's electoral triumph at the subnational level (Turnbull-Dugarte, 2019), it is not clear that the initial boost that the party enjoyed because of its tough line on devolution in the first "post-referendum" election translates into explaining its support at the national level.

As part of the CIS's post-electoral survey (November),[10] respondents are asked what the most important problems facing Spain are. Of some 4,800 respondents, 8 per cent of respondents reported that they felt the Catalan conflict or the crisis with the autonomous communities was one of the top three most important issues in Spain. A smaller, yet sizeable proportion, claimed the same of immigration and the refugee crisis (5.78 per cent). Should, as we argue, these issues be central to VOX's assent to become the third largest party in Spain, we would expect a greater proportion of VOX supporters to identity these issues as central problems.

Figure 4.8 displays the electoral choices (including abstention) exercised by voters who, in November 2019, cited the ongoing problem in Catalonia as one of the three most important problems facing Spain at the time of the election (right-hand panel), and those who did not (left-hand panel). Amongst those who included the independence conflict as one of the country's most pressing issues, 13.55 per cent voted for VOX. VOX only gained 9.97 per cent of the vote from those who didn't list the Catalan issue within their top three concerns. The gap in these preferences is important with a 3.58 percentage-point gap equating to an increase in support for VOX 33.6 per cent higher for those who identified the Catalan conflict as one of their most important issues.

Given the highly politicized nature of the Catalan issue at the height of the two elections that took place in April and November, the CIS included an explicit question surveying respondents regarding the extent to which the events in Catalonia had any effect in their voting calculus.[11] One in four voters (23.15 per cent) report that it did (Figure 4.9). This is a sizeable proportion of the electorate. Comparing the distribution of the electoral choices exercised among individuals that identify the Catalan issue as having an effect in deciding their vote with those who claim that it did not, we see a sizeable gap in the level of support for the populist radical right.

Who votes for VOX? **95**

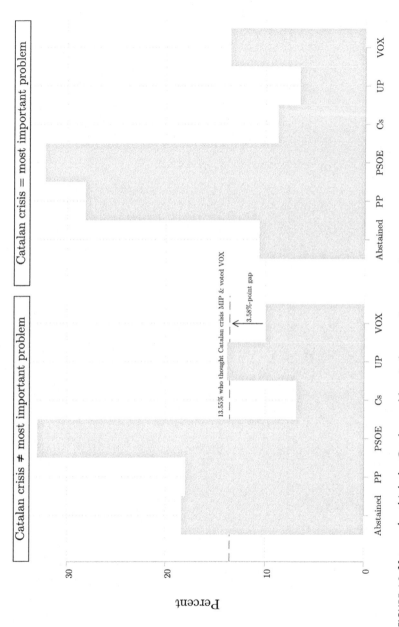

FIGURE 4.8 Voters who think the Catalan problem is the most important issue

Source: elaboration of the authors based on CIS (2019b)

96 Who votes for VOX?

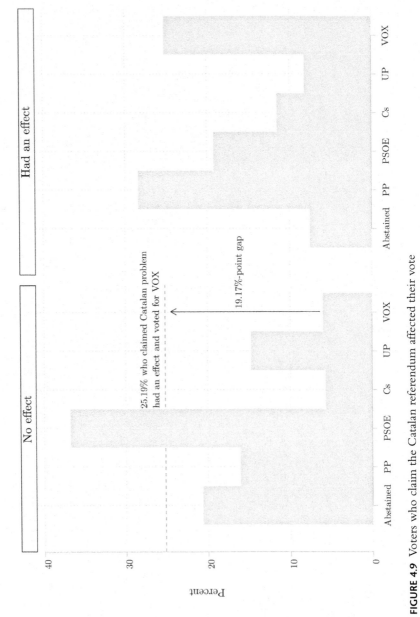

FIGURE 4.9 Voters who claim the Catalan referendum affected their vote

Source: elaboration of the authors based on CIS (2019b)

For those who report that their vote was not influenced by the Catalan situation, only a small proportion voted for VOX: 6.02 per cent. VOX's vote revenue from those who claim they were affected is substantially greater at 25.19 per cent. The 19.17 percentage-point gap is sizeable and equates to an increase of more than 318 per cent.

Exploring the role of the nationalism (internal threat), our descriptive comparison shows that the Catalan conflict mattered in helping to understand the support for VOX. Those who identified the issue as being one of the most important problems facing the country at the time host a significantly greater proportion of VOX voters than those who did not identify this issue. Moreover, citizens themselves cite the Catalan issue as one of the driving forces behind their choice at the ballot box, with one in four signalling the conflict over the question of Catalan separatism as influential in their choices.

We now turn to another "threat" politicized by VOX: immigration. As mentioned above, 5.78 per cent of Spanish voters in November 2019 cited either concerns over immigration or the refugee crisis as one of the top three issues facing Spain (Figure 4.10). The distribution of support for VOX among voter attitudes on the immigration issue gives us a key insight into the importance of this concern for VOX's electorate. VOX took home 28.05 per cent of the votes among voters citing immigration as one of Spain's top three problems, whilst banking only 6.41 per cent from those who did not share the same concern. The gap in VOX's support between these two groups is far from trivial and a 19.44 percentage-point gap translates into an increase of 303 per cent.

Attitudes towards immigration are complex (Ruedin, 2020) and in many cases indicative of multidimensional preferences regarding what type of immigration should be permitted. In order to disentangle the multidimensional nature of immigration preferences, we model the support for different immigration types, including immigrants that belong to the ethnic out-group, immigrants from the ethnic in-group, and those from poor countries (Turnbull-Dugarte, 2020). VOX's political opposition to immigration in Spain is richly embalmed with nativist rhetoric that seeks to demonize ethnic others who are distinct from the (white) Spanish majority. Should VOX's supporters be drawn to the party because of rejectionist rhetoric, we might expect these same voters to be more likely to endorse the rejection of immigrants who belong to different ethnic groups over those who are ethnically similar to themselves (in-group).

Nativist messages, however, are often tied up with economic concerns. VOX itself has often attempted to rationalize its opposition to immigration by portraying the arrival of both legal and illegal migrants to Spain as i) a destabilizing force on the economy and a threat to a precarious labour market for Spanish locals, and ii) a drain on public finances. Opposition to immigration amongst the populist radical right's electoral revenue may be also driven by aporophobia rather than purely ethnic out-group rejection (nativism). We test this by analysing the probability of opposing the entry of different migrant types amongst the parties' different supporters.

98 Who votes for VOX?

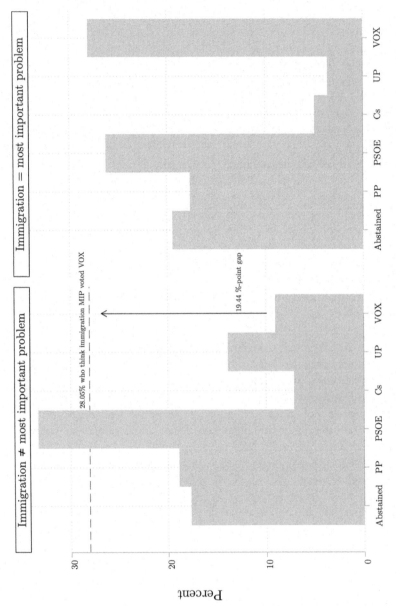

FIGURE 4.10 Voters who think immigration is the most important issue

Source: elaboration of the authors based on CIS (2019b)

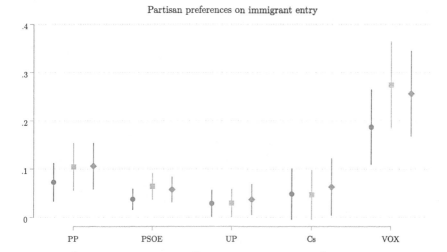

FIGURE 4.11 Partisan preferences for different immigration types

Source: elaboration of the authors based on ESS (2020)

Relying on data from wave nine of the ESS (2019), we assess the extent to which party voters' preferences on immigration and different immigration types are distinct. Figure 4.11 reports the probability of refusing entry to Spain to immigrants from i) an ethnic in-group, ii) and ethnic out-group, and iii) a poor country, conditioned on having voted for each of the five parties. Across these different immigration types, we observe that the supporters of VOX are significantly more likely to oppose immigration, regardless of the immigrant type, compared to the supporters of any other political party. Comparing VOX's supporters to those closest to the party within the political right, we see that VOX's voters are almost twice as likely to reject all types compared to those of the PP. Immigration preferences then, in contrast to initial findings in the subnational case of Andalucía (Turnbull-Dugarte, 2019), *do* in fact diverge substantially between VOX's voters and those of other partisan supporters.

In terms of variation in immigrant types within VOXs supporters, there appears to be slightly more support for ethnic in-groups than out-groups. The probability that a VOX voter would reject an ethnic in-group individual is .187 whereas it is greater is the case of an out-group (.275) or poor individual (.256). Note, however, that these predicted probabilities are not statistically distinguishable from one other. Whilst the percentage-point gaps suggest, in line with our expectations on the nativist preferences of VOX supporters, that opposition to immigration is driven by xenophobia and nativism, we cannot conclude (statistically) that the role of immigrant *type* plays a significant role. What we can be sure of, however, is that in

100 Who votes for VOX?

comparison to those who vote for other parties, those who cast a ballot for VOX are far less sympathetic to immigration than all others.

Modelling ideological support for VOX

So, we know that nativism (immigration) and nationalism (state unity) play a large role in understanding VOX's electoral success, but so too do concerns over religiosity and general left–right ideological positions. To take stock of all of the ideological determinants of voting for VOX, we produce a multivariate model using CIS data from the November 2019 election to ascertain which factors retain their explanatory role in understanding votes for VOX when all of these issues are considered.

As above in the case of our multivariate analysis of the socio-demographic predictors of voting for VOX (recall Figure 4.3), the coefficients visualized in Figure 4.12 can be interpreted as the percentage-point change in the probability of voting for VOX associated with a one-unit change in the value of the variable we are looking at. Whilst the figure here only reports the coefficients for the political variables, the model used to estimate these coefficients includes all of the socio-demographic variables presented in Figure 4.3 as controls.

Let us first consider the effect of traditional left–right ideological positions. Moving one step along the left–right scale increases the probability of voting for VOX by 4.2 percentage points. This is a sizeable effect. As an example, an individual who places themselves near the ideological centre with a left–right value of 5 would be 12.6 percentage points less likely to vote for VOX than an individual with and ideological value of 8, holding all else equal. Frequent church attendance is positively associated with voting for the populist radical right-wing party, but the effect fails to gain significance. As demonstrated in initial assessments (Turnbull-Dugarte et al., 2020), those who are politically interested are, on average, more inclined to vote for VOX over other alternatives.

Turning towards our variables of internal (Catalan) and external (immigration) threats, we observe that they play a substantive role in understanding support for Abascal's nativist flag-waving party. Those who claimed that the events in Catalonia played an influential role in their voting decision were 6.4 percentage points more likely to vote for VOX. The predicted probability of voting for VOX amongst those who claimed that the Catalan events had no effect on their vote choice is .07, so a 6.4 percentage-point increase in the probability is a substantive change of 91.4 per cent. Note that including this variable results in an insignificant coefficient for the variable measuring internal treat measured as one of the most important issues. Among these issue-important variables, we see that those who identified immigration in the list of top three concerns were 7.1 percentage points more like to support VOX. There is, therefore, an independent effect of both internal and external threats to Spain in determining what drives VOX's voters at the ballot box.

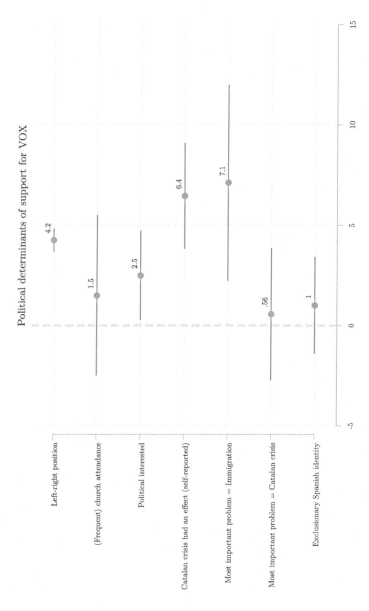

FIGURE 4.12 Average marginal effect of political determinants

Source: elaboration of the authors based on CIS (2019b)

VOX voters compared: still an Iberian exception?

In the final section of this chapter, we take a step back from our insular view of Spain and take a more comparative approach. We ask: "how do VOX's voters compare to those of other populist and radical right-wing parties across Western Europe?" To do this we compare VOX's supports to those of the populist radical right in Germany with Alternative for Germany [*Alternative für Deutschland*] (AfD); Austria with the Austrian Freedom Party [*Freiheitliche Partei Österreichs*] (FPÖ); Finland with the Finns Party, formerly True Finns [*Perussuomalaiset*] (PS); Italy with League [*Lega*], formerly Northern League until 2018 [*Lega Nord*]; and France with the National Rally [*Rassemblement national*] (RN), formerly National Front until June 2018 [*Front national*] (FN). We select the supporters of these parties for our comparison given the consistent categorization of these parties within the populist radical right party family (Norris, 2020; Rooduijn et al., 2020).

Figure 4.13 gives us an idea of where VOX's voters fall across these numerous issue dimensions in comparison to their peers in other Western European states. The left-hand panel shows the spatial position of VOX's voters on the question of immigration (vertical axis) and the general left–right ideological space (horizontal axis). Those who support VOX are strongly opposed to immigration. Note that the placement of VOX's voters within this two-dimensional distribution places them neatly within the same lower-right quadrant where the voters of the other populist radical right-wing parties lie. This reflects the spatial position of the party itself within the conservative-right space making it, in Norris's words (Norris, 2020), an example of the "class profile" of the populist radical-right.

Our analysis of the support for Spain's exit from the EU provided us with an image of VOX's supporters as somewhat Eurosceptic. Alongside UPs, with both parties operating at the polar ends of the traditional left–right space, a sizeable amount of VOX's supporters would, given the chance, vote in favour of Spexit. The Euroscepticism propagated by the party, however, is very much dwarfed in comparison to that advocated by the Western European peers, so we have reason to expect that the Eurosceptic tendencies of their voters will also overshadow that of VOX.

Looking at the data, we find that this is very much the case. First the right-hand panel of Figure 4.13 shows that VOX's electoral base is on the verge of the Europhile–Eurosceptic dichotomy, which places it somewhat apart from their contemporaries in Germany, France, Finland, and Austria. Taking a closer look specifically on support for disintegration from the supranational polity, Table 4.10 shows that percentage of support for leaving the EU in a hypothetical referendum on this question amongst the supporters of VOX, the AfD, RN, FPÖ, Lega, and Finns Party. The supporters of VOX's Western European contemporaries are significantly more Eurosceptic than VOX. Whilst less than one-fifth of VOX's voters would support Spain's exit from the EU, the majority of AfD (52 per cent), RN (56 per cent), and FPÖ (56 per cent) voters would vote for the same in their respective country. Whilst

Who votes for VOX? **103**

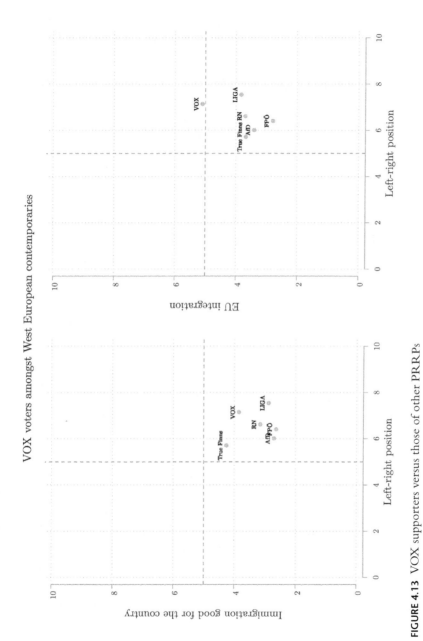

FIGURE 4.13 VOX supporters versus those of other PRRPs
Source: elaboration of the authors based on ESS (2020)

104 Who votes for VOX?

TABLE 4.10 Support for European Union exit compared

Partisan voters	Support for EU exit (percentages)		
	Remain	Leave	Total
VOX	85.42	14.58	100
AfD	48.08	51.92	100
RN	44.21	55.79	100
FPÖ	43.61	56.39	100
Lega	67.59	32.41	100
Finns Party	56.49	43.51	100
Total	56.17	43.83	100

Source: elaboration of the authors based on ESS (2020)

TABLE 4.11 Religiosity compared

Religious practice	Partisan voter						
	VOX	AfD	RN	FPÖ	Lega	Finns Party	Total
Daily	26.88	16.72	5.15	11.76	25.00	17.16	15.96
More than weekly	8.06	4.82	2.21	5.88	8.65	4.48	9.29
Weekly	10.22	2.89	1.47	7.35	4.81	2.24	5.05
Monthly	8.06	8.36	6.62	8.82	3.85	5.97	6.26
Religious holidays	3.76	3.22	0.00	5.88	1.92	0.00	4.95
Less often	17.20	17.68	9.56	13.24	18.27	35.82	22.22
Never	25.81	46.30	75.00	47.06	37.50	34.33	36.26
Total	100	100	100	100	100	100	100

Notes: Question: "How often pray apart from at religious services (percentages)?"

Source: elaboration of the authors based on ESS (2020)

the Euroscepticism of VOX's voters might break with the mould of Spain's pro-EU consensus (Turnbull-Dugarte and Devine, 2021), it does not (yet) approximate the more rampant levels of Euroscepticism observed among their neighbours.[12]

Beyond the issue of immigration and EU integration, we do not find any notable divergence between VOX voters and their radical right peers on the questions of the environment or LGBT+ right (see Appendix). Amongst the parties included here, we observe that voters of Italy's Lega remain those most opposed to the introduction of same-sex marriage. This is not altogether surprising given both the higher levels of opposition to LGBT+ rights in Italy (Dotti Sani and Quaranta, 2020) and the higher levels of (Catholic) religiosity. Indeed, comparing the levels of religious observation amongst the voters of the six parties we consider, those of Lega are the most religious. Importantly, however, we see a clear mirroring between the religiosity observed among Lega voters and those of VOX in Spain. Around one in four of both VOX and Lega voters claim to pray on a daily basis, a rate that surpasses the level of self-reported devotion displayed amongst the supporters of the AfD, RN, and the FPÖ by a substantive amount.

Modelling support for the populist radical right

In order to provide a comprehensive overview of the role of these different determinants in explaining the support for VOX and the other right-wing populists we consider, we estimate a battery of multivariate regression models analysing the voter profiles of each party's supporters. Figure 4.14 displays a model which includes only socio-demographics, whereas Figure 4.15 replicates it with the inclusion of additional attitudinal variables. The coefficients reported in these figures indicate the AMEs of different variables on the probability of voting for each of the parties. The reported coefficients should be interpreted as the percentage-point change in the probability associated with an increase in the variable value from the baseline.[13]

We focus our discussion on the political variables reported in Figure 4.15, which includes measures of religiosity, support for EU integration, attitudes towards immigration, acceptability of LGBT+ minorities, voters' overall left–right position, as well as evaluations of the state of the economy and satisfaction with democracy.

Self-reported religiosity does not exhibit any independent effect in explaining the electoral support for *any* of the parties under consideration, including VOX, with the exception of the FPÖ. A one-unit increase in self-reported religiosity (scaled 0–10) reduces the probability of voting for the Austrian populist radical right by about one percentage point.

In terms of the role of Euroscepticism, VOX is the only party whose electoral support is *not* influenced by voter preferences on EU integration. Across all other parties, increased support for the EU is significantly associated with reduced support. Euroscepticism, then, does not appear to be a driving force behind VOX's success, at least when these other ideological measures are considered.

We do see, however, that in the case of immigration, the connection between these concerns and support for VOX is largely mirrored by that observed among the supporters of the party's contemporaries. A one-unit increase in support for immigration (scaled 0–10) reduces the probability of voting for VOX by 1.2 percentage points, which is comparable to the effects of immigration in driving support for the populist radical right in the other Western European contexts displayed in Figure 4.15. Concerns over immigration amongst VOX's voters using our national -level data from the Spanish election study is replicated in the comparative context.

Whilst tolerance of LGBT+ individuals is negatively correlated with support for the AfD in Germany or the RN in France, there is no significant connection between these attitudes and support for VOX. This non-effect is also observed in the case of voting for the FPÖ, Lega, or True Finns. We, therefore, do not find any uniform consensus among the supporters of the populist radical right on this question.

106 Who votes for VOX?

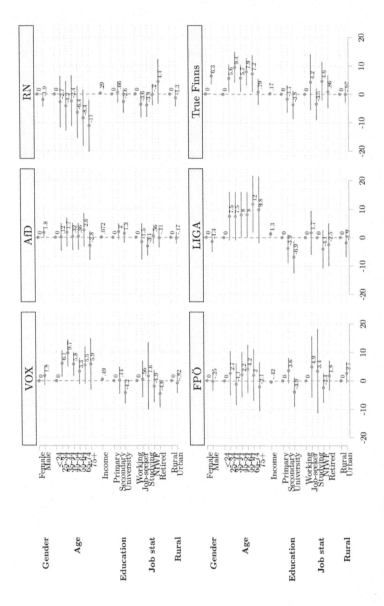

FIGURE 4.14 Sociological profile of VOX compared

Source: elaboration of the authors based on ESS (2020)

Who votes for VOX? **107**

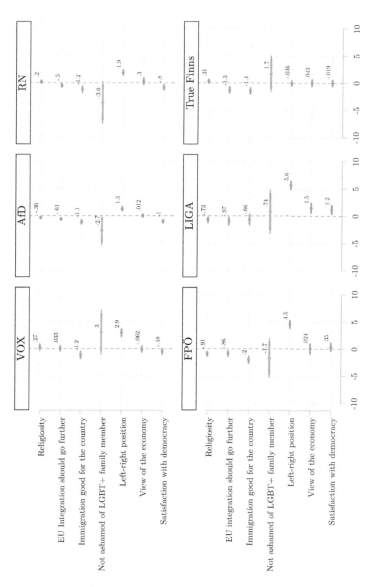

FIGURE 4.15 Political profile of VOX compared

Source: elaboration of the authors based on ESS (2020)

108 Who votes for VOX?

As one would expect, voters who identify further to the right are more likely to vote for VOX than another alternative. A one-unit increase across the left (0)–right (10) scale heightens the probability of voting for the populist radical right by 2.9 percentage points. This effect is larger than that associated with voting for the AfD (1.3) and the RN (1.9), but smaller than that observed for the FPÖ (4.5) or Lega (5.6). If we use these coefficients as a benchmark of the "radicalism" of the radical-right support, we can see that VOX falls somewhere between the right-leaning tendencies of the party voters we consider here.

Interestingly, evaluations of economic performance and satisfaction with democracy do not present us with any significant effects in the voting for VOX. The non-effect of the former is important for our comparative understanding of VOX's success. One of the core explanations signalled to explain the rise of populist parties (be that of the left or the right) is the issue of economic discontent or belonging to the so-called "losers of globalization" (Rama and Cordero, 2018; Santana and Rama, 2018; Vittori, 2016). In the case of the VOX, concerns over the economic performance of the state have no relationship of substance or significance in explaining which voters support the populist radical right-wing party.

Conclusions

Our analysis of the electoral support for VOX, both in comparison to the voters of Spain's existing political parties, as well as those of the populist radical right over neighbouring countries in Europe, have sought to provide a picture of the voter profile of Spain's new right-wing challenger and to answer the question: who votes for VOX?

One of the most substantive take-aways of our comparative analysis is the apparently counter-intuitive effect observed in the case of age. Political pundits commenting on the ever-expanding list of op-eds on the rise of populism across a number of countries have often pointed towards the low level of electoral support for these parties amongst the young as a sign of the future health and longevity of liberalism among Western electorates. Placing faith in the argument that the young will inherit the Earth and the future shape of democratic governments does not, however, necessarily paint an optimistic picture for Spain. Whilst a majority of the country's youngest voters elected to vote for a party other than VOX, a sizeable proportion of the same age demographic did. Given the powerful habit-shaping role that early partisan socialization can have on electoral preferences, the strong level of electoral support that VOX was able to bank from the Spain's young may signal troubling times ahead for those who defend socio-liberal and cosmopolitan values in Spain.

Notes

1 Details of how the authors operationalize support for populism as a latent concept are provided in Spierings and Zaslove (2017). Essentially, these authors create an index

composed of different direct instruments that aim to capture feelings of political efficacy, political trust, and perceptions of democratic responsiveness.

2 Available on YouTube at: www.youtube.com/watch?v=RaSIX4-RPAI&list=WL&index=7&t=0s

3 Output from a logistic regression model, regressing support for VOX on age and age-squared using a sub-sample of right-wing voters only.

4 We say "new" in comparison to the more established parties of PP and the PSOE but, given that both Cs and UP have been competing nationally in Spanish elections since 2014, they cannot be considered newcomers anymore.

5 Data on the ideological position of the voters of We Can and Cs is available since the 2017 ESS wave.

6 In the case of both the PP and Cs, the mean ideological position became larger (more right wing) but the confidence intervals in each year overlap substantially, so we cannot conclude that the distribution of ideological support for each party's voter base is significantly different in 2019 compared with 2017.

7 To measure support for same-sex marriage and environmental measures, we rely on data from the European Election Study (2019) as opposed to the ESS, given that the former scales individuals' attitudes on these questions on the same 11-point scale as the CIS.

8 The party's leadership, particularly Rocío Monasterio, played a significant participatory role in the Make Yourself Heard (*HazteOir*) campaign that challenged LGBT+ rights. The campaign gained notoriety in 2017 after it launched a travelling bus campaign which was branded with the words "Boys have penises. Girls have vaginas. Don't let anybody fool you!" [*Los niños tienen pene. Las niñas tienen vulva. Que no te engañen!*]

9 Leaving aside the Catalan snap elections convoked by the Spanish government after having suspended the Catalan autonomy, and which took place only two months after the ephemeral declaration of independence by the Catalan parliament.

10 The CIS did not solicit information on the most important issue facing voters during the April 2019 pre- or post-electoral surveys.

11 "Have the recent events in Catalonia had any influence on your voting decision in the November 10th elections?" [*Lo que ha ocurrido últimamente en Cataluña ¿ha tenido alguna influencia en su decisión de voto en las elecciones del 10 de noviembre?*]

12 The lower levels of Euroscepticism of VOX's voters (as compared to the levels of other PRRP voters) may be related to the territorial problem. The presence of Spain in the EU, and the support of EU institutions to the central government facing the Catalan challenge, may be behind this difference.

13 Note that the comparative analysis here relies on data from the ESS, so the coefficients report different (yet similar) values to the measures used in our Spain-only analysis above, which relied on data from the Spanish post-electoral study of the CIS.

References

Akkerman T (2005) Anti-immigration parties and the defence of liberal values: The exceptional case of the List Pim Fortuyn. *Journal of Political Ideologies* 10(3): 337–354.

Akkerman T (2015) Gender and the radical right in Western Europe: A comparative analysis of policy agendas. *Patterns of Prejudice* 49(1–2): 37–60.

Alonso S and Rovira Kaltwasser C (2015) Spain: No Country for the Populist Radical Right? *South European Society and Politics* 20(1): 21–45.

Arian A and Shamir M (1983) The Primarily Political Functions of the Left–Right Continuum. *Comparative Politics* 15(2): 139–158.

Bakker R, Jolly S and Polk J (2012) Complexity in the European party space: Exploring dimensionality with experts. *European Union Politics* 13(2): 219–245.

Bessant J (2018) Young precariat and a new work order? A case for historical sociology. *Journal of Youth Studies* 21(6): 780–798.

Betz H-G (1994) *Radical Right-Wing Populism in Westerm Europe*. Basingstoke: MacMillan.

Brinkmann HU and Panreck C-I (2019) Migration und Rechtspopulismus – zwei Seiten einer Medaille? Eine gängige These der Rechtspopulismusforschung auf dem Prüfstand. Brinkmann HU and Panreck C-I (eds) *Rechtspopulismus in Einwanderungsgesellschaften. Die Politische Auseinandersetzung Um Migration Und Integration*. Ebook: Springer, pp. 1–21.

Campbell R and Erzeel S (2018) Exploring Gender Differences in Support for Rightist Parties: The Role of Party and Gender Ideology. *Politics & Gender, 14*(1), 80–105. doi:10.1017/S1743923X17000599

Caughey D, O'Grady TOM and Warshaw C (2019) Policy ideology in European Mass Publics, 1981–2016. *American Political Science Review* 113(3): 674–693. DOI: 10.1017/S0003055419000157.

Cavaille C and Marshall J (2019) Education and Anti-Immigration Attitudes: Evidence from Compulsory Schooling Reforms across Western Europe. *American Political Science Review* 113(1): 254–263.

CIS. 2019b. *Estudio 3269. Postelectoral Elecciones Generales Noviembre (November) 2019*. Madrid: Centro de Investigaciones Sociológicas (CIS). www.cis.es/cis/opencm/ES/1_encuestas/estudios/ver.jsp?estudio=14479

Converse PE (2006) The nature of belief systems in mass publics (1964). *Critical Review* 18(1–3): 1–74.

Cordero G (2017) Three Decades of Religious Vote in Europe. *World Political Science* 13(1): 77–98.

Cordero G and Montero JR (2015) Against Bipartyism, Towards Dealignment? The 2014 European Election in Spain. *South European Society and Politics* 20(3): 357–379.

Dalton RJ and Wattenberg MP (2002) *Parties Without Partisans*. Oxford: Oxford University Press.

della Porta D, Kouki H and Fernández J (2017) Left's Love and Hate for Europe: Syriza, Podemos and Critical Visions of Europe During the Crisis. Caiani M and Guerra S (eds) *Euroscepticism, Democracy and the Media*. Basingstoke: Palgrave MacMillan, pp. 219–240.

De Vries C (2018) *Euroscepticism and the Future of European Integration. Euroscepticism and the Future of European Integration*. Oxford: Oxford University Press.

De Vries CE and Hobolt SB (2020) *Political Entrepeneurs. The Rise of Challenger Parties in Europe*. Princeton, New Jersey: Princeton University Press.

Díez Medrano J (2003) *Framing Europe: Attitudes to European Integration in Germany, Spain, and the United Kingdom*. Princeton: Princeton University Press.

Dotti Sani GM and Quaranta M (2020) Let Them Be, Not Adopt: General Attitudes Towards Gays and Lesbians and Specific Attitudes Towards Adoption by Same-Sex Couples in 22 European Countries. *Social Indicators Research* 150(1): 351–373.

ESS Round 9: European Social Survey Round 9 Data (2020). Data file edition 3.0. NSD - Norwegian Centre for Research Data, Norway – Data Archive and distributor of ESS data for ESS ERIC. doi:10.21338/NSD-ESS9-2018.

Fernández-Albertos J (2015) *Los Votantes de Podemos*. Madrid: La Catarata.

Fernández-Albertos J and Manzano D (2012) The Lack of Partisan Conflict over the Welfare State in Spain. *South European Society and Politics* 17(3): 427–447.

Givens TE (2004) The radical right gender gap. *Comparative Political Studies* 37(1): 30–54.

Goodwin M and Milazzo C (2017) Taking back control? Investigating the role of immigration in the 2016 vote for Brexit. *British Journal of Politics and International Relations* 19(3): 450–464.

Hainmueller J and Hiscox MJ (2006) Learning to love globalization: Education and individual attitudes toward international trade. *International Organization* 60(2): 469–498. DOI: 10.1017/S0020818306060140.

Hainmueller J and Hiscox MJ (2007) Educated preferences: Explaining attitudes toward immigration in Europe. *International Organization* 61(2): 399–442.

Hakhverdian A, Van Elsas E, Van der Brug W, et al. (2013) Euroscepticism and education: A longitudinal study of 12 EU member states, 1973–2010. *European Union Politics* 14(4): 522–541.

Halikiopoulou D, Nanou K and Vasilopoulou S (2012) The paradox of nationalism: The common denominator of radical right and radical left euroscepticism. *European Journal of Political Research* 51(4): 504–539.

Harteveld Eelco, Van der Brug Wouter, Dahlberg Stefan and Kokkonen Andrej (2015) The gender gap in populist radical-right voting: examining the demand side in Western and Eastern Europe, *Patterns of Prejudice*, 49(1-2): 103-134, DOI: 10.1080/0031322X.2015.1024399

Heinisch R and Werner A (2019) Who Do Populist Radical Right Parties Stand for? Representative Claims, Claim Acceptance and Descriptive Representation in the Austrian FPÖ and German AfD. *Representation* 55(4): 475–492.

Hooghe L, Marks G and Wilson CJ (2002) Does left/right structure party positions on European integration? *Comparative Political Studies* 35(8): 965–989.

Im ZJ, Mayer N, Palier B, et al. (2019) The "losers of automation": A reservoir of votes for the radical right? *Research and Politics* 6(1): 1–7. DOI: 10.1177/2053168018822395.

Immerzeel, Tim, Hilde Coffé, and Tanja van der Lippe (2015) Explaining the Gender Gap in Radical Right Voting: A Cross-National Investigation in 12 Western European Countries, *Comparative European Politics* 13(2), 263–286. 10.1057/cep.2013.20

Inglehart R and Klingemann HD (1976) Party Identification, Ideological Preference and the Left–Right Dimension among Western Mass Publics. *Party Identification and beyond: Representations of Voting and Party Competition.*

Inglehart RF (2008) Changing values among western publics from 1970 to 2006. *West European Politics* 31(1–2): 130–146.

Keith D (2017) Opposing Europe, Opposing Austerity. Radical Left Parties and the Eurosceptic Debate. Leruth B, Startin N, and Usherwood S (eds) *The Routledge Handbook of Euroscepticism.* London: Routledge, pp. 86–99.

Kitschelt H (1995) *The Radical Right in Western Europe.* Michigan: University of Michigan Press.

Konstantinidis N, Matakos K and Mutlu-Eren H (2019) "Take back control"? The effects of supranational integration on party-system polarization. *Review of International Organizations* 14(2): 297–333. DOI: 10.1007/s11558-019-09355-z.

Kunst S, Kuhn T and Van de Werfhorst HG (2020) Does education decrease Euroscepticism? A regression discontinuity design using compulsory schooling reforms in four European countries. *European Union Politics* 21(1): 24–42.

Lancaster CM (2019) Not So Radical After All: Ideological Diversity Among Radical Right Supporters and Its Implications. *Political Studies* EarlyView. DOI: 10.1177/0032321719870468.

Lauterbach F and DeVries CE (2020) Europe belongs to the young? Generational differences in public opinion towards the European Union during the Eurozone crisis. *Journal of European Public Policy* 27(2): 168–187.

Lefkofridi Z, Wagner M and Willmann JE (2014) Left-Authoritarians and Policy Representation in Western Europe: Electoral Choice across Ideological Dimensions. *West European Politics* 37(1): 65–90. DOI: 10.1080/01402382.2013.818354.

Lijphart A (1984) *Democracies: Patterns of Majoritarian and Consensus Government in Twenty-One Countries.* New Haven: Yale University Press.

Lipset Seymour Martin and Rokkan S (1967) Cleavage Structures, Party Systems, and Voter Alignments. Lipset Seymour M. and Rokkan S (eds) *Party Systems and Voter Alignments: Cross-National Perspectives.*

Lupu N (2015) *Party Brands in Crisis. Partisanship, Brand Dilution, and the Breakdown of Political Parties in Latin America.* Cambridge: Cambridge University Press.

McLaren L and Paterson I (2020) Generational change and attitudes to immigration. *Journal of Ethnic and Migration Studies* 46(3): 665–682.

Montero JR. (1987) Los fracasos políticos y electorales de la derecha española: Alianza Popular, 1976–1986. *Revista Española de Investigaciones Sociológicas* 39: 7–43.

Mudde C (2007) *Populist Radical Right Parties in Europe.* Cambridge: Cambridge University Press.

Norris P (2020) Measuring populism worldwide. *Party Politics* 26(6): 697–717. EarlyView. DOI: 10.1177/1354068820927686.

Oesch D (2008a) Explaining workers' support for right-wing populist parties in Western Europe: Evidence from Austria, Belgium, France, Norway, and Switzerland. *International Political Science Review* 29(3): 349–373.

Oesch D (2008b) The changing shape of class voting. *European Societies* 10(3): 329–355. DOI: 10.1080/14616690701846946.

Oesch D and Rennwald L (2018) Electoral competition in Europe's new tripolar political space: Class voting for the left, centre-right and radical right. *European Journal of Political Research* 57(4): 783–807. DOI: 10.1111/1475-6765.12259.

Orriols L and Cordero G (2016) The Breakdown of the Spanish Two-Party System: The Upsurge of Podemos and Ciudadanos in the 2015 General Election. *South European Society and Politics* 21(4): 469–492.

Payne SG (1993) *Spain's First Democracy. The Second Republic, 1931–1936.* Madison: University of Wisconsin Press.

Pitt A, Qu H, Rhee A, et al. (2018) *Inequality and Poverty across Generations in the European Union.*

Portillo J and Bracero A (2020) Así te manipula Vox con su lenguaje. *Huffington Post,* 28 June.

Ralph-Morrow E (2020) The Right Men: How Masculinity Explains the Radical Right Gender Gap. *Political Studies* EarlyView. DOI: 10.1177/0032321720936049.

Rama J and Cordero G (2018) Who are the losers of the economic crisis? Explaining the vote for right-wing populist parties in Europe after the Great Recession. *Revista Espanola de Ciencia Politica* 48: 13–43.

Rooduijn, M., Van Kessel, S., Froio, C., Pirro, A., De Lange, S., Halikiopoulou, D., Lewis, P., Mudde, C. & Taggart P (2020) The PopuList: An Overview of Populist, Far Right, Far Left and Eurosceptic Parties in Europe.

Rooduijn M (2018) What unites the voter bases of populist parties? Comparing the electorates of 15 populist parties. *European Political Science Review* 10(3): 351–368. DOI: 10.1017/S1755773917000145.

Royo S (2000) *From Social Democracy to Neoliberalism. The Consequences of Party Hegemony in Spain, 1982–1996.* New York: Palgrave MacMillan.

Ruedin D (2020) Do we need multiple questions to capture feeling threatened by immigrants? *Political Research Exchange* 2(1): 1–24. DOI: 10.1080/2474736x.2020.1758576.

Sampietro A and Sánchez-Castillo S (2020) Building a political image on Instagram: A study of the personal profile of Santiago Abascal (Vox) in 2018. *Communication and Society* 33(1): 169–184.

Sánchez-Cuenca I (2000) The Political Basis of Support for European Integration. *European Union Politics* 1(2): 147–171.

Santana A and Rama J (2018) Electoral support for left wing populist parties in Europe: addressing the globalization cleavage. *European Politics and Society* 19(5): 558–576.

Siedler T (2011) Parental unemployment and young people's extreme right-wing party affinity: Evidence from panel data. *Journal of the Royal Statistical Society. Series A: Statistics in Society* 174(3): 737–758.

Siegel SN (n.d.) Rightwing Populism in a Post-Marriage World: The Varieties of Backlash. DeVries-Jordan H and Anderson E (eds) *The Politics of LGBTQ Equality: Marrige and Beyond.* University Press of Kansas.

Spierings N and Zaslove A (2017) Gender, populist attitudes, and voting: explaining the gender gap in voting for populist radical right and populist radical left parties. *West European Politics* 40(4): 821–847.

Spierings N, Zaslove A, Mügge LM, et al. (2015) Gender and populist radical-right politics: An introduction. *Patterns of Prejudice* 49(1–2): 3–15.

Standing G (2013) Defining the precariat: A class in the making. Available at: www.eurozine.com/defining-the-precariat/ (accessed 20 October 2020).

Stanley B (2008) The thin ideology of populism. *Journal of Political Ideologies* 13(1): 95–110.

Stockemer, D, Lentz, T, and Mayer, D (2018) Individual Predictors of the Radical Right-Wing Vote in Europe: A Meta-Analysis of Articles in Peer-Reviewed Journals (1995–2016). *Government and Opposition, 53*(3), 569–593. doi:10.1017/gov.2018.2

Stubager R (2009) Education-based group identity and consciousness in the authoritarian-libertarian value conflict. *European Journal of Political Research* 48(2): 204–233.

Stubager R (2013) The Changing Basis of Party Competition: Education, Authoritarian-Libertarian Values and Voting. *Government and Opposition* 48(3): 372–397.

Turnbull-Dugarte SJ (2019) Explaining the end of Spanish exceptionalism and electoral support for Vox. *Research & Politics* 6(2): 1–8. DOI: 10.1177/2053168019851680.

Turnbull-Dugarte SJ and Devine D (2021) Can EU judicial intervention increase polity scepticism? Quasi-experimental evidence from Spain. *Journal of European Public Policy.* Online First. DOI: 10.1080/13501763.2021.1901963

Turnbull-Dugarte SJ, Rama J and Santana A (2020) The Baskerville's dog suddenly started barking: voting for VOX in the 2019 Spanish general elections. *Political Research Exchange* 2(1). DOI: 10.1080/2474736X.2020.1781543.

Turnbull-Dugarte SJ (2020) Multidimensional issue preferences of the European lavender vote. *Journal of European Public Policy* Online First. DOI: 10.1080/13501763.2020.1804987.

Van De Wardt M, De Vries CE and Hobolt SB (2014) Exploiting the cracks: Wedge issues in multiparty competition. *Journal of Politics* 76(4): 986–999. DOI: 10.1017/S0022381614000565.

Van der Brug W and Van Spanje J (2009) Immigration, Europe and the 'new' cultural dimension. *European Journal of Political Research* 48(3): 309–334.

Vittori D (2016) European populism in the shadow of the great recession. *Acta Politica*, pp. 400–402. DOI: 10.1057/ap.2016.7.

Wodak R (2015) *The Politics of Fear: What Right-Wing Populist Discourses Mean. The Politics of Fear: What Right-Wing Populist Discourses Mean.* London: SAGE.

Zanotti L and Rama J (2020) Spain and the populist radical right: Will Vox become a permanent feature of the Spanish party system? *LSE European Politics and Policy (EUROPP) blog.*

5

VOX AND SUPPORT FOR DEMOCRACY

Legacies from an authoritarian past

¡Por España!
y el que quiera defenderla,
honrado muera.
Y el traidor que la abandone,
no tenga quien le perdone,
ni en Tierra Santa cobijo,
ni una cruz en sus despojos,
ni las manos de un buen hijo
para cerrarle los ojos.

Diego Hernando de Acuña, Captain of Spanish Tercios – a
military unit active from 1534 until 1704 (toast by
Javier Ortega Smith to celebrate VOX electoral result,
11 November 2019)[1]

This chapter aims to be a first approximation of the study of VOX's stance on democracy both from the supply and the demand perspective. More in detail, this chapter analyses both the discourse of VOX leaders and the profile of its voters regarding their attitudes toward democracy.

In the introduction to this book, we maintained that VOX belongs to the populist radical right party family (PRRP), even with its peculiarities. Considering VOX as a *radical* instead of an *extreme* party means that, at least in theory, it is not semi-loyal or disloyal to the principal tenets of democracy (see Linz, 1978; Mudde, 2007; 2019). However, we maintain that due to some features of its leaders' discourse that act as cognitive shortcuts to invoke nostalgic images of pre-democratic politics, it is possible that the party attracts voters who are not fully engaged with the democratic regime or even activate anti-democratic attitudes in a part of the electorate. In this penultimate chapter we turn towards this question.

The chapter is structured as follows. In the first section, we examine the relationship between PRRPs and democratic support at the theoretical level. The second section focuses on the supply side, analysing the relationship between VOX and democracy by examining its leaders' public interventions and the party's electoral programme. The third part of the chapter is dedicated to the analysis of the relationship between the populist radical right and democracy from the perspective of voters. This *demand-side* analysis combines a descriptive and explanatory perspective to help understand the relationship between support for democracy and voting for PRRPs and, in particular, VOX.

Here, we start with a comparative perspective, identifying the effect of both satisfaction with democracy and democratic support upon the probability of casting a vote for four well-known Western European PRRPs: the Freedom Party of Austria [*Freiheitliche Partei Österreichs*] (FPÖ); the National Rally in France [*Rassemblement national*] (RN), formerly National Front until June 2018 [*Front national*] (FN); the German Alternative for Germany [*Alternative für Deutschland*] (AfD); and the Italian League [*Lega*], formerly Northern League until 2018 [*Lega Nord*]. Then we deal with the analysis of VOX voters concerning their attitudes toward the democratic regime.

The conclusions discuss the possible relationship among a recent authoritarian past, anti-democratic sentiments, and the propensity to vote for VOX. To the best of our knowledge, this finding contributes to the literature on the vote determinants for the populist radical right and helps us to better understand the potential anti-democratic penchants within the electoral revenue of PRRPs.

Democracy and the populist radical right

The relationship between populism and democracy is far from being settled (Rama and Casal Bértoa, 2020; Rovira Kaltwasser and van Hauwaert, 2020; Zanotti and Rama, 2020; Zaslove et al., 2020). Disentangling this relationship is even more difficult since the majority[2] of populist forces in Europe belong to the family of populist radical right parties. Following Mudde (2007), we maintain that this set of parties shares at least three ideological features: nativism, authoritarianism, and populism (see Figure 5.1). Nativism, a combination of xenophobia and nationalism, is the core ideological characteristic of these parties. Moreover, as we mentioned in the introduction, nativism is an ideology that holds that states should be inhabited exclusively by members of the native in-group ("the nation"), and that the non-native out-group, their beliefs, and their ideas are fundamentally threatening to the homogeneous nation-state (Mudde, 2007).

The starting point on this matter is that radical parties differ from extreme parties. The latter are those parties that reject democracy as the best political regime and aim to change it (Mudde, 2007: 22–24). By contrast, radical parties are situated near the extremes of the left–right axis, but their aim is not overthrowing democracy. In other words, whilst radical parties may advocate policies that are unpalatable for moderates and that fall at the polar ends of the ideological spectrum, they remain

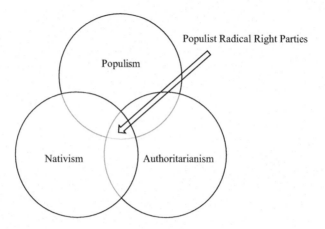

FIGURE 5.1 Populist radical right ideological traits

Source: Elaboration of the authors based on Mudde (2007)

loyal to the democratic system and view it as the best viable conduit through which they can achieve their policy objectives. In short, PRRPs are radical yet democratic whilst extreme right parties are radical and *anti*-democratic.

However, given its exclusionary features, PRRPs may have a more dangerous effect on *liberal* democracy. The distinction between inclusionary and exclusionary populism has become increasingly common in the academic literature since it helps to characterize the two different versions of populism that are predominant in the contemporary world. This distinction is based on three dimensions: material, political, and symbolic (Betz, 2001; Filc, 2010; Mudde and Rovira Kaltwasser, 2013).

The material dimension is linked to the distribution of material resources to various groups in society. While in the majority of cases exclusionary populism tends to exclude people from the distribution of these resources, in the case of inclusionary populism some groups are targeted to receive more of state resources (Mudde and Rovira Kaltwasser, 2013: 158). The political dimension refers to Dahl's (1971) concept of democracy, which is based on political participation and public contestation. While exclusionary populism prevents the full participation and contestation of some groups, inclusionary populism targets some groups to extend their participation and contestation. Lastly, the symbolic dimension alludes to the boundaries set on both "the people" and "the elite". Although this dimension looks less straightforward, it does not mean that it is less relevant (Mudde and Rovira Kaltwasser, 2013). When populist actors define "the people" with certain symbols and values, those who do not share these symbols and values are implicitly excluded and therefore become "the others". In line with this, Margulies (2018) points out that "at best nativist parties have a conflicted attitude toward liberal values; at worst, these parties deploy such values instrumentally to serve ethnonationalist and illiberal purposes". Indeed, whilst one might view the rejection and the demonization of the ethnic out-groups as morally questionable, and at odds with liberal values, these views are not anti-democratic per se. In sum, we can say that PRRPs, due to their nativist feature, pose a severe strain on principles of liberal democracy, without being anti-democratic.

Because of the predominance of populist radical right parties in Europe, at the empirical level it is difficult to differentiate the effect of the nativist and the populist component, even if nativism, not populism, seems to be more dangerous for the democratic regime.[3]

Moreover, even if the populist radical right is not anti-democratic, we cannot forget that some of these parties have their roots in authoritarian movements, as is the case of the 1970s National Front or the Freedom Party of Austria (Biorcio, 2003: 7). McDonnell and Werner (2019: 83–84), for example, explain that the decision of the Danish People's Party [*Dansk Folkeparti*] (DF) and the Finns Party [*Perussuomalaiset*] (PS) not to join the transnational Europe of Nations and Freedom group in the European Parliament, a group mostly integrated by PRRPs, was because "parties like the Front National, Austrian Freedom Party, Sweden Democrats and Vlaams Belang all have extreme right histories and associations with fascism". This is particularly relevant for this chapter since Spain has a relatively recent authoritarian past, belonging to the so-called third wave of democratization (Huntington, 1991).

VOX and democracy

In this section, we will analyse the discourse of VOX's leaders to assess the stance of the party toward democracy. As mentioned before, we consider that VOX fits well the populist radical right characterization as it exhibits, especially in the last years, a *polyhedral* speech that combines nationalism, nativism, and populism (Casals, 2020: 32). Therefore, and assuming that PRPPs, at least at the ideological level, are not per se against democracy, we do not expect a lack of support for democracy among the party leaders. However, as seen in Chapter 3, the party presents a romanticized and nostalgic image that is sympathetic to Spain's pre-democratic regime under Franco and the party has made constant allusions to a "better" past and more "glorious times" in Spain's history.[4] Since voters are assumed to vote for parties closest to their views, for Spaniards a radical right option is probably the best option that voters with low attachment to democracy are going to get.

Because of the constant references to the pre-democratic period, VOX's discourse deserves a closer examination. In this sense, it is important to note that the authoritarian Spanish regime was characterized by a strong nationalistic rhetoric and by its organic anti-liberal conception of democracy (Ribera Payá and Díaz Martínez, 2020). Also, the pre-democratic corporate government sought to assemble the "living forces" of the nation around a common goal: restoring the grandeur of Spain (Ribera Payá and Díaz Martínez, 2020). All these elements are present in the discourse of VOX. Especially the references to "the Living Spain" ("*la España Viva*") in opposition to the "Anti Spain" ("*Anti España*") are present both in the electoral manifesto and in the public speeches of the party's leaders (see Casals, 2020). Indeed, the manifesto for the November 2019 election (the one that the party used as well in other electoral calls) is called "100 measures for the Living Spain" ("*100 Medidas para la España Viva*") (VOX, 2019). Even during the electoral campaign for the April 2019 general election, the slogan of the party was "It is the time of the Living Spain" ("*Es la hora de la España Viva*").[5] Moreover, during the rally in the Colón square, in Madrid that closed the electoral campaign for the April elections of 2019, the party's leader Santiago Abascal claimed:

> *The 28th April we will not see common elections. On the 28th we decide what matters the most: a patriotic alternative or an agreement of betrayal. Either the disaggregation or the historical continuity of our homeland. Either socialist misery, or the prosperity of our children and grandchildren. Either the progressive dictatorship or freedom for the Spaniards. Furthermore, more clearly, on the 28th [election of April 2019] we choose, either the anti-Spain or the living Spain.*

Those who oppose VOX's *Living Spain* represent the *anti-Spain* – those who are not willing to take patriotic actions in the interest of the country but are driven by some other individualistic interest. VOX depicts the mainstream media as an ally of the anti-Spain. They are characterized as a "lying machine"[6] that "crafts fake news from progressive bureaus of radios and televisions,"[7] which help to prop up the "progressive dictatorship" (Ribera Payá and Díaz Martinez, 2020: 15).

It was during the campaign for the general election in April 2019 when the party started to intensify its nationalist message with constant references to the recent Spanish authoritarian past conveyed through a populist discourse. VOX presented itself as the representative of the *real Spain*, against those who are allegedly the enemies of Spain. The term anti-España was employed in the Spanish Civil War by the *Bando Nacional* (sympathizers of the authoritarian dictator Francisco Franco) in reference to those whom they regarded as "enemies of the Homeland" ("*enemigos de la Patria*", the Republicans). Another example of this recurrent use of the Living Spain discourse was on 1 December 2018, just one day before the Andalusian regional elections, in the rally for "the unity of Spain" organized by the Foundation for the Defence of the Spanish Nation [*Fundación para la Defensa de Nación Española*] (DENAES), where Santiago Abascal claimed:[8]

> *Spain is alive and claims the inheritance that our parents have given us. Spain is alive and is fighting for the future and the freedom that we have to give to our children. Spain is alive and is much stronger than its enemies. Spain is alive and is much stronger than what its enemies thought Spain was.*

This rhetorical presentation of an imagined antagonistic confrontation between the real Spain and the anti-Spain clearly represents an example of populism. The idea further projects a Spain that is simultaneously reborn through the fight against the nation's secular enemies (Casals, 2019). It is important to remark again that the opposition between the real Spain and the anti-Spain became "especially frequent in the general elections of 1936", so that it was "a clear indication of the political division of the country and a prelude to the upcoming war"[9] (García-Santos, 1980). In this sense, VOX re-uses a metaphor employed in the pre-constitutional Spain and certainly employed by National-Catholicism (Casals, 2019).

Besides the rhetoric of the Living Spain, the Francoist period was characterized by the fusion of revolutionary fascism with conservative, traditional, and monarchist parties that supported the Nationalist side of the civil war. As we pointed out in Chapter 3, VOX is a deeply conservative party concerning issues of traditional (Catholic) morality. In a 2019 interview, Santiago Abascal expressed his view on abortion, maintaining that "there are women who claim that they own their bodies but what is inside [i.e. the fetus] is not theirs".[10]

As part of their reaffirmation of traditional values, the issue that VOX's leader tends to politicize the most is the role of the women. The rejection of feminism as a legitimate ideology is clearly expressed in the manifesto that VOX's female leaders wrote and presented to mark the occasion of International Women's Day in March 2020. As far as they are concerned, such commemorative events "[are] created by the extreme left".[11] Other examples of the rejection of feminism also abound. Francisco Serrano, one of the party representatives in the Andalusian Parliament, showed his rejection of what he defines "gender ideology". In 2015, he claimed in his Twitter account that "the radical left feminism is composed of violent lesbians and resentful misandrists who take away public funds".[12] Furthermore, in 2017, he claimed that "the issue with feminism is that it is led by women who are not [females], from their gender perspective. They hate the man, their competitor", and in 2014 "feminism has turned into a fundamentalism that hates femininity, maternity, family, and life as the fruit of the love between man and woman".

A polemic image uploaded to VOX's official Twitter account on 28 April 2019, the day of the Spanish general elections, summarizes these ideas.[13] This image represents the Living Spain (the knight with the sword) versus the anti-Spain ("leftist" media like El País, La SER, and La Sexta, radical left formations, Catalan nationalists, and both LGBT+ and feminist movements).[14] It was very polemical as the image comes from the film The Lord of the Rings, and displayed VOX as one the protagonists, Aragorn (interpreted by Viggo Mortensen), and the anti-Spain as the villainous Orcs of Mordor. Both Warner Brothers (who own the rights of the film) and Viggo Mortensen, publicly denounced the use of their image by VOX's electoral campaign.[15]

Lastly, VOX has defended the Spanish Crown on numerous occasions. VOX Andalucía has registered two non-legislative proposals ("Proposiciones no de Ley", PNLs) in the Andalusian Parliament for the regional government to demand the "social-communist" government of Pedro Sánchez "defend and protect the institution of the Crown" and "prevent the impunity of the coup plotters" of 1 October 2017, the day of the Catalan independence unauthorized referendum.[16] For the Andalusian MPs who presented these proposals, it was incredibly important that "the Parliament of Andalusia defended and protected the institution of the Crown, the highest representation of our form of government, the parliamentary monarchy, as well as the dignity and figure of His Majesty King Felipe VI, who embodies

120 VOX and support for democracy

the indissoluble unity and historical continuity of the Spanish Nation". Also, as mentioned in Chapter 3, the party has committed itself "to provide the maximum possible legal protection to the symbols of the nation, especially the Flag, the Anthem and the Crown". To increase the penalties for offences and outrages against Spain and to its symbols or emblems, "no affront to them must remain unpunished" (VOX manifesto: 2). However, as Casals (2020: 28) underlines, VOX's support to the Crown is not as straightforward. Indeed, Abascal claimed, "I'm Spanish. Neither monarchical nor republican. […] Spain, its sovereignty and its unity are above the monarchy, the republic, the Constitution and democracy". Thus, it can be inferred from this that VOX is potentially disruptive, as it may consider itself legitimated to explore non-democratic political forms that preserve Spain as a nation if it judges that it is in danger.

In sum, discursively VOX's leaders do not express themselves against the democratic regime, at least coherently and in an explicit manner. However, they adopt many of the positions of the Francoist regime in terms of the defence of traditional moral values exalting the alleged past grandeur of Spain.

Although it is true that VOX does not explicitly assume an ideological affiliation with the dictatorship, it *is* also true that the recurrent speech alluding to the authoritarian legacy with rose-tinted glasses might attract former voters of far-right parties or activate latent anti-democratic attitudes among those voters who previously only had the option of voting for the mainstream right (if they wanted their vote to translate into seats in representative institutions).

Figure 5.2 shows the evolution of the vote share for all far-right parties in Spain from 1977 to November 2019 (excluding VOX).

The figure clearly shows that the support for this set of parties in Spain has always been residual, with the exception of 1979, where Blas Piñar won one seat for the circumscription of Madrid as the leader of National Union [*Unión Nacional*] (UN), which took home 378,964 or 2.11 per cent of the votes, and ended up as the sixth most voted party.[17] In fact, the average of votes for far-right parties between 1977 and 2019 was 77,000, and the average vote share for this parties was only 0.4 per cent of the total. On the whole, if we focus on the post-1982 period, the trend shows low support for far-right parties in Spain, with just the exception of 2011, when Platform for Catalonia [*Plataforma per Catalunya*] (PxC) obtained close to 60,000 or 0.25 per cent of the votes, although even this result was far more modest than the one achieved in 1979.[18] The curious thing is that in the last election the support for far rightist parties descended to less than 1,000 votes, coinciding with the emergence of VOX at the national level. For that reason, it is plausible to interpret that VOX was able to attract former voters of far-right forces with *extreme*-right preferences. Additionally, VOX attracted former PP voters who, when compared with the voters of other Spanish parties are, under certain circumstances, more sympathetic towards an authoritarian regime (Torcal and Medina, 2002; Torcal, 2008).

However, we still know very little about the profile of VOX's voters in terms of their democratic regime preferences. This is relevant because, as we have seen, one of the specificities of the discourse of VOX is the exaltation of the national

VOX and support for democracy 121

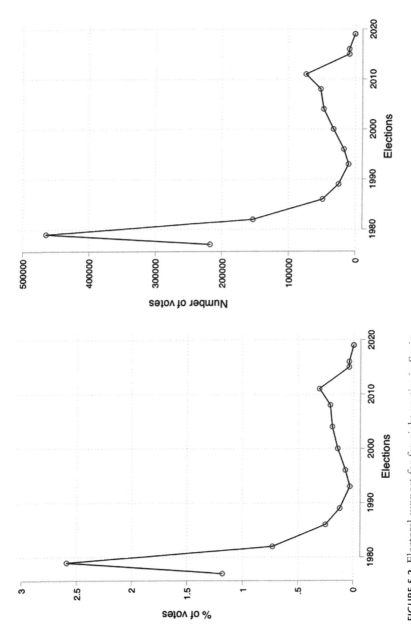

FIGURE 5.2 Electoral support for far-right parties in Spain

Note: Right-hand panel (number of votes). Left-hand panel (percentage).

122 VOX and support for democracy

FIGURE 5.2 Cont.

1977: Falange Española de las Jons Auténtica (FJONSA); Alianza Nacional 18 de Julio (AN18); Reforma Social Española (RSE); Falange Española de las Jons (FJONS); Asociación Círculos José Antonio (CJA); Fuerza Nueva (FN); Falange Española Independiente (FEI). *1979:* Partido Carlista (PCARL); Falange Española de las Jons Auténtica (FJONSA); Falange Española Auténtica (FEA); Falange Española Independiente – Unidad Falangista (UF-FI-AT); Falange Española-Unidad Falangista (FE-UF); Unión Nacional (UN). *1982:* Fuerza Nueva (FA); Solidaridad Española (SE); Movimiento Falangista Español (MFE); Falange Española – JONS (FE-JONS); Falange Española Independiente (FEI); Movimiento Católico Español (MCATE); Falange Asturiana (FA); Partido Carlista (PC). *1986:* Falange Española – JONS (FE-JONS); Coalición de Unidad Nacional (CUN); Partido Español Cristiano (PEC). *1989:* Falange Española – JONS (FE-JONS); Falange Española Independiente (FEI). *1993:* Falange Española – JONS (FE-JONS); Movimiento Católico Español (MCE); Falange Española Auténtica FE(A). *1996:* Falange Española Auténtica FE(A); Alianza por la Unidad Nacional (AUN); Falange Española Independiente (FEI). *2000:* La Falange (FE); Plataforma España 2000 (ES2000); Falange Española Independiente – Falange 2000 (FEI-FE 2000); Partido Carlista (PC). *2004:* Democracia Nacional (DN); Falange Española – JONS (FE-JONS); Falange Española Falange (FE Falange); Falange Auténtica (FA); España 2000; Alianza por la Unidad Nacional (AUN). *2008:* Falange Española – JONS (FE-JONS); Democracia Nacional (DN); Alternativa Española (AES); España 2000 (ES 2000); Falange Auténtica (FA); Alianza Nacional (AUN); Partido Carlista (PC); FRENTE – Frente Español; Comunión Tradicionalista Carlista (CTC); Movimiento Falangista de España (MFE). *2011:* Plataforma por Catalunya (PxC); España 2000 (ES2000); Falange Española – JONS (FE-JONS); Democracia Nacional (DN). *2015:* Falange Española – JONS (FE-JONS); Democracia Nacional (DN). *2016:* Falange Española – JONS (FE-JONS); La Falange (FE). *2019 April A*: Falange Española – JONS (FE-JONS). *2019 November:* Falange Española – JONS (FE-JONS).

Source: (1977–2019) Elaboration of the authors based on Spanish Ministry of Interior website data (see: www.infoelectoral.mir.es/)

way of life. This highly salient aspect of the party ideology is linked to concepts and symbols of the authoritarian past. These constant references to the pre-democratic period might be a way to attract the portion of the electorate who is not entirely loyal to democracy.

Taking all of this into account and to shed some light on the extent to which those electors who show less support for democracy also exhibited a higher propensity to vote for VOX in both the April and November 2019 elections, we test the effect of regime preference upon the probability to vote for VOX instead of another political opponent.

We divide the following section of the chapter in two parts. In the first, we show descriptive information about the relationship between satisfaction with democracy *and* democratic support with voting for four well-known Western European

PRRPs. Additionally, we test the effect of these same variables upon the likelihood to vote for these parties instead of other political options. The second part replicates this approach for the case of VOX, analysing in a descriptive and analytical way the effect of regime support upon the electoral support for VOX in the April and November 2019 Spanish general elections.

Attitudes towards democracy and vote for populist radical right parties in comparative perspective

We have analysed the relationship between PRRPs and democracy at a conceptual level. We now turn to analysing the democratic profile of their voters. Thus, trying to fill this gap we assess to what extent those who vote for populist radical right parties are those who display lower levels of support for democracy as well as less satisfaction with democracy. In doing this, we draw on the European Elections Studies (EES) dataset (see Schmitt et. al., 2019) to examine the *democratic profile* of AfD, FPÖ, Lega, and FN voters (following the same idea defended in Chapter 4). We opt for the EES instead of the European Social Survey (Round 9) because of the absence of any questions regarding regime preference or other proxies in the latter dataset.

On the basis of the respondents' position regarding satisfaction with the way democracy works (low = unsatisfied, high = satisfied) and the extent to which living in a democracy is essential (low = non-essential to live in a democracy, high = essential to live in a democracy), we created a number of voter categories. These include: i) *the non-democratic unsatisfied voter*, who under certain circumstances is willing to support an authoritarian regime and at the same time is dissatisfied with the way democracy works; ii) *the democratic unsatisfied voter*, who supports democracy but is dissatisfied with the way it works; iii) *the non-democratic satisfied voter*, who under certain circumstances is willing to support an authoritarian regime but is satisfied with the way democracy works; and iv) *the democratic and satisfied voter*, who shows support for democracy and is also satisfied with the way democracy works (Gonzalez et al., 2019). These four categories, pulling on the work of Gonzales et al (2019), are summarized in Table 5.1.

TABLE 5.1 Scheme of the democratic/undemocratic and satisfied/unsatisfied voter

		Support for democracy	
		Low	*High*
Satisfaction with democracy	*Low*	Non-democratic unsatisfied voter	Democratic unsatisfied voter
	High	Non-democratic satisfied voter	Democratic and satisfied voter

Source: own elaboration based on González et al. (2019)

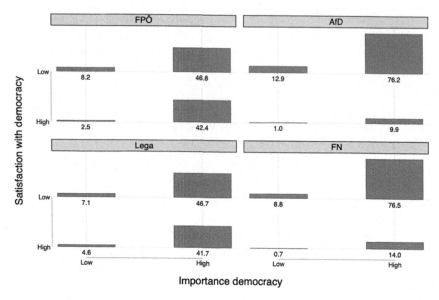

FIGURE 5.3 The democratic/undemocratic and satisfied/unsatisfied voter

Source: Elaboration of the authors based on EES data

We now turn to show the distribution of these categories amongst the voting blocks of European PRRPs. Figure 5.3 shows that although the majority of PRRP's voters in Europe are unsatisfied with how democracy works, they consider it essential to live under a democratic political system. The party with the highest percentage of non-democratic unsatisfied voters is AfD, followed by FN, FPÖ, and the Lega. In turn, FN ranks at the top of political parties with democratic yet unsatisfied voters, followed by AfD. Interestingly, both FPÖ and Lega host a high percentage of democratic and satisfied voters: 42.4 and 41.7 per cent, respectively. In the case of Lega, this could be due to the presence in the system of a more radical alternative, Brothers of Italy [*Fratelli d'Italia*] (FdI). The latter is the heir of the former fascist party and it is discursively more radical than the Lega. As a consequence, it seems reasonable to believe that those voters who show less support for democracy might opt for Brothers of Italy (in fact, in the same database we find that 12.5 per cent of the voters of Brothers of Italy display low levels of both satisfaction with and support for democracy).

These findings seem to confirm that although PRRP's voters tend to be unsatisfied with democracy, their levels of support for democracy are *not* substantially lower than those of other parties' voters (the mean percentage of voters who display low levels of support for democracy for all the parties is 8.27).

Going a step further, Figure 5.4 displays the effects of both satisfaction with democracy and the importance ascribed to the fact of living in a democracy, upon the likelihood to vote for the abovementioned PRRPs instead of other political

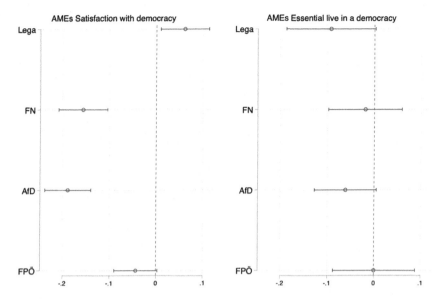

FIGURE 5.4 Attitudes towards democracy and support for populist radical right parties

Source: Elaboration of the authors based on EES data

options in the different countries (Italy, France, Germany, and Austria). Here we run logistic regression models estimating the average marginal effects (AMEs) of both variables on the probability of voting for one of the PRRPs. Whilst not reported here, the models also control for a vector of potential, confounding sociodemographic and political variables including sex, age, education, and left–right self-placement on the ideological spectrum.

For the interpretation of Figure 5.4 we have to assume that each horizontal line represents an independent variable of the model (*satisfaction with democracy* for the left-hand panel and the importance of *living in a democracy* for the right-hand panel), the point standing for the best estimation of its effect upon the dependent variable, and the horizontal line around it, for its 95 per cent confidence interval. If a confidence interval crosses the vertical line drawn at the origin (zero) of the horizontal axis, the effect of the variable is not statistically significant, i.e. there is no effect distinguishable from zero that we are able to identify given the data. If it does not cross it and is located at its right, the effect is positive and statistically significant, whereas if it is located at its left, the effect is negative and statistically significant.

The results are clear: whereas the likelihood to cast a vote for the FN and AfD over all other French or German alternatives increases amongst those who are less satisfied with the way democracy works, we *do not* find any relationship between anti-democratic voters and the support for the four analysed PRRPs. This means that those with higher anti-democratic values are *not* more likely to support a PRRP over other political options. But what about the case of VOX?

126 VOX and support for democracy

Modelling support for VOX as a function of non-democratic regime preferences

As we have previously mentioned, this part of the chapter aims to study the impact of political system preferences upon the probability to cast a vote for VOX over other political parties both in the last April and November 2019 Spanish elections separately and also merging both datasets. As in the case of Chapter 4, we employ post-electoral datasets by the *Centro de Investigaciones Sociológicas* (CIS), which is the Spanish national, public institution responsible for survey data collection at the national level.[19]

We divide our analysis in two blocks. Firstly, we examine the distribution of regime preferences among the electorate of the main political parties in Spain: PSOE, PP, Cs, UP, and VOX. Then, following the same idea of Figure 5.5, we build a profile of Spanish political parties' voters, by considering both their satisfaction with democracy and their support for democracy as a regime type. Secondly, we model the electoral support for VOX through a binary logistic regression in which the dependent variable (the variable we wish to explain) is vote recall and the main independent variable is regime support.

Distribution of voters' regime preference in Spain

We first provide a descriptive overview of the percentage of electors that cast a vote for VOX in the general elections of April and November 2019 and those who voted for other parties, regarding their distribution in three categories of the variable regime preference: 1 "A democratic system is always preferable"; 2 "the political system is indifferent"; 3 "sometimes an authoritarian regime is necessary". Thus, Figure 5.5 displays the average levels of support for each one of these categories. The results indicate that those respondents who chose the third category (sometimes an authoritarian regime is necessary) were more common among VOX voters than among those of all the other political forces. Notably, in the last general election, the one of November 2019, the percentage of this third category increases until it reaches more than 21 per cent. More precisely, whereas in the April 2019 election the percentage of VOX voters that positioned themselves on the second and third categories were 7.22 and 16.25 respectively, in November 2019, 5.70 per cent regard the type of regime as irrelevant and 21.65 per cent consider that, sometimes, an authoritarian regime is preferable. This means that a combined proportion of 1 in 4 (27.35 per cent) have preferences that do not explicitly endorse democracy as a necessarily desirable regime type. If we compare the graph of VOX displayed in Figure 5.5 with the one that represents the whole electorate (labelled "Total") the distribution clearly illustrates that, whereas the third category is residual in the whole Spanish electorate, it is notable in VOX.

Finally, with data from the April 2019 elections, which include both satisfaction with democracy and political system preferences (unfortunately, the CIS's November post-electoral survey does not ask about satisfaction with democracy),

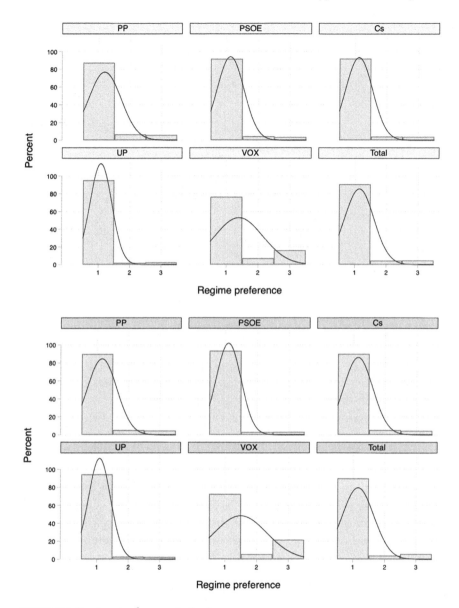

FIGURE 5.5 Regime preferences in Spain

Source: CIS (2019a) and CIS (2019b)

we replicated the typology of citizens who voted for the main five parties with respect to their democratic profile (see Figure 5.6). Again, we distinguish among four categories: *unsatisfied authoritarians, satisfied authoritarians, unsatisfied democrats,* and *satisfied democrats*. Clearly, VOX's electoral pool is conformed by a higher percentage (12.1 per cent) of unsatisfied authoritarian voters than those of any of the

128 VOX and support for democracy

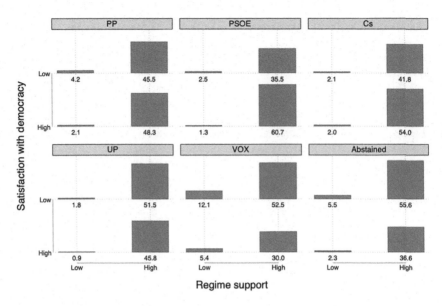

FIGURE 5.6 Regime preferences in Spain by party

Note: for satisfaction with democracy, *low* means lower satisfaction with the way democracy works (positions from 1 to 5) and high means *higher* satisfaction with the way democracy works (positions from 6 to 10). On the other hand, for regime support, *low* means support for an authoritarian regime while *high* means support for a democratic political system.

Source: Elaboration of the authors, based on the CIS's April post-election survey (CIS, 2019a)

other parties. The rest of their electoral support is made up of satisfied authoritarians (5.4), unsatisfied democrats (52.5), and satisfied democrats (30.0). PSOE voters display the highest percentage of satisfied democrats, whereas abstainers display the second largest category of unsatisfied authoritarians (5.5 per cent), followed by the PP (4.2 per cent). Abstainers are also those with the highest proportion of unsatisfied democrats.

The next section presents the multivariate analysis, with an emphasis on the political variables and on the effect of regime preferences upon the likelihood to cast a vote for VOX.

Measuring the effect of regime preference upon the probability to vote for VOX

We run three logistic models: the first one with the CIS post-electoral survey for the Spanish general elections April 2019; the second one with the CIS post-electoral for the Spanish November 2019 elections; and the third one with a pooled dataset including both elections (conditioned with fixed effects). As in the case of the models we have presented elsewhere, we report the average marginal effects (AMEs). These can be interpreted as the percentage-point change in the probability of voting for VOX associated with a one-unit change in the value of the explanatory variable (see Table 5.A1 in the Appendix section, for the coefficients of the logistic regressions).

Our main independent variable, *regime preference*, is coded as 0 for those who consider that the political system is indifferent or those who believe that in some circumstances an authoritarian option is preferable, and as 1 for those electors who declare that democracy is always preferable. Additionally, we included sociodemographic and political variables to avoid problems of false correlations.[20]

With respect to the dependent variable, we assigned the value 1 for those who report to have voted for VOX and the value 0 for those who report to have cast a vote for any other party. We recoded abstainers, null and blank votes as missing. As previous research shows, the majority of VOX's April 2019 voters came from former voters (2016) of the PP, followed by a smaller portion of former Ciudadanos's voters, 58.9 and 13.5 per cent, respectively (Zanotti et al., 2020). Also, in the snap elections of November 2019, 19.1 per cent of VOX voters were former PP voters (i.e. voted for the PP in April 2019), while 10.1 were former Cs. For this reason, we also ran logistic binary regressions with two alternative dependent variables (1 = voted for VOX, 0 = voted for PP) and (1 = voted for VOX, 0 = voted for PP or Cs) in order to check the robustness of the effect of the main independent variable upon the probability to cast a vote for VOX (see Table 5.A2 in the Appendix section and Figure 5.9). For the sake of simplicity, Figure 5.7 below shows the coefficients of AMEs of the three statistical models.

Figure 5.7 clearly shows that, even after controlling for a battery of sociodemographic as well as political variables, the support for VOX instead of other parties increases among those which consider that the political regime does not matter or that an authoritarian regime is preferable to a democratic one. Interestingly, the results also underline that the profile of VOX voters shares some similarities and differences with the traditional radical right parties (see also Chapter 4). Thus, men, middle aged (between 30 and 45 years old), those with upper secondary educational level (see Table 5.A1 in the Appendix section), those who identify more with the right, those who display a higher level of attachment to Spanish national identity, and those who perceive that the Spanish political and economic conditions are bad, exhibit a higher propensity to cast a vote for VOX than for other political parties. In this regard, ideology really matters to understand the support for VOX. In fact, the probability to vote for VOX in April 2019 was 32 per cent higher for those placed on the right and 46 per cent higher in November snap election.

Figure 5.8 highlights the results displayed on the last rows of Figure 5.7, concerning our variable of interest, regime support. Here we can see that the likelihood to vote for VOX instead of other political options increases two percentage points for those voters with an authoritarian sentiment in April and seven percentage points in November.

130 VOX and support for democracy

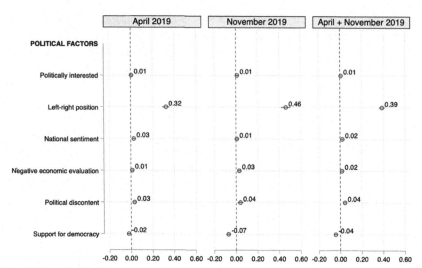

FIGURE 5.7 Probability to vote for VOX instead of other parties

Source: Elaboration of the authors, on the basis of the CIS's April and November post-election surveys (CIS, 2019a; CIS, 2019b)

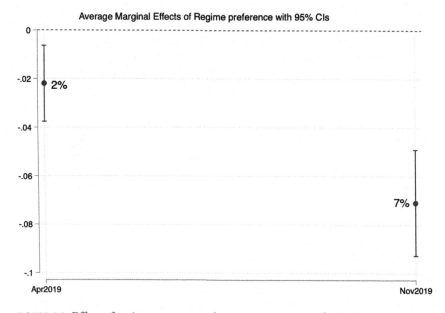

FIGURE 5.8 Effect of regime support on the propensity to vote for VOX

Source: Elaboration of the authors, based on the CIS's April and November post-election surveys (CIS, 2019a; CIS, 2019b)

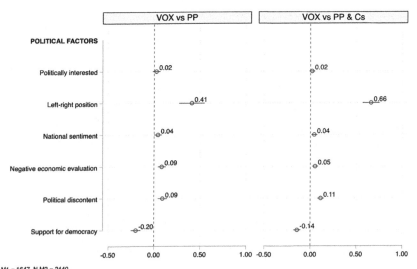

FIGURE 5.9 Probability of voting for VOX instead of other right-wing parties

Note: April and November post electoral CIS surveys merged. Left-hand baseline: PP. Right-hand baseline: Cs.

Source: Elaboration of the authors, based on the CIS's April and November post-election surveys (CIS, 2019a; CIS, 2019b)

In Figure 5.9, we replicate the estimation used to compile Figures 5.7 and 5.8 but explicitly compare the voters of VOX with those who voted for the other right-wing parties (PP and Cs). Regime preference still matters: the probability of voting for VOX vis à vis the PP and vis à vis PP and Cs increases for those with authoritarian attitudes. The average marginal effects reported in Figure 5.9 highlight that the likelihood to support VOX increases by a substantive 20 percentage points among those with non-democratic regime preferences compared with those who voted for the PP. On the other hand, the likelihood to support VOX increases 14 percentage points compared with the PP *and* Cs.

Given that in Chapter 4 we provide evidence showing that age plays an important role in determining the probability of voting for VOX, we seek to test the conditionality of the effect of regime preferences across different age cohorts. To do this, we model an interaction effect of age with democratic support. Foa and Mounk's (2016; 2017) findings suggest that young cohorts are more likely to support a non-democratic regime. In fact, they argue, this trend has increased in the last years. The results of their analysis are straightforward: "Only one in three Dutch millennials accords maximal importance to living in a democracy; in the United States, that number is slightly lower, around 30 per cent" (Foa and Mounk 2016: 8). Moreover, the share of citizens who approve the statement "having a strong leader who does not have to bother with parliament or elections", for example, has gone

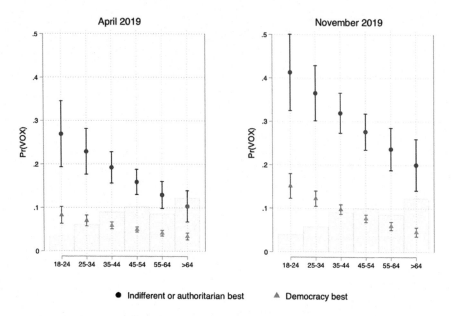

FIGURE 5.10 System preferences, age and voting for VOX

Source: Elaboration of the authors, based on the CIS's April and November post-election surveys (CIS, 2019a; CIS, 2019b).

up markedly in countries such as Germany, the United States, and Spain (Foa and Mounk, 2017: 7) and mostly among the young cohorts. There is, therefore, reason to expect that the effect of anti-democratic feelings on the support for VOX at the ballot box will be higher among younger Spanish cohorts than among older ones.

Figure 5.10 shows that younger cohorts with anti-democratic feelings were more likely to vote for VOX instead of other parties, especially in the November elections (right-side graph on Figure 5.10). The probability of voting for VOX in November 2019 was 0.41 for the 18–25 age cohort and was 0.20 for those aged older than 64. All in all, our empirical findings signal that age and democratic preferences matter. Younger cohorts are more prone to support VOX but the greatest amount of support for Spain's new PRRP is enjoyed amongst those of the young who are not necessarily supportive of democracy as a regime type.

Conclusion

The relationship between democratic support and the vote for populist radical right parties (PRRPs) is not clear. Although at the theoretical level radical right parties are not anti-democratic but rather at odds with the *liberal* component of democracy, in the case of VOX the recurrent allusions to the pre-democratic past of Spain in different arenas such as their public discourse, manifesto, and social media let us question the extent to which their voters' attitudes toward democracy are crucial in determining the vote for the party.

To assess this matter, first we analysed the discourse of the parties in those arenas as well as its voters with respect to their democratic profile. Then, we carried out a descriptive analysis regarding the distribution of democratic preferences and the support for the different Spanish political parties, finding that those with high *anti-democratic* sentiments constituted 23.5 per cent of VOX's electoral bases in April 2019 and more than 27 per cent in the snap elections of November (these *anti-democratic* sentiments are residual in the rest of political options). The take-home message from this analysis is clear: one in four of VOX's voters hold regime preferences that are, at best, volatile.

Last, we tested the effect of regime support upon the probability to cast a vote for VOX instead of other political forces in Spain for the two general elections of 2019. Our findings suggest that those that consider that the political system is indifferent or that sometimes an authoritarian regime is necessary were the most likely to support VOX. More in detail, controlling for other relevant variables (see Turnbull Dugarte et al., 2020), regime preferences are still crucial for explaining the support for VOX.

When we model support for VOX via multivariate regression, which allows us to assess the effect of these preferences whilst controlling for other potential confounders, we find that voters with anti-democratic preferences are more likely to vote for VOX over any other political party or when paired up against the other established parties on the right.

These findings are of note for various reasons. On the one hand, the relationship between democratic regime support and vote for other Western European PRRPs (e.g. the French National Front, Italian Lega, Austrian Freedom Party, and Alternative for Germany) is not statistically significant. This goes in line with the conceptualization and distinction between extreme and radical right parties: supporters of the radical right are not necessarily anti-democratic. However, as we demonstrated in the first part of this chapter, VOX's flirtation with a romanticized image of pre-transition Spain, consciously or not, attracts the support of those voters who do not fully endorse democracy. In other words, the discursive emphasis of some aspects of the Spanish recent authoritarian legacy could have activated anti-democratic attitudes in some voters as well as attracted those who before voted for far-right options.

Crucially, our findings suggest that VOX voters, both in the April and November general elections, are motivated by their political regime preferences. Thus, this finding suggests that the regime preference of its supporters move beyond radicalism into the realms of extremism. More importantly, we also find that young cohorts with authoritarian or indifferent preferences about the political regime, were more prone to vote for VOX. This goes in line with the findings of previous studies (see Foa and Mounk, 2016: 8) that underline that "the decline in support for democracy is not just a story of the young being more critical than the old; it is, in the language of survey research, owed to a 'cohort' effect rather than an 'age' effect". Thus, whereas voters born before the 1960s consider that living in a democracy is essential or that it is good or very good to live in a democratic political system, the ones born in the 1990s and the millennials are the most "anti-democratic" (Foa and Moun, 2016).

134 VOX and support for democracy

These findings might be a consequence of the country's relatively recent authoritarian past. The many references to Spain's pre-republican period in the discourse of the party's leaders may have a role in activating authoritarian attitudes in a portion of the electorate. In this sense, the emergence of a populist radical right party in a context like the Spanish one, could have the consequence of enhancing not only ideological polarization in terms of preferred policies, but also a much more dangerous effect in regards to the loyalty or disloyalty towards the democratic system.

Notes

1 See: https://twitter.com/Ortega_Smith/status/1193802059021213697.
2 Following the PopuList (Rooduijn et al., 2019), in Europe there are 80 populist radical right parties out of 121 populist parties.
3 See the article: www.theguardian.com/commentisfree/2017/dec/07/cambridge-dictionary-nativism-populism-word-year.
4 Recently VOX's leader, Santiago Abascal, claimed that the Socialist government of Pedro Sánchez represents the worst government in the last 80 years, including in this time range the authoritarian government of Francisco Franco. See: www.europapress.es/nacional/noticia-abascal-senala-gobierno-peor-ultimos-80-anos-sanchez-le-acusa-anorar-dictadura-franquista-20200909093217.html.
5 See: www.voxespana.es/noticias/es-la-hora-de-la-espana-viva-20190215.
6 See: www.youtube.com/watch?v=4mFnJ02zocM&feature=youtu.be&t=2128&fbclid=IwAR2Qg36BQSNZzkH8pFkPgnpVk1uMDSop405d0BBlhqsk4EbISeTtXBPMSL.
7 See: www.youtube.com/watch?v=i6Fwxu8zSjk.
8 In Spanish: *España está viva y reivindica la herencia que nos han dado nuestros padres. España está viva y pelea por el futuro y la libertad que tenemos que entregar a nuestros hijos. España está viva y es mucho más fuerte que sus enemigos. España está viva y es mucho más fuerte de lo que sus enemigos pensaban que era España* (See: www.youtube.com/watch?v=nzYd4Hsh2qw&t=300s).
9 See also the declarations of VOX's secretary, Javier Ortega Smith, alluding to the Spanish Reconquista of Granada against the Islamic invasion: www.youtube.com/watch?v=_sO0zZXA3Oc.
10 See: www.lasexta.com/noticias/nacional/santiago-abascal-aborto-hay-mujeres-que-dicen-que-cuerpo-suyo-pero-que-llevan-dentro-cuerpo_201910115da037b10cf2cf2d3c2d55b0.html.
11 See: www.youtube.com/watch?v=BrTil80mMTg.
12 See: www.elconfidencial.com/elecciones-andalucia/2018-12-03/elecciones-andaluzas-vox-francisco-serrano_1682634/.
13 See:www.elconfidencial.com/elecciones-generales/2019-04-28/vox-tuit-bandera-lgtb-feminismo-medios-comunicacion_1968750/
14 They also refer to the mainstream Spanish conservative party, PP, as "the coward little right" [*la "derechita cobarde"*].
15 See: https://cadenaser.com/ser/2019/05/07/politica/1557219107_939430.html
16 See: https://okdiario.com/andalucia/vox-andalucia-insta-junta-defender-corona-exige-que-no-haya-impunidad-golpistas-del-1-o-6207449.
17 See: www.infoelectoral.mir.es/.
18 See: www.infoelectoral.mir.es/. At the local and regional level, Pardos-Prado and Molins (2009) find that the largest share of supporters of PxC comes from the Socialists' Party of Catalonia [*Partit dels Socialistes de Catalunya*] (PSC-PSOE) and from abstainers.

19 The datasets which are based on a nationally representative sample. For the April survey the sample consisted of 5,943 interviews (out of 6,000 designed interviews) among the Spanish voting age population with the right to vote in general elections (i.e., Spanish nationals aged 18 years or more) who were residing in Spain (including the two autonomous cities of Ceuta and Melilla in North Africa). The design was the same for the November elections, with just the exception of the number of cases: 4,804 interviews out of 5,000 designed.

20 Regarding the control variables, we have selected a series of indicators that commonly capture the main drivers of support for PRRPs (see Chapter 4), as well as other social and demographic factors usually employed to explain electoral behaviour. Thus, we include indicators of age (in years); a dichotomous indicator of sex (1 = female); a measure of education level (1 = primary, 2 = secondary, and 3 = university degree), and the size of the place of residence (1 = urban dweller, 0 = rural). In addition to the objective measure of socio-economic status, we also include a binary measure of individuals' sociotropic perception of the economic situation (1 = negative evaluation of the economy, 0 = neutral or positive economic evaluation) and a binary indicator of political discontent (1 = political situation bad, 0 = political situation neutral/good); a scale of respondents' ideological positions on the left–right dimension (1–10), and a binary indicator of political interest (1 = high political involvement, 0 = low).

References

Betz H-G (2001) Exclusionary Populism in Austria, Italy, and Switzerland. *International Journal: Canada's Journal of Global Policy Analysis* 56(3): 393–420. DOI: 10.1177/002070200105600302.

Biorcio R (2003) Italian populism: from protest to governing party, paper presented at the Conference of the European Consortium for Political Research, Marburg 18–21 September.

Casals X (2019) Selection of VOX articles published in the last years. Available at: https://xaviercasals.wordpress.com/2019/03/30/aqui-puede-accederse-a-todos-nuestros-articulos-sobre-VOX/ (accessed 17 October 2020).

Casals X (2020) El Ultranacionalismo de VOX. Cinco claves para comprender "La España viva", *Grand Place, Pensamiento y Cultura* 13(2): 27–35.

CIS (2019a) *Estudio 3248. Postelectoral Elecciones Generales Abril (April) 2019.* Madrid: Centro de Investigaciones Sociológicas (CIS). Available at: http://www.cis.es/cis/opencm/ES/1_encuestas/estudios/ver.jsp?estudio=14453.

CIS (2019b) *Estudio 3269. Postelectoral Elecciones Generales Noviembre (November) 2019.* Madrid: Centro de Investigaciones Sociológicas (CIS). Available at: http://www.cis.es/cis/opencm/ES/1_encuestas/estudios/ver.jsp?estudio=14479

Dahl RA (1971) *Polyarchy: Participation and Opposition.* New Haven; London: Yale University Press.

Filc D (2010) *The Political Right in Israel: Different Faces of Jewish Populism.* London: Routledge.

Foa RS and Mounk Y (2016) The Danger of Deconsolidation. The Democratic Disconnect. *Journal of Democracy* 27(3): 5–17.

Foa RS and Mounk Y (2017) The Signs of Deconsolidation. *Journal of Democracy* 28(1): 5–15.

García-Santos JF (1980) *Léxico y Política de la Segunda República.* Salamanca: Ediciones Universidad de Salamanca.

González R, Bagsted M, Carvacho H, Miranda D, Muñoz B, Plaza A (2019) Radiografía del cambio social. Análisis de Resultados Longitudinales Estudio Longitudinal Social de Chile ELSOC 2016-2018. Available at: https://coes.cl/encuesta-panel/ (accessed 17 October 2020).

Huntington SP (1991) Democracy's Third Wave. *Journal of Democracy* 2(2): 12–34.

Linz JJ (1978) *The breakdown of democratic regimes. Vol. 1 Crisis, breakdown and reequilibration.* Baltimore: The Johns Hopkins University Press.

Margulies B (2018) Exchange: Nativists are Populists, Not Liberals. *Journal of Democracy* 29(1): 141–147.

McDonnell D and Werner A (2019) *International Populism. The Radical Right in the European Parliament.* London: C. Hurst & Co.

Mudde C (2007) *Populist Radical Right Parties in Europe.* Cambridge, UK; New York, NY: Cambridge University Press.

Mudde C (2019) *The Far Right Today.* Cambridge, UK: Polity Press.

Mudde C and Rovira Kaltwasser C (2013) Exclusionary vs. Inclusionary Populism: Comparing Contemporary Europe and Latin America. *Government and Opposition* 48(2): 147–174. DOI: 10.1017/gov.2012.11.

Pardos-Prado S and Molins JM (2009) The emergence of right-wing radicalism at the local level in Spain: the Catalan case. *International Journal of Iberian Studies* 22(3): 201–218. DOI: 10.1386/ijis.22.3.201/1.

Rama J and Casal Bértoa F (2020) Are Anti-Political-Establishment Parties a Peril for European Democracy? A Longitudinal Study from 1950 till 2017. *Representation* 56(3): 387–410. DOI: 10.1080/00344893.2019.1643770.

Ribera Payá and Díaz Martínez (2020) The end of the Spanish exception: the far right in the Spanish Parliament. *European Politics and Society* 0(0): 1–25. DOI: 10.1080/23745118.2020.1793513.

Rooduijn M, Van Kessel S, Froio C, Pirro A, De Lange S, Halikiopoulou D, Lewis P, Mudde, C and Taggart P (2019) The PopuList: An Overview of Populist, Far Right, Far Left and Eurosceptic Parties in Europe.

Rovira Kaltwasser C and Van Hauwaert SM (2020). The populist citizen: Empirical evidence from Europe and Latin America. *European Political Science Review* 12(1): 1–18. DOI: 10.1017/S1755773919000262.

Schmitt H, Hobolt SB, Van der Brug W and Popa, SA (2019) *European Parliament Election Study* 2019, Voter Study.

Torcal M and Medina L (2002) Ideología y voto en España 1979–2000: los procesos de reconstrucción racional de la identificación ideológica. *Revista Española de Ciencia Política* 6: 57–96. Available at: https://recyt.fecyt.es/index.php/recp/article/view/37328 (accessed 17 October 2020).

Torcal M (2008) El origen y la evolución del apoyo a la democracia en España. La construcción del apoyo incondicional en las nuevas democracias. *Revista Española de Ciencia Política* 18: 29–65. Available at: https://recyt.fecyt.es/index.php/recp/article/view/37457 (accessed 17 October 2020).

Turnbull-Dugarte SJ, Rama J and Santana A (2020) The Baskerville's dog suddenly started barking: voting for VOX in the 2019 Spanish general elections. *Political Research Exchange* 2(1). Routledge: 1781543. DOI: 10.1080/2474736X.2020.1781543.

VOX España (2019) 100 medidas para la España Viva. Available at: www.VOXespana.es/biblioteca/espana/2018m/gal_c2d72e181103013447.pdf (accessed 17 October 2020).

Zanotti L, Santana A, Rama J and Turnbull-Dugarte S (2020) There are good reasons to be unfaithful: Explaining support for VOX and vote switching amongst the Spanish right. Manuscript.

Zanotti L and Rama J (2020) Support for Liberal Democracy and Populist Attitudes: A Pilot Survey for Young Educated Citizens. *Political Studies Review* 0(0). DOI: 10.1177/1478929920945856.

Zaslove A, Geurkink B, Jacobs K and Akkerman A (2020) Power to the people? Populism, democracy, and political participation: a citizen's perspective. *West European Politics* 0(0): 1–25. DOI: 10.1080/01402382.2020.1776490.

Appendix

TABLE 5.A1 Probability of voting for VOX instead of other parties

	April 2019	*November 2019*	*Merge*
Sex	−0.65★★★	−0.71★★★	−0.65★★★
	(0.17)	(0.15)	(0.11)
18–24	0.70★	1.88★★★	1.50★★★
	(0.42)	(0.31)	(0.24)
25–34	1.47★★★	1.97★★★	1.74★★★
	(0.30)	(0.29)	(0.21)
35–44	1.64★★★	1.53★★★	1.62★★★
	(0.27)	(0.28)	(0.19)
45–54	1.12★★★	1.36★★★	1.25★★★
	(0.28)	(0.27)	(0.19)
55–64	0.42	1.06★★★	0.77★★★
	(0.31)	(0.28)	(0.21)
Secondary	0.67★★	1.07★★★	0.85★★★
	(0.28)	(0.31)	(0.21)
University	0.24	0.17	0.18
	(0.32)	(0.35)	(0.23)
Rural	−0.20	−0.39★★★	−0.31★★★
	(0.16)	(0.15)	(0.11)
Political interest	0.15	0.19	0.16
	(0.17)	(0.15)	(0.11)
LR ideology	8.55★★★	7.59★★★	7.98★★★
	(0.48)	(0.43)	(0.32)
National sentiment	0.73★★★	0.13	0.43★★★
	(0.16)	(0.16)	(0.11)
Economic current situation	0.33★	0.49★★★	0.35★★★
	(0.18)	(0.15)	(0.11)
Political situation	0.84★★★	0.64★★★	0.88★★★
	(0.18)	(0.23)	(0.13)
Regime preference	−0.58★★★	−1.17★★★	−0.90★★★
	(0.21)	(0.19)	(0.14)
Constant	−9.39★★★	−8.15★★★	−8.75★★★
	(0.52)	(0.50)	(0.35)
N	4,245	3,210	7,455

Standard errors in parentheses
★★★ $p<0.01$, ★★ $p<0.05$, ★ $p<0.1$

Source: Elaboration of the authors, on the basis of the CIS's April and November post-election surveys (CIS, 2019a; CIS, 2019b)

138 VOX and support for democracy

TABLE 5.A2 Probability of voting for VOX instead of other parties, merged dataset

	VOX vs PP	VOX vs PP &Cs
Sex	−0.65***	−0.65***
	(0.12)	(0.11)
18–24	1.97***	1.35***
	(0.28)	(0.25)
25–34	2.07***	1.62***
	(0.23)	(0.21)
35–44	1.78***	1.52***
	(0.21)	(0.20)
45–54	1.29***	1.14***
	(0.20)	(0.20)
55–64	0.77***	0.70***
	(0.21)	(0.21)
Secondary	0.88***	0.89***
	(0.21)	(0.21)
University	0.19	0.15
	(0.25)	(0.24)
Rural	−0.33***	−0.24**
	(0.12)	(0.11)
Political interest	0.14	0.13
	(0.13)	(0.11)
LR ideology	2.39***	4.76***
	(0.43)	(0.39)
National sentiment	0.25**	0.30***
	(0.13)	(0.12)
Economic current situation	0.50***	0.37***
	(0.13)	(0.12)
Political situation	0.54***	0.82***
	(0.15)	(0.14)
Regime preference	−1.15***	−1.04***
	(0.17)	(0.15)
Constant	−3.46***	−5.74***
	(0.42)	(0.39)
N	1,647	2,440

Standard errors in parentheses
*** $p<0.01$, ** $p<0.05$, * $p<0.1$

Source: Elaboration of the authors, on the basis of the CIS's April and November post-election surveys (CIS, 2019a; CIS, 2019b)

6

CONCLUSIONS

"What we are all about is giving a voice to the average Spaniard, the Spaniard on the street. For those who aren't ashamed of our history, of our national symbols, or our traditions, of our King, or of all what our country represents"

(Rocío Monasterio, Vistalegre II, October 2019)

Who is VOX?

VOX is the brand-new Spanish populist radical right party. VOX is a party who was destined to be small but ended up being one of the biggest fishes in the political party pool. VOX is a party that was born at the wrong time, but which grew at the right time. Where other parties of a radical and extreme right flavour failed, VOX succeeded, and the party now boasts the position of being that which brought an end to Spain's previously Spanish-exceptional status as a country free of the populist radical right.

VOX is a small group of (gentle)men (and a tiny group of women) who take the bulk of the party's decisions. Santiago Abascal and his four horse(wo)men – Javier Ortega Smith, Iván Espinosa de los Monteros, Rocío Monasterio, and Jorge Buxadé – constitute the inner circle of the party on the front line. VOX has institutional power at all levels of government in Spain's vast layers of multilevel governance. The party counts on, at present, some 644 elected representatives who take advantage of their elected office to give voice to anti-abortion proposals, criticize gender equality measures, advocate for radical tax cuts, and glorify a better (predemocratic) past. These representatives are no small number as this translates into 52 MPs in Spain's national Congress, 61 regional parliamentarians, eight members in the autonomous cities of Ceuta and Melilla, three senators, four members of the European Parliament, 526 local councillors, and five mayors, all advocating for a more radical and more right-wing Spain.

140 Conclusions

VOX is a potential kingmaker and the party has leveraged its position as an actor with a sizeable amount of elected representatives to influence policy-making by becoming a reliable and legitimate external supporter of sub-national governments that have been fronted by the more established right-wing parties: the People's Party (PP) and Citizens (Cs). VOX is an electoral machine that boasts more than 54,000 affiliated party members (Martín, 2020) and obtained over 3.6 million votes in the last national election, that is to say, 15 per cent of the votes cast in November 2019.

How did Spain get here?

VOX is a party who was born in the wrong time (or in the wrong place). VOX was born in late 2013, when the traditional party systems of other Southern European countries, like Italy or Greece, had already been affected by challenger parties. However, Spain was not *yet* ripe for something similar to take place. In Spain, the first election after the beginning of the Great Recession of 2008 only produced the replacement of the governing Spanish Socialist Workers' Party (PSOE) by the mainstream opposition party, the PP (Torcal, 2014). VOX thus came onto the scene as a populist radical right-wing challenger to the PP when the latter's institutional power was on the rise.

The party system change that was sweeping through Europe's party systems (Magalhães, 2014; Hernández and Kriesi, 2016) only took place in the subsequent elections of 2015, which shook the hitherto stable Spanish party system. At that point we saw the emergence of a populist radical left party, We Can (UP), a centre-right liberal formation, Citizens (Cs) and, recently, a populist radical right force, VOX (see Anduiza et al., 2018; Rodríguez Teruel and Barrio, 2016 and Turnbull-Dugarte et al., 2020). Still, the 2015 *quake*, and the ensuing window of opportunity opened for new parties to enter the system, was asymmetric. While the PSOE was still in a much poorer shape than the PP, the first successful *political entrepreneurs* were those at its flanks, We Can and Cs. VOX seemed destined to be yet another example of the failed far-right challengers that had, until then, proven incapable of perforating the PP's monopolistic hold on right-wing voters (Alonso and Rovira Kaltwasser, 2015) .

However, VOX is a party that was able to ride the wave of structural opportunities available for the populist challenger at the right time. Indeed, in late 2017 and early 2018, everything changed, and the window of opportunity opened for VOX. The territorial conflict with Catalan nationalists, reconverted as secessionists, intensified, reaching climactic levels with the unauthorized referendum called on 1 October 2017. Regional autonomy in Catalonia was suppressed for several months in application of article 155 of the Spanish constitution. Additionally, many Catalan independentist leaders faced serious judicial charges. Some of them fled whilst others stood trial. Building on one of the cornerstones of its discourse and programme, the quest for recentralization and the fight to combat sub-national statehood, VOX joined the lawsuit against the Catalan independence leaders as a popular prosecutor, gaining considerable media attention. Many were inclined to positively evaluate the party's contributions to the trial. The situation in Catalonia had generated a feeling of inequality among Spaniards when Catalan nationalist sectors imposed their objective of breaking away from Spain. VOX profited from this situation by presenting itself as the party most reliably devoted to face the secessionist challenge and stand up for the unity of Spain. This allowed it to fill the spatial gap on the extremes of the territorial issue that were increasingly important for voters but uncatered by the established parties.

The main driver behind the system-rupturing rise of VOX was the secessionist process initiated in Catalonia in 2012.[1] Other events, such as serious corruption scandals involving high-rank PP's officials, further contributed to the growth of VOX. The removal of PP's Prime Minister Mariano Rajoy from office after a successful motion of no confidence that installed the Socialist Pedro Sánchez in government eroded the image of the PP, the natural pool of prospective voters of VOX. Thus, neither the quasi-majoritarian electoral system, nor the supposed concentration of the right-wing vote on the traditional PP could keep on acting as a barrier to the emergence of VOX, firstly at the regional level (Andalusia 2018), and then at all the levels of government.

What does VOX want?

After analysing VOX's manifesto, at least three things are straightforward: (1) the party has a strong anti-immigration stance and advocates for stricter law and order policies as the majority of PRRPs; (2) it strongly defends the unity of Spain against all those who allegedly want to break or undermine it; and (3) it is against what it labels the "progressive dictatorship" and aggressively seeks to defend the Catholic religion and traditional moral values. This last element attests to VOX's extreme conservatism, which is displayed by the recurrent allusions to the Spanish traditional way of life and to the religious Catholic tradition, such as anti-abortion stances, as well as via the emphasis on traditional gender roles. These issues are repeated in VOX's discourses in an almost obsessive way with the party framing the crisis of COVID-19 and the state of emergency imposed by the government as an attack against Spanish values. To give but one example, in June 2020, Abascal criticized the feminist movement claiming: "[Shouting] long live March 8th, is the same as shouting long live disease and long live death", referring to the 2020 demonstrations in favour of gender equality on 8 March (Women's Day) that took place in Spain despite the detection of an increasing number of COVID-19 cases during the previous days. This example illustrates not only the high salience of traditional values in VOX's discourse but also its leaders' frequent resort to an antagonistic discourse, which is contributing to affective polarization in Spain (Torcal and Comellas, forthcoming). Incidentally, the "Long live death" [*"Viva la Muerte"*] phrasing is an allusion to a famous expression of José Millán-Astray, the founder of *La Legión* (an elite military unit) and a personal friend of the dictator Francisco Franco.

142 Conclusions

Who votes for VOX?

You do not become the third largest party in Spain without gaining a sizeable amount of support from the electorate. Both in April and November 2019, millions of people voted for VOX, and in November the party's vote share rose to 15.1 per cent, meaning that it succeeded in supplanting both UP and Cs as the third largest party in the country, only behind the traditionally hegemonic PP and PSOE.

In Chapter 4 we painted a picture of the sociological profile of VOX's supporters. Of note is that VOX's supporters tend to break away from those of the traditional populist right-wing parties as well as those of the (relatively) new parties in substantive ways. In line with a robust body of comparative work that profiles the socioeconomic constitution of the populist radical right's electorate, VOX's supporters are predominantly young and male (Rooduijn, 2018). The strong performance of the party amongst the young in the electorate also continues a precedent established with the eruption of Ciudadanos and Unidas Podemos (then Podemos) who were able to rely on their entrepreneurial novel status and message of change in order to mobilize support from the young (Orriols and Cordero, 2016).

In comparison to the supporters of the other parties in Spain, VOX's electorate is significantly less educated. It is the party with the lowest share of degree-holding voters and is largely supported by those with mid-level high school or vocational training. VOX, therefore, wins the support of whom they pen the "Spain that gets up early" [*La España que madruga*]. A deficit of support amongst university graduates is something that may develop into an issue of concern that the party will need to address should it seek to expand upon its existing electoral success in future electoral competitions. Spain's population, as in other advanced democracies, is increasingly composed of degree holders, so banking votes from those without a university education means that – in the long run – the party will be seeking support from an increasingly smaller pool of voters. Gaining enough votes to form a key coalition-forming or government-leading role in the future will require the party to make inroads amongst the degree-holding class and expand the voting coalition that has fuelled their electoral victories up until now.

VOX is the party of Spain's wealthy. Their supporters are, on average, more well off than the average citizen, and we find that their voters tend to care a lot about matters of status and wealth. Beyond the individual-level data that shows this aspect, we see this reflected in the distribution of VOX's support across different localities. Let us illustrate this with an example. The party's support in the Salamanca quarter of Madrid, one of the most luxurious neighbourhoods in the capital, is notably high. Salamanca has also hosted the majority of the right-wing protests held against the socialist-led coalition government during the height of the Coronavirus lockdown. These protests, endorsed by VOX, along Madrid's "Golden Mile" were made up of flag-waving protestors, some of which carried Spain's pre-constitutional Francoist emblems (Gabilondo, 2020), and individuals taking part in *caceroladas*[2] against the government, whilst residents played the national anthem from their balconies. Mirroring the maldistribution of wealth between less well-off democrats

Conclusions **143**

and well-to-do authoritarians during Spain's pre-democratic years, we find that the supporters of the country's populist and radical right-wing party are, economically, part of the former camp.

These nationalist demonstrations amongst the residents of Madrid's wealthiest residents tap into one of the core determinants of VOX's electoral support: nationalism. As previously demonstrated (Turnbull-Dugarte et al., 2020), VOX's electorate is highly clustered around those who identify strongly with Spain and, primarily, those who view the country to be "under attack" from internal secessionist forces (in Catalonia) and external cosmopolitanism mainly in the form of immigration (Mendes and Dennison, 2021) but also in relation to the EU (see Chapter 4).

Other than the canonical link between individuals' ideological preferences on the left–right space, we show that VOX voters are significantly more inclined to oppose Spain's membership of the EU and substantially more opposed to immigration than the voters of all other parties. Stereotypes of the "typical" voter of the populist radical right as radically right-wing, flag-waving, Eurosceptic, anti-immigration nativists tend to abound in popular discourse yet, in the case of VOX, we find that this stereotypical image is very much a true reflection of who votes for VOX.

Is VOX a threat to democracy?

We have gone to lengths to make clear the distinction between extreme right and radical right-wing parties within the overarching concept of the "far right" and where VOX lies on this dichotomy. The distinction between extreme right and radical right is important and we echo it here.

We define VOX as a populist radical right party. That is, we view the party to be ideologically radical but not extreme since discursively it *does not* go against the central tenets of democracy. However, belonging to the populist radical right family means that the party communicates and advocates for policies that are somewhat at odds with some of the core principles of *liberal* democracy such as the rule of law, individual liberties, or the rights of minorities.

Whilst VOX falls within the radical, as opposed to the extreme, party category, our analysis shows that there are latent anti-democratic tendencies within its voting constituents. Empirically, controlling for a battery of other important determinants of the vote such as ideology or national sentiment, we find that preferences for an alternative *non-democratic* regime are positively and significantly correlated with choosing VOX at the ballot box. Moreover, analysing the party public discourse in different arenas, we find that this flirtation with non-democratic regime types is not only the product of nostalgic reflections amongst older cohorts who may harbour a romanticized image of pre-democratic Spain to which VOX very much alludes to in their discourse. Rather, it is also sizeable and notable amongst the party's younger supporters. This means that amongst most of VOX's younger voters there is an observable lack of support for democracy. It may be the case that, when VOX rallies its supporters with shouts of "Long live Spain!" [¡*Viva España!*], reminiscent of the

144 Conclusions

pre-democratic rallying cry, and with calls to "Make Spain Great Again!", for some of the party's voters, the time when Spain was great refers to the pre-democratic period.

Consequences of the rise of VOX

Government formation in Spain, particularly at the regional and municipal level, is no stranger to complex party negotiations over government formation (Field, 2014) and both minority governments, supported via confidence and supply arrangements, and formal coalitions are commonplace (Field, 2016). With VOX's dramatic ascendency on the national level after the party's 2018 inaugural success in Andalusia, Spain's mainstream right-wing party has set itself apart from some of its European counterparts by breaking the cordon sanitaire that had previously kept out populist radical right-wing parties from government institutions (Akkerman et al., 2016; Akkerman and Rooduijn, 2015), given that they were not viewed as *koaltionsfähig*. At the time of writing, VOX supports right-wing minority governments in three autonomous communities (Andalusia, Madrid, and Murcia) via confidence and supply arrangements and governs in isolation in five of Spain's 8,131 municipalities. Interestingly enough, the five municipalities in which VOX enjoys an absolute majority are municipalities with less than 115 inhabitants: Barruelo del Valle (Valladolid), Vita (Ávila), Cardeñuela Riopico (Burgos), and Navares de las Cuevas (Segovia) – all four in the Castilla y León region – and Hontecillas (Cuenca) in the region of Castilla-La Mancha. Additionally, VOX gives external support in two major municipalities, Madrid, and Zaragoza.

These confidence and supply agreements have, as one would expect, not come without any cost and VOX has been able to exercise a non-trivial amount of influence over the policy programmes adopted by the PP-led governments in those municipalities and regions where VOX's support was necessary for government formation. In Andalusia, for example, they were able to cut €600,000 earmarked for associations related to the promotion and insertion of immigrants, now earmarked for buildings and other judicial constructions.[3] In the City of Madrid, it is not an anecdotic fact that 2019 was the first time without an institutional agreement of all the political parties with representation in Madrid Assembly [*Asamblea de Madrid*] against gender violence [*Violencia Machista*] – something that not happened since 2005. The coalition government of PP and Cs decided to not join this agreement with Mas Madrid and PSOE given VOX's opposition.[4] These are just two examples of a series of measures that VOX imposed in regions where conservative political forces need the party's support. These measures include repealing LGTBI laws, eradicating the historical memory of classrooms, and intensifying immigrant deportations.[5]

Beyond the role of VOX in shaping legislative outcomes via its capacity as external government-supporting partner for PP-led minority government coalitions with Cs, there is also very real potential for VOX's presence in the national-level institutions to shape policy and political events. Despite much protest from the

Conclusions **145**

PSOE and UP, VOX managed to gain a seat on the Congressional Committee [*Mesa del Congreso*] with Ignacio Gil Lázaro, a former member of the PP, becoming one of the chamber's vice-presidents.[6] The parliamentary party has also been extremely active in parliament. During Spain's 13th legislature (May 2019–September 2019), between the April and November elections, a total of 5,716 parliamentary motions were brought forward and 4,767 of these were tabled by the five main parties. While VOX's 24 MPs made up 6.9 per cent of the legislature, their motions made up 11 per cent of all those made (Merelo Campos and Pérez Miro, 2019). The party's MPs therefore appear to be punching above their weight in an attempt to make their voice in the chamber heard.

VOX and Spain tomorrow: where do we go from here?

Politics is in a constant state of flux with parties, voters, governments, institutions, states, and supranational and international organizations often trying to keep up with political events as they occur. This makes the writing of a book on politics challenging, even more so when the rate of political change is increasing, and levels of instability are unusually high.

At the time of first writing these final pages, Spain was beginning its de-escalation of the lockdown measures imposed by the national government in response to the Coronavirus outbreak. Through a highly antagonistic discourse, VOX's leaders penned the Sánchez-led government's management of the pandemic as "dire", "criminal", and "illegitimate", and officially called for a vote of no confidence against the government. There was no chance of the motion being successful and resulting in the removal of Sánchez from office: it makes sense to conclude that its aim was to ensure a media and public focus centred on VOX. Central to the party's longevity is the party's ability to portray itself as the primary party of the opposition and the legitimate right-wing party in waiting that can take up the reins of government at the next election. In short, their vote of no confidence was every bit a legislative manoeuvre aimed at damaging Pablo Casado and the PP, as much as it was aimed at damaging Sánchez and the Socialist government.

The party's inaugural success relied on its anti-establishment rhetoric which presented a two-pronged attack. The first was to signal its role as the defender of the "ordinary" Spaniard against the "progressive dictatorship" of the mainstream elite. The second was to attack Spain's governing class, on both the left and the right, for failing to provide simple, "common sense" solutions to the Catalan crisis. The populist rhetoric of fighting for the "will of the people" was, therefore, coalesced with attacks against the (lack of) competence[7] within the mainstream.

This two-pronged attack is likely to be fruitful for the party as the temporal horizon of the health and economic shock triggered by the Coronavirus pandemic extends over a longer period of time. By propping up right-wing governments outside of formal coalitions, VOX has been able to retain its challenger party status (Zulianello, 2019). This is important as it facilitates the party's continued use of anti-system and anti-elite rhetorical messages that attack all parties with governing

146 Conclusions

experience. This is evidenced even more in the case of the Coronavirus in which VOX has often stood alone as the *only* right-wing party to refuse to ratify the government's state of emergency proclamations.[8] Whilst the exigency of being responsible has forced the PP into recognizing the exceptional need to moderate its opposition to the government and vote favourably to ratify the state of alarm declarations – at least during the early peak of the pandemic – VOX has been able to clearly differentiate itself from the governing class by remaining the "lone wolf" that exists to keep the government, and the wider governing class, in check.

Fuelling the flames of this anti-elite messaging is of course the fact that the performance of the Socialist-led coalition in responding to the pandemic has not been free of critique, and international benchmarking between Spain and the country's European neighbours suggests that the country is performing far worse than elsewhere. This has paved the way for VOX to present itself as the only alternative and government in waiting that can i) throw out an incompetent and "criminal" government, and ii) "get the job done".

Will VOX and the populist radical right replace the PP as the hegemonic party of the right-wing block? Our expectation is that, whilst improbable, this is not impossible. On the one hand, we could assume that, if the conservative PP intensifies its strategy of ideological moderation, it could absorb a significant fraction of those voters placed around the centre which, currently, make up close to 30 per cent of VOX's voters. On the other hand, and as we explore in detail in Chapter 4, the constituents of the PP and VOX also display a high amount of symmetry in their ideological preferences. For example, whilst we note that, on average, attitudes towards immigration are most negative among those who vote for VOX, they are not all that different from those harboured within the voters of the PP. Similar low-level spatial divergence between the two parties' voting blocks are observed on other socio-cultural dimension issues such as LGBT+ rights or concerns over the environment. Thus, if the PP proves capable of catering to the policy preferences of the conservative Spanish electorate, this may well function as a circuit-breaker that can stymie VOX's potential growth and long-term longevity.

It is worth noting that electoral competition in recent years has, on the whole, taken place *within* ideological blocks, rather than *across* them. In other words, whilst, as detailed in Chapter 2, Spain has experienced a substantive increase in electoral volatility and the rise of voter promiscuity, vote-switching between political forces is largely among parties on either end of the ideological space. VOX has not, for example, been able to appeal much to the PSOE's voters who, unlike their peers in other Western European states, have resisted the siren call of the populist radical right. Put simply, if the electorate remains firmly entrenched in the traditional pattern of left–right electoral competition, VOX will find it difficult to maintain and increase its basis of support.

Much of this discussion, however, places a lot of faith in the ability of the PP to effectively manage, as they have done in the past (Alonso and Rovira Kaltwasser, 2015), to cater to the needs of the "broad church" of voters on the right. The PP is not, however, in government. Should VOX's strategy of monopolizing the public discourse by placing itself front and centre as the primary alternative to the left in

Conclusions **147**

the face of an inactive and lacklustre PP, our (reasoned) speculation does not paint a bleak picture for the populist radical right. The results of the recent Catalan regional elections in February 2020, in which VOX obtained more seats than PP and Cs combined, should serve as a warning that the possibility of a *sorpasso* in the right-wing block should not be understated.

Noteworthy also is that VOX's current constituency of voters are not only the voters of today but also those of tomorrow. Some analysts have placed their hopes in the populist radical right's demise on generational replacement and the emergence of a new (younger) liberal electorate. The evidence from Spain casts doubt on this optimism. Hopes of an emerging liberal youth appear largely misplaced and do not appear to be the silver bullet that commentators assumed. The electoral choices of today's young paint a picture of the voting behaviour of Spain's emerging future electorate, and that picture, as we detail in Chapter 4, votes a lot for VOX.

A final optimistic note for VOX is the organizational features of the party, mainly in terms of its leadership. Populists, of both the left and right, have often fuelled their success on the back of an individualist, charismatic and front-facing leader. Pim Fortuyn in the Netherlands and Alberto Fujimori in Peru are classic examples of populist personalist leadership.

On the contrary, the leadership of VOX is not concentrated in one man's hands. Instead, it is based on the presence of a number of potential successors to Abascal in the case that his political career should end. In other words, personality-based mobilization and idol-like adoration is something that we do not observe in the case of VOX. This might actually be functional in terms of the survival of the party in the long run. When the time comes for a new leader to bang the drums and rally the troops, the party leadership has ensured there are soldiers with household names that will be able to answer the call.

Notes

1 Although immigration is usually one of the main drivers of support for populist radical right formations and could therefore be expected to constitute a necessary condition for the emergence of a populist radical right party in Spain (Alonso and Rovira-Kaltwasser, 2015), the available data suggest that it did not play an important role in VOX's electoral success (at least in the first phase), whereas it was the territorial conflict that stood out as the main driver of support for Abascal's party, given the weak position of conservative Mariano Rajoy's PP on this issue.

2 *Caceroladas* are a traditional form of protest in Spain, in which protesters make their discontent known through accompanied noise, typically hitting pans, pots, or other household utensils. Protesters can go out into the streets and concentrate on a specific square or participate from their homes, thus being able to achieve a high degree of adherence and participation in the protest. Some of the most famous *caceroladas* in Spain were the ones against the Iraq War (government of PP's José María Aznar, in 2003); the Movement of *indignados* during the government of PSOE's Jose Luis Rodríguez Zapatero against the economic measures adopted by the Socialist government to stop the recession or, more recently, against the management of the COVID-19 pandemic by the Pedro Sánchez Socialist government.

3 See: https://elpais.com/politica/2019/06/13/actualidad/1560412854_648671.html.

148 Conclusions

4 See: https://elpais.com/ccaa/2019/11/20/madrid/1574254076_494028.html.
5 Thus, the proposal of agreement handed out by VOX to PP and Cs in exchange for its external support to a PP and Cs coalition government in Murcia included most of these measures: www.eldiario.es/murcia/politica/vox-murcia-lgtbi-erradicacion-memoria_1_ 1464742.html. The same applies to VOX's proposal of agreement for its support to a similar government in the region of Madrid: https://www.eldiario.es/madrid/medidas-irrealizables-vox-comunidad-madrid_1_1483510.html.
6 See: https://elpais.com/politica/2019/12/03/actualidad/1575359820_193278.html.
7 For an excellent discussion of the role of government competence on electoral preferences and mass attitudes, see Green and Jennings (2017).
8 Of the total of seven extensions to the state of alarm that the government had to put to a vote in Congress, VOX only voted in favour on the first occasion; the other six times, it voted against (as did a large part of the regionalist/independentist parties, e.g. ERC, JxCat or Bildu). See: www.diariovasco.com/politica/seis-prorrogas-estado-alarma-20200602144255-ntrc.html

References

Anduiza E, Guinjoan M and Rico G (2018) Economic Crisis, Populist Attitudes, and the Birth of Podemos in Spain. Giugni M and Grasso M. (eds) *Citizens and the Crisis. Palgrave Studies in European Political Sociology.* Palgrave Macmillan, Cham. https://doi.org/ 10.1007/978-3-319-68960-9_3.

Akkerman T and Rooduijn M (2015) Pariahs or Partners? Inclusion and Exclusion of Radical Right Parties and the Effects on Their Policy Positions. *Political Studies* 63(5): 1140–1157.

Akkerman T, de Lange SL and Rooduijn M (2016) Inclusion and mainstreaming? Radical right-wing populist parties in the new millenium. Akkerman T, de Lange SL, and Rooduijn M (eds) *Radical Right-Wing Populist Parties in Western Europe: Into the Mainstream?* London: Routledge, pp. 1–28.

Alonso S and Rovira Kaltwasser C (2015) Spain: No Country for the Populist Radical Right? *South European Society and Politics* 20(1): 21–45.

Field BN (2014) Minority parliamentary government and multilevel politics: Spain's system of mutual back scratching. *Comparative Politics* 46(3): 293–312.

Field BN (2016) *Why Minority Governments Work: Multilevel Territorial Politics in Spain.* Basingstoke: Palgrave MacMillan.

Gabilondo P (2020) Las caceroladas en la milla de oro de Madrid: 100 personas bajo la lluvia y tráfico cortado. *El Confidencial,* 13 May. Available at: www.elconfidencial.com/espana/ madrid/2020-05-13/coronavirus-cacerolada-gobierno-madrid-milla-oro-salamanca-madrid_2592095/.

Green J and Jennings W (2017) *The Politics of Competence. Parties, Public Opinion and Voters.* Cambridge: Cambridge University Press.

Hernández E and Kriesi H (2016) The electoral consequences of the financial and economic crisis in Europe. *European Journal of Political Research* 55(2): 203–224.

Magalhães PC (2014) Introduction – Financial Crisis, Austerity, and Electoral Politics. *Journal of Elections, Public Opinion and Parties* 24:2: 125–13.

Martín AI (2020) Vox duplica su número de afiliados en un año y vuelve a Vistalegre triunfal. *EsDiario,* 4 March.

Mendes MS and Dennison J (2021) Explaining the emergence of the radical right in Spain and Portugal: salience, stigma and supply. *West European Politics* 44(4): 752–775. EarlyView. DOI: 10.1080/01402382.2020.1777504.

Merelo Campos J and Pérez Miro J (2019) El PP, el partido más trabajador de la legislatura, Vox supera a Podemos y el PSOE se duerme en los laureles. *COPE*, 19 September.

Orriols L and Cordero G (2016) The Breakdown of the Spanish Two-Party System: The Upsurge of Podemos and Ciudadanos in the 2015 General Election. *South European Society and Politics* 21(4): 469–492.

Rodríguez Teruel J and Barrio A (2016) Going National: Ciudadanos from Catalonia to Spain. *South European Society and Politics* 21(4): 587–607. DOI: 10.1080/13608746.2015.1119646.

Rooduijn M (2018) What Unites the Voter Bases of Populist Parties? Comparing the Electorates of 15 Populist Parties. *European Political Science Review* 10(3): 351–368.

Torcal M (2014) The Incumbent Electoral Defeat in the 2011 Spanish National Elections: The Effect of the Economic Crisis in an Ideological Polarized Party System. *Journal of Elections, Public Opinion and Parties* 24:2: 203–221

Torcal M and Comellas JM (forthcoming) Affective Polarization in Spain in Comparative Perspective. *South European Society and Politics*

Turnbull-Dugarte SJ, Rama J and Santana A (2020) The Baskerville's dog suddenly started barking: voting for VOX in the 2019 Spanish general elections. *Political Research Exchange* 2(1). DOI: 10.1080/2474736X.2020.1781543.

Zulianello M (2019) *Anti-System Parties. From Parliamentary Breakthrough to Government.* London: Routledge.

INDEX

Abascal, S. 1, 2, 5, 32, 118, 141; founding of VOX and **18**, 18–19; PP and 17–18
age and support for VOX 72–4, **73**, *74*
Austrian Freedom Party *[Freiheitliche Partei Österreichs]* (FPÖ) 22
authoritarianism 4–5, 115–17, *116*
Aznar, J. M. 13–14, 50, 59

Basque Country Unite *[Euskal Herria Bildu]* (EH Bildu) 17
Bolsonaro, J. 43, 60
Buxadé Villalba, J. 2, 139

Calvo-Sotelo, L. 13
Canarian Coalition *[Coalición Canaria]* (CC) 13–14
candidate selection by VOX 28–30, **30**
Casado, P. 28
Catalan Republican Left *[Esquerra Republicana de Catalunya]* (ERC) 14
centre-periphery index 59, *60*
Chacón, C. 29
Citizens *[Ciudadanos]* (Cs) 11, 76
class and support for VOX 74–7, **75**, *76*, **77**
cleavage-based analysis of emergence of VOX 54–5; polarization in the left-right divide and 55–9, *56–7*, **58**
consequences of rise of VOX 144–5
Coronavirus pandemic 145–6

Danish People's Party *[Dansk Folkeparti]* (DF) 22

democracy 114–15, 132–4; comparative perspective of vote for populist right parties and attitudes toward **123**, 123–5, *124–5*; modelling support for VOX as function of non-democratic regime preferences and 126–32, *127–8*, *130–2*; populist radical right and 115–17, *116*; VOX and 117–23, *121–2*, 143–4
democratic consolidation 13
democratic transition 11, 13
Demonstration for the Unity of Spain 3

education and support for VOX 77–9, **78**
Electoral Committee, Vox 26–8, **27**
electoral growth of VOX 23–6, *24–6*
electoral manifesto of VOX 42–3, 63–4, 141; immigration 44, **44**, 48–51, *50*, *68*; law and order 44, **44**, 46–8, **47**; national way of life: positive 44, **44**, **45**, 45–6; salient categories in 44, **44**, **61**; traditional morality 44, **44**, 51–2, **52**; welfare state: expansion 44, **44**, 52–4, **53**
Espinosa de Los Monteros, I. 2, 139

Felipe VI, King 119–20
5 Star Movement *[Movimento 5 Stelle]* (M5S) 11
Foundation for the Defence of the Spanish Nation *[Fundación para la Defensa de Nación Española]* (DENAES) 118
Franco, F. 11, 141

French National Rally [Rassemblement National] (RN) 22

Galician National Block [Bloque Nacionalista Galego] (BNG) 14
gender and support for VOX **70**, 70–2
Gonzalez, F. 13
Great Recession of 2008 10

ideology of VOX voters 82–4, **83–4**; modelling of 100, *101*
immigration 44, **44**, 48–51, *50, 68*

La Legión 141
law and order 44, **44**, 46–8, **47**
LGBT+ rights 91, *92*
Living Spain 118–19

Manifesto Project (MARPOR) 43, 44
market liberalism 57–8, **58**
Millán-Astray, J. 141
Monasterio, R. 2, 5, 139

nationalism 93–100, *95–6, 98–9*
national way of life: positive 44, **44**, **45**, 45–6
nativism 4, 93–100, *95–6, 98–9*, 115–17, *116*
Navarre Yes [Nafarroa Bai] (NaBai) 14

Pérez Rubalcaba, A. 29
polarization in the left-right divide 55–9, *56–7*, **58**
political hegemony 13
Popular Alliance [Alianza Popular] (AP) 13
Popular Party [Patrido Popular] (PP) 10; Abascal as member of 17–18; demise of bipartisanship and precarious governance and 14; extraordinary intensification of electoral competition between PSOE and 13; party system dimensions and 15–17
populism 4, 5, 115–17, *116*
populist radical right: comparative perspective of attitudes toward democracy and vote for **123**, 123–5, *124–5*; democracy and 115–17, *116*; modelling support for 105–8, *106–7*; VOX as party of 4–6, 42, 114–15

Radical Right-Wing Populism in Western Europe 70
Rajoy, M. 18, 31, 141

regime preferences of voters 126–32, *127–8, 130–2*
RILE index 55–9, *56–7*, **58**

Sáenz de Santamaría, S. 28
Sánchez, P. 14, 29, 119, 141
Serrano, F. 119
sexual values 90–1
Smith, J. O. 2, 114, 139
socio-cultural preferences of VOX voters 87–91, **89**, *90, 92*, **93**
socio-demographics of VOX voters 69–81; age 72–4, **73**, *74*; class 74–7, **75**, *76*, **77**; education 77–9, **78**; gender **70**, 70–2; modelling of 79–81, *80*
Spanish politics: alternation in power in 13–14; demise of bipartisanship and precarious governance and 14; democratic consolidation in 13; democratic transition in 11, 13; extraordinary intensification of electoral competition in 13; future of VOX and 145–7; Great Recession of 2008 and 10; largest political parties in 10–11; party system dimensions in 15–17, *16*; patterns of party system and electoral cycles in 11–15, **12**; political hegemony in 13; precarious governance in 14
Spanish Socialist Worker's Party [Partido Socialista Obrero Español] (PSOE) 3, 10, 11; extraordinary intensification of competition between PP and 13; party system dimensions and 15–17; political hegemony of 13; primaries and 29
Spexit 88–9, **89**, *90*
Suárez, A. 11, 13

Third Way, Europe 55
Together We Can [Unidos Podemos] (UP) 11, 28, 29, 142
traditional morality 44, **44**, 51–2, **52**
Trump, D. 43, 60, 61–2

Union, Progress and Democracy [Unión, Progreso y Democracia] (UPyD) 14
Union of the Democratic Centre [Unión de Centro Democrático] (UCD) 11, 13
United Left [Izquierda Unida] (IU) 14

Vidal-Quadras, A. 19
voters, VOX 142–3; compared to other populist and radical right-wing parties across Western Europe 102–5, *103*, **104**; on the economy 84–7, *85–6*; ideology of

152 Index

82–4, **83–4**, 100, *101*; modelling support for populist radical right and 105–8, *106–7*; motivations of 81–100; nativism vs nationalism and 93–100, *95–6, 98–9*; probability of voting for VOX instead of other parties **137–8**; religious profile of **93**; socio-cultural preferences of 87–91, **89**, *90, 92*, **93**; socio-demographic profile of 69–81; support as function of non-democratic regime preferences 126–32, *127–8, 130–2*

VOX 1–2, 30–2; ascension to third position in government 10–11; Catalan independence and 19; cleavage-based analysis of emergence of 54–9, *56–7*, **58**; in comparative perspective 59–63, **61**; consequences of rise of 144–5; democracy and 117–23, *121–2*, 143–4; electoral growth of 23–6, **24–6**; electoral manifesto of (*see* electoral manifesto of VOX); explaining the rise of 2–4, 140–1; founders of **18**, 18–19; future of Spain and 145–7; internal organization of 26–8, **27**; official founding of 18–19; origins in PP split 17–23; political landmarks related to emergence of 19, 22; as populist radical right party 4–6, 42, 114–15; seats in the Congress of Deputies **39–41**; selection of candidates by 28–30, **30**; shares in the Congress of Deputies **36–8**; support for, as function of non-democratic regime preferences 126–32, *127–8, 130–2*; who is 139–40

We Can *[Podemos]* 11, 14, 72
welfare chauvinism 62
welfare state: expansion 44, **44**, 52–4, **53**

Zapatero, J. L. R. 13–14, 50